Growing Up American

Growing Up American

*How Vietnamese Children Adapt
to Life in the United States*

Min Zhou
Carl L. Bankston III

Russell Sage Foundation • New York

Library of Congress Cataloging-in-Publication Data

Zhou, Min, 1956–
   Growing up American : how Vietnamese children to adapt to life in the United States
    / Min Zhou, Carl L. Bankston, III.
     p.   cm.
   Includes bibliographic references and index.
   ISBN 0-87154-994-8 (cloth)   ISBN 0-87154-995-6 (paper)
   1. Vietnamese American children—Cultural assimilation.
I. Bankston, Carl L. (Carl Leon), 1952– . II. Title.
E184.V53Z48   1998   97-36932
305.23'0973—dc21   CIP

Copyright © 1998 by Russell Sage Foundation. First papercover edition 1999. All rights reserved. Printed in the United States of America. No part of this publication may be reproduced, stored in a retrieval system, or transmitted in any form or by any means, electronic, mechanical, photocopying, recording, or otherwise, without the prior written permission of the publisher.

Reproduction by the United States Government in whole or in part is permitted for any purpose.

The paper used in this publication meets the minimum requirements of American National Standard for Information Sciences—Permanence of Paper for Printed Library Materials. ANSI Z39.48-1992.

Text design by Suzanne Nichols.

RUSSELL SAGE FOUNDATION

112 East 64th Street, New York, New York 10021

10 9 8 7 6 5 4 3 2 1

For Philip Jia, Marikit, Andrew, and Victor:
Children of Immigrants

Contents

Min Zhou is associate professor of sociology and Asian American studies at the University of California, Los Angeles.

Carl L. Bankston III is assistant professor of sociology at Tulane University.

Acknowledgments

More people have helped us with this research than we can possibly mention here, but we would like to recognize and thank a few of them, with apologies to all those whom we have unintentionally left out. Scott Feld, Nancy Foner, John R. Logan, Robert K. Merton, Alejandro Portes, Rubén G. Rumbaut, Alex Stepick, Carol Dutton Stepick, and Roger Waldinger were major sources of inspiration, insight, ideas, and encouragement throughout this research.

We would like to thank the Russell Sage Foundation for its support in much of the writing of this book. We would also like to express our gratitude to our current institutions—the University of California, Los Angeles, and the University of Southwestern Louisiana as well as our former institutions—Louisiana State University and Loyola University.

The book would not have been possible without the cooperation and assistance of the people of the Versailles Vietnamese community of New Orleans and other informants in the larger Vietnamese communities elsewhere in the United States. Monsignor Dominic Luong, Joseph Vuong, Margaret Nguyen, and Ngoc Thanh Nguyen were particularly helpful to us in our fieldwork. On this note, we owe a great deal to the employees of Associated Catholic Charities, above all to Dr. Susan Weishar and Anthony Tran, for taking time from their hectic work schedules to help us. For assistance in gathering data on Vietnamese youths in the public school system, we would like to thank a number of school administrators and teachers, notably Susan Egnew, Tom Rigsby, and Joseph Peccarrere. Our gratitude also goes to Stephen J. Caldas who played a key part in introducing us to people in the schools and in enabling us to obtain achievement test results.

We especially thank Roger Waldinger who read and commented on each chapter of the book in great detail during revision, helping us to give shape to an initially unwieldy manuscript. We thank David Haproff, the director of publications, and Suzanne Nichols, the production manager, at the Russell Sage Foundation, for patiently steering us along the way and Nina Gunzenhauser for her painstaking and meticulous editing of the final manuscript. We also thank the two anonymous reviewers for their helpful comments and suggestions.

We thank Paula Maher, Hong Xu, Camille Yezzi, and other staff members at the Russell Sage Foundation and Diana Lee, Pham Tram, Linda Tran, Nancy Wang, for their assistance through various phases of this research. Our special appreciation goes to Philip Jia Guo who provided assistance in preparing graphics and tables.

We would like, finally, to express our deepest gratitude to each member of our families whose love, care, and faith sustained us from beginning to end.

MIN ZHOU
CARL L. BANKSTON III

─── Introduction ───

The Children of Vietnamese Refugees

Hai Nguyen, 17, and his family arrived in Versailles Village from a refugee camp in Malaysia when he was 11. His family settled in New Orleans because his mother, who was born and raised in the Vietnamese village of Vung Tau, had a brother there. Hai is a high school junior now, and he is planning to attend college after another year. He says he wants to go to Tulane or Loyola because he has friends from the neighborhood at both universities and he expects they will help him with any problems he may have.

Cuong Dang, 17, left Vietnam by boat with his mother when he was 8. Now he lives with his mother and stepfather in Versailles Village. His stepfather, a fisherman, is frequently away from home for weeks at a time on his boat in the Gulf of Mexico. His mother works as a checkout clerk at a grocery store. Cuong is still in school and intends to graduate, but he has no intention of going on to college. All his friends are Vietnamese, but none of them are interested in Vietnam or things Vietnamese. "All that, that's all old stuff," he says. When asked whether he considers himself Vietnamese or American, he simply shrugs; he doesn't really care.

For the children of immigrants in the United States, the passage to adulthood involves growing up American. That's no easy thing; it adds the conflicting pressures of assimilation and the demands of familial or ethnic loyalty to the common problems of adolescence. The children of refugees have it harder still, carrying the additional burdens associated with sudden flight from the homeland and all the losses that the search for safe haven entails.

This book tells the story of America's single largest group of refugee children—the children of Vietnamese refugees—as they have experienced growing up American. The Vietnamese are members of a larger Southeast Asian refugee population that emerged on the American scene in sizable numbers shortly after the withdrawal of American troops from Vietnam and the fall of Southeast Asian governments allied to the United States. The Vietnamese form the core of this refugee population;

1

between 1975 and 1990, the number of Vietnamese in America increased from an insignificant number to 614,547.

The arrival of the Vietnamese represents the advent of an entirely new ethnic group on the American scene. With the emergence of the second generation—some born in Vietnam and brought to the United States as young children; others born after the parents' flight from Vietnam—we have a phenomenon of greater significance still: the refugees' children will be the first generation to grow up largely or entirely on American soil. In contrast to their parents, the children of the Vietnamese immigrants—like all immigrant children—are unlikely to think of their parents' home country as a place to which they might return, nor will they use it as a point of reference by which to assess their progress in the new land. Rather, their expectations will be governed by the same standards to which other Americans aspire, and it is by those standards that young Vietnamese Americans will assess themselves and be assessed by others. While these young people launch on a quest for social and economic progress to take them well beyond the lower levels of their immigrant parents, it's not clear whether that quest will succeed. In the answer to that question lies the future of Vietnamese America. It is also the issue with which this book is concerned.

VIETNAMESE CHILDREN AND THE "NEW SECOND GENERATION"

The children of Vietnamese immigrants belong to the "new second generation"—those U.S.- or foreign-born children of contemporary immigrants growing up in the United States and currently moving into maturity in rapidly growing numbers. Now, as in the past, the emergence of a second generation involves a new, decisive chapter in the ethnic experience. After the first generation moves to America seeking a better life for their families, their children either realize or smash those hopes. For the most part, American history is a story of immigrant children fulfilling their parents' dreams. But the past may not provide a reliable guide to the second generation experience unfolding before us today.

Contemporary immigrants have encountered an America different from the one encountered by the earlier immigrants. Today America has an emerging "hourglass" economy in which opportunities for movement from bottom to top have gotten harder for all (Zhou 1997a). Ever since the late 1960s, just when the United States began receiving larger numbers of non-European newcomers, economic restructuring has been profoundly altering the employment base of the American economy. In major urban centers, the industrial plants and their assembly-line operations that used to rely on a large force of semiskilled workers have migrated from high-wage countries to the Third World (Kasarda 1983; Piore 1979; Wilson 1978, 1987). As a result, urban labor markets have become highly segmented. One segment is a growing sector of knowledge- or capital-intensive jobs, offering high wages, good working conditions, career stability, and promotional opportunities, but requiring a college education and sophisticated job and interpersonal skills. The other segment is made up of burgeoning tiers of low-skilled, labor-intensive service jobs, offering low wages, poor working conditions, and few chances for upward mobility (Averitt 1968; Tolbert, Horan, and Beck 1980). Stable blue-collar jobs of the sort that used to pay adequate wages for a family and thus enabled many earlier immigrants to earn a decent living have become increasingly rare. Consequently, economic restructuring has undone the traditional ladder of social mobility, creating new obstacles for those newcomers who are poorly educated and lack marketable skills.

This new economic reality defines the world that confronts the children of immigrants. That encounter, as the sociologist Herbert Gans (1992) has suggested, is likely to involve one of two scenarios: the child either succeeds in school and moves ahead, or falls behind the modest, often low status of the parents' generation. Gans has labeled the latter scenario "second-generation decline." Children growing up in households headed by poor, low-skilled immigrants face uncertain prospects for moving ahead through school success. The parents, of course, have few of the economic resources that can help children do well in school. The environment does not help when neighborhoods are poor, beset by violence and drugs, and local schools do not function well. To add to this difficulty, immigrant children receive conflicting signals, hearing at home that they should achieve at school while learning a different lesson—that of rebellion against authority and rejection of the goals of achievement—on the street. At the same time, both real life and the television screen expose children to the wage and consumption standards of U.S. society, and children come to expect more than their parents ever had. As a result, Gans points out, children of the foreign born are unwilling to work at low-paying, low-status jobs of their parents, but they do not have the education, skills, or opportunities to do better.

This mismatch between rising aspirations and shrinking opportunities will either lead to second-generation decline or provoke "second-generation revolt" (Perlmann and Waldinger 1997). This is the daunting dilemma that Vietnamese parents and their children face; how they negotiate it shapes their adaptation to American society.

In absolute numbers, the Vietnamese make up a relatively small component of today's emerging second-generation population. Demographic characteristics and the American experience of the Vietnamese make this case ideally suited for assessing the problems and prospects of the children of immigrants growing up as the twentieth century comes to a close. The second generation to which the Vietnamese children belong reflects the influence of the migration waves that have transformed immigrant America over the past thirty years. The children of this generation of immigrants are linked mainly to source countries in Latin America and Asia. In 1990, Latinos comprised 52 percent of all foreign-born children under 18, with Asians accounting for another 27 percent; those proportions fell to 48 percent and 24 percent, respectively, among U.S.-born children with at least one immigrant parent (Oropesa and Landale 1997). And for most Latino and Asian groups—the Mexicans and Japanese Americans excepted—the second generation represents the largest part of the population born or raised in the United States.

Among today's second generation, Vietnamese children are the newest of the new. As of 1990, 79 percent of all Vietnamese children could be classified as members of the second generation, having either been born in the United States or arrived here prior to the age of 5. Another 17 percent could be labeled as members of the "1.5 generation," those who arrived in the United States between the ages of 5 and 12. Only 4 percent arrived as adolescents, and thus appropriately belong to the first generation.[1]

Like their counterparts among the other immigrant groups, today's Vietnamese children will be the first to see whether they can really "make it in America." The conditions under which many immigrants live, however, put that goal in doubt. Immigrant children are far more likely than their non-Hispanic white counterparts to live in poverty, to depend on public assistance, and to grow up in households where wage earners are disproportionately underemployed.

But the situation of the Vietnamese has even more problems. First, they arrived under circumstances quite different from those encountered by today's typical newcomers. Unlike most other contemporary immigrants, the Vietnamese were pushed out of their homeland, forced to leave without adequate preparation and with scant control over their final destination. Many possessed little in the way of assets—formal education, skills, English-language proficiency, or familiarity with the ways of an advanced society—that would ease the passage into America. No ethnic community, eager to help out with assistance of varying sorts, was ready to greet the early refugees; instead, the government, working in tandem with individual or institutional sponsors, decided where the Vietnamese would resettle. Consequently, many of the Vietnamese found themselves involuntarily dispersed, pushed into urban or suburban neighborhoods of a wholly unfamiliar type, often deteriorating areas where the residents were poor and the schools were inadequate. Although the two decades from the mid-1970s to the mid-1990s saw the establishment and consolidation of Vietnamese communities throughout the country, many of the newcomers have not moved up far economically. As of 1990, poverty affected almost half the first- and 1.5-generation Vietnamese children, and just under a third of the second generation, as opposed to one tenth of the general U.S. population. Over a quarter of the Vietnamese depended on public assistance, in comparison with 8 percent among all Americans.

Thus, the prospects seem dim. But there is evidence that the future is looking much better. As will be shown in the chapters to follow, Vietnamese children seem to be doing exceptionally well in school. Though a significant minority is lagging behind, for reasons that will also be discussed, the school success of the Vietnamese suggests that ethnic progress depends on more than the human and financial capital with which the immigrant parents begin. Instead, the ingredients of success seem bound up with "ethnicity," a term that will later be discussed in more detail but that now serves as shorthand for a group's distinctive cultural and social-organizational traits. Since the circumstances of their immigration appeared to spell trouble, understanding the Vietnamese experience promises to shed light on the conditions that influence prospects for the much larger second-generation population, of which the Vietnamese are so clearly an emblematic case.

But if a study of the Vietnamese is likely to generate broader lessons, this group deserves attention for reasons of its own. Southeast Asian refugees arrived and were resettled under the auspices of the U.S. government; whatever the moral case for refugee admission and resettlement, the taxpayer might want to know whether his or her dollars were well spent. The size and ubiquity of the Vietnamese population make this a matter of more than academic interest. The Vietnamese have been dispersed to every state and can be found in almost every major city, including those that have historically received very few immigrants. Numerically, the Vietnamese are on an upward curve, in large measure because of the population's youth; by the year 2000, the Vietnamese are expected to constitute the nation's third-largest Asian group, ranking just after the Filipinos and the Chinese (Lee 1992).

Notwithstanding the group's size, its growth, and its recent history, it has attracted less than its fair share of scholarly attention. Recent years have seen the publication of a few excellent studies of Vietnamese children and the Vietnamese family (see, for example, Caplan, Choy, and Whitmore 1991; Kibria 1993; Muzny 1989; Rutledge 1985; Starr and Roberts 1985). Most of this work, however, has been concerned with specific issues associated with resettlement and attendant changes in Vietnamese family life, providing important baseline information but not fully exploring the complex process of adaptation among the newer generation. These earlier studies have also tended to focus on the role of the family and the importance of the Vietnamese ethnicity, paying less attention to the ethnic community. By contrast, a concern with the community, its organization, and its impact on socioeconomic adaptation lies at the heart of our work, adding an entirely new dimension to an understanding of the process by which the Vietnamese have sought to get ahead.

FRAMEWORK FOR ANALYSIS

The Effects of Social Class and Race/Ethnicity

Individual traits, family socioeconomic backgrounds, and racial or ethnic characteristics are the crucial ingredients of second-generation adaptation. Since childhood is a time of acquiring skills, the most important individual characteristics influencing their adaptation are those associated with exposure to American society, such as English language ability, place of birth, age upon arrival, and length of residence in the United States. Conventional theories of immigrant assimilation predict that proficiency in English, native birth or arrival at a young age, and longer U.S. residence should lead to adaptive outcomes.

But this is not always how it seems to work. Recent studies have revealed an opposite pattern: regardless of national origin, the longer the U.S. residence the more maladaptive the outcomes, whether measured in terms of school performance, aspirations, or behavior (Kao and Tienda 1995; Rumbaut and Ima 1988; Suárez-Orozco and Suárez-Orozco

1995). Clearly, the outcomes of adaptation vary according to where immigrants settle, whether in affluent middle-class suburbs or in impoverished inner-city ghettos. While the emergence of a middle-class population is a distinctive aspect of today's immigration, a disproportionately large number of immigrant children converge on underprivileged and linguistically distinctive neighborhoods. There, the immigrants and their children come into direct daily contact with the poor rather than with the middle class; they are also apt to encounter members of native minorities and other immigrants rather than members of the dominant majority. At the school level, many immigrant children find themselves in classrooms with other immigrant children speaking a language other than English or with native minority children who either have problems keeping up with schoolwork or consciously resist academic achievement. Under these circumstances, exposure to American society can either lead to downward mobility or confine immigrant offspring to the same slots at the bottom level from which they began (Ogbu 1974; Perlmann and Waldinger 1997; Portes 1995; Portes and Zhou 1993).

Family socioeconomic status shapes the immediate social conditions for adaptation, because it determines the type of neighborhood in which children live, the quality of school they attend, and the group of peers with whom they associate. Immigrant children from middle-class backgrounds benefit from financially secure families, good schools, safe neighborhoods, and supportive formal and informal organizations, which ensure better life chances for them. Children with poorly educated and unskilled parents, in contrast, often find themselves growing up in underprivileged neighborhoods subject to poverty, poor schools, violence, drugs, and a generally disruptive social environment.

The sociologist James S. Coleman and his associates, in what has become well known as the Coleman report (1966), reported that children did better if they attended schools where classmates were predominantly from higher socioeconomic backgrounds. Children who live in poor inner-city neighborhoods confront social environments drastically different from those who live in affluent suburban neighborhoods. These children suffer from the unequal distribution of educational resources, which seriously curtails their chances in life, trapping them further in isolated ghettos (Davis 1993; Jencks and Mayer 1990). Ghettoization, in turn, produces a political atmosphere and mentality that preserve class division along racial lines, leading to the greater alienation of minority children from American institutions and further diminishing their chances for upward mobility (Fainstein 1995).

However, recent research has revealed that immigrant children tend to do better than their U.S.-born peers of similar socioeconomic backgrounds who attend public schools in the same neighborhoods (Portes 1995). How can one account for this peculiar phenomenon? The anthropologist John U. Ogbu (1974) attributed varying outcomes to the social status of groups in the receiving society. He distinguished between immigrant minorities (whose arrival in the United States is by choice) and castelike minorities (whose arrival is forced or whose disadvantaged social status is imposed). He reasoned that group members of racial minorities can either accept an inferior caste status and a sense of basic inferiority as part of their collective self-definition, or they can create a positive view of their heritage on the basis of cultural and racial distinction, thereby establishing a sense of collective dignity (see also De Vos 1975). This choice is available to both immigrant minorities and castelike minorities; the difference in the direction taken, Ogbu found, lay in the advantageous or disadvantageous aspects of racial or group identity. Ogbu (1989) showed in his research on Chinese-American students in Oakland, California, that in spite of cultural and language differences and relatively low economic status, these students had grade point averages that ranged from 3.0 to 4.0. He attributed their academic success to the integration of these students into the family and the community, which placed high value on education and held positive attitudes toward public schools.

Ethnic or racial status influences the social adaptation of immigrant children in ways closely connected to family socioeconomic status. Indeed, the sociologist William Julius Wilson (1978) argued that contemporary racial inequality became largely a matter of social class. Past racism, in his view, essentially delayed the entry of racial minority members into full participation in the American economy until the old blue-collar opportunities largely disappeared, leaving nonwhites in jobless neighborhoods. This perspective emphasizes the impact of economic restructuring, but we place more emphasis on the effect of continuing racial discrimination. Minority status systematically limits access to social resources such as opportunities for jobs, education, and housing, with the result that racial/ethnic disparities in levels of income, educational attainment, and occupational achievement persist (Lichter 1988; Tienda and Lii 1987; Wilson 1978; Zhou 1993; Zhou and Kamo 1994). The sociologists Douglas S. Massey and Nancy A. Denton (1987) provided convincing evidence that the physical and social isolation of many black

Americans was produced by ongoing conscious, discriminatory actions and policies, and not simply by racism in the past.

Race and ethnicity may be related to school performance for cultural reasons, as well as for purely socioeconomic reasons. It is possible that Vietnamese cultural values, such as a tradition of respect for teachers, affect how young people respond to the American institution of public education. The experience of immigration, moreover, can reshape cultural values. Ogbu (1974, 1983, 1989, 1991) pointed out that immigrant groups frequently sought upward mobility, so that education often came to occupy a central place in immigrant aspirations. But the deliberate cultivation of ethnicity may also be a factor. The anthropologist Margaret A. Gibson 1989, for example, found that the outstanding performance of Punjabi children in a relatively poor rural area of northern California derived from parental pressure on children to adhere to their own immigrant families and to avoid excessive Americanization. Similarly, the psychologist Nathan Caplan and his associates found that Indochinese refugee children (except for Cambodians and Hmongs) excelled in the American school system, despite the disadvantaged location of their schools and their parents' lack of education and facility with English (Caplan, Whitmore, and Choy 1989). These researchers, too, attributed refugee children's academic achievement to cultural values and practices unique to Indo-Chinese families. While more recent studies of the educational experiences of Asian American children have shown that parents' socioeconomic status, length of U.S. residence, and homework hours significantly affected academic performance, they also found that controls for such factors did not eliminate the effect of ethnicity (Kao and Tienda 1995; Portes and Rumbaut 1996; Rumbaut 1995b, 1996; Rumbaut and Ima 1988). More significantly, the sociologists Alejandro Portes and Dag MacLeod (1996), using National Educational Longitudinal Survey data, reported that the negative effect of disadvantaged group memberships among immigrant children was reinforced rather than reduced in suburban schools, but that the positive effect of advantaged group memberships remained significant even in inner-city schools.

Racial or ethnic group membership can entail serious disadvantages in the American public school system. The inequalities of race and class that plague American society are carried into the American educational system where minority group members often attend schools that provide poorer resources than those available in other schools. Schools may thus become "arenas of injustice" that provide unequal opportunities on the basis of race and class (Keniston et al. 1977). Ethnicity may therefore be of limited advantage for castelike minorities. If a socially defined racial minority group wishes to assimilate but finds that normal paths of integration are blocked because of race, the group's members may be forced to use alternative survival strategies that enable them to cope psychologically with racial barriers but that do not necessarily encourage school success. Further, the historically oppressed group, such as castelike/involuntary minorities, may react to racial oppression by constructing identities in the form of conformity—"unqualified acceptance of the ideological realm of the larger society"—and, more frequently, in the form of avoidance—"willful rejection of whatever will validate the negative claims of the larger society" (Fordham 1996, 39). As a consequence, it may be the willful refusal to learn, not the failure to learn, that affects the academic outcomes of the children of castelike/involuntary minorities (Kohl 1994). Under the pressure of the oppositional youth subculture, then, minority children who do well in school may be forcefully rejected by their peers as "turnovers" acting "white" (Bourgois 1991; Gibson 1989; Portes and Stepick 1993; Waters 1996).

The Ethnic Factor: Sources of Social Capital or Liability

Refugee resettlement and family socioeconomic situations place Vietnamese children in specific neighborhoods and facilitate contacts with specific peer groups. If growing up in poor neighborhoods has adverse social consequences for native-born minority children, how, then, do neighborhood and peer-group settings affect Vietnamese children? One common response to the disadvantages imposed on a minority group by the larger society is group solidarity among the members of that minority. We therefore first examined to what extent the Vietnamese were able to use their common ethnicity as a basis for cooperation to overcome socioeconomic disadvantages. To explore this question, we ventured into a typical poor urban minority neighborhood to investigate how the children of Vietnamese refugees managed to overcome their class disadvantages to adapt to American schools. The focus on Vietnamese children from poor socioeconomic backgrounds enabled us to examine the ethnic effect while controlling for the social-class factor. Specifically, we perceived that the ethnic factor as a social context that influenced children's adaptation through support as well as control.

We do not believe that it can be assumed that the Vietnamese, as members of a new ethnic minority group, are necessarily always victims of racism. In some situations, they may even be involuntary beneficiaries. While they often settle in minority neighborhoods, it is quite possible that they experience fewer obstacles of prejudice and institutional discrimination than native-born children of American minorities. Racial stereotypes such as the stereotype of Asians as the "model minority" may conceivably even work in favor of individual Vietnamese. We argue that while structural and individual factors are certainly important determinants of immigrant adaptation, these factors often work together with immigrant culture and group characteristics to shape the fates of immigrants and their offspring. An immigrant culture may be referred to as the "original" culture, consisting of an entire way of life, including languages, ideas, beliefs, values, behavioral patterns, and all that immigrants bring with them as they arrive in their new country. This original culture may be seen as hindering the adaptation of members of the ethnic group (the assimilationist perspective) or as promoting this adaptation (the multiculturalist perspective).

To see an immigrant culture as an American microcosm of the country of origin, however, is to overlook the historically dynamic nature of all cultures. As the historian Kathleen N. Conzen (1991) recognizes, immigrant cultures are constantly changing and adapting to new environments. Cultures may persist while adapting to the pressures of American society, resulting in many similar patterns of cultural orientation among different immigrant groups. These newly adapted cultural patterns are often confused with those of their original cultures. American ethnic foods offer an example of this cultural reshaping. Each type of ethnic food—Italian, Mexican, or Chinese, for example—is distinctive in itself, but they are quite similar in fitting the taste of the general American public. If a particular dish does not appeal to the public taste, it will not be known or accepted as an ethnic dish no matter how authentic it may be.

Similarly, the cultural traits that characterize a group depend not only on how the group selects these traits as its identifying characteristics but also on how the larger society responds to them. If the cultural characteristics an immigrant group selects for display in America are approved by the mainstream, the group will generally be considered to have an advantageous culture; otherwise its culture will be deemed deficient. For example, most of the Asian subgroups whose original cultures are dominated by Confucianism, Taoism, or Buddhism—such as the Chinese, Koreans, Japanese, and Vietnamese—often selectively unpack from their cultural baggage traits such as two-parent families, a strong work ethic, delayed gratification, and thrift that are suitable to the new environment. They either leave packed or keep strictly to themselves other traits not so well considered, such as nonconfrontation, passivity, submissiveness, and excessive obligation within the family. Since the things unpacked resemble the ideals of the mainstream culture, these "proper" original cultures create an image that elicits favorable treatment from the larger society, which may give the group more help in dealing with the difficulties of adjustment and enable group members to capitalize on the ethnic resources.

On the other hand, if a group displays characteristics that are not comparable to the ideals of the mainstream, or that resemble characteristics identified with or projected onto native-born minorities, such as matriarchal families, these traits will be combined with the race/ethnic factor and seen as deficient cultural characteristics and stigmatized. The groups so stigmatized will receive unfavorable treatment from the larger society, exacerbating their problems and trapping them in a vicious cycle. Therefore, the effect of an immigrant culture varies depending not only on the social structures of the ethnic community on which the immigrant culture is based, but also on the social structures of the larger society of which the immigrant culture is a part.

Immigrant cultures may be defined as patterns of social relations involving shared obligations, social supports, and social controls. When, for example, Korean Americans obtain from other Korean Americans low-interest loans requiring little collateral, or Chinese American students in after-school Chinese language classes receive encouragement and approval for their general academic orientations, these are forms of social support inherent in particular patterns of social relations. When, on the other hand, an Asian Indian American or a Japanese American receives disapproval, or even ostracism, from coethnics for failing to attain a respected occupation, this is a form of social control.

Clearly, social support and social control may channel individuals into particular forms of behavior through material and social-psychological means; both support and control, however, stem from relationships based on value-orientations brought from the home country and adapted to the circumstances of the host country. Two sociological concepts are useful in a consideration of the issue: James S. Coleman's concept of social capital and Emile Durkheim's concept of social integration. Coleman (1987) defines social capital as the existence of a system of relationships that promotes advantageous outcomes for participants in the system. More specifically, he explains that "what I mean by social capital in the raising of children is the norms, the social networks, and the relationships between adults and children that are of value for the child's growing up. Social capital exists within the family, but also outside the family, in the community" (p. 34; see also Coleman 1988, 1990b).

Norms, social networks, and relationships between adults and children may have absolute value; that is, some types of relationships or norms may be of value to children in any environment. In the present context, certain general characteristics of Vietnamese families, such as two-parent families and respect for elders, may help children advance in any segment of contemporary American society. If, however, these families live in social environments that are not conducive to academic achievement and upward mobility, then these characteristics may take on even greater importance. Therefore, the importance of accepting community-prescribed norms and values and cultivating social relationships depends largely on the opportunities offered to immigrants in their host country. In disadvantaged neighborhoods where difficult conditions and disruptive elements dominate, immigrant families may have to consciously strive to preserve traditional values by means of ethnic solidarity to prevent the next generation from acculturating into the underprivileged segments of American society in which their community is located.

Moreover, as Coleman observes, the community provides a context in which social capital is formed. The adult society surrounding a family can reinforce familial support and direction. In this sense, an ethnic community can be perceived simply as consisting of various sets of social ties among members of an ethnic group. Membership in any group, however, is a matter of degree; individuals may belong to social groups to varying extents. If norms, values, and social relationships within an ethnic group do influence the adaptation of group members, the influence should logically depend on the extent to which individuals hold the norms and values and participate in the social relationships. Hence, participation in social relationships and acceptance of group norms and values are interrelated; the more individuals associate with a particular group, the greater the normative conformity to behavioral standards and expectations prescribed by the group. At the same time, ethnic communities may also hinder the adaptation of young members of immigrant groups. The writer Richard Rodriguez, in his eloquent memoir *Hunger of Memory* (1982), maintains that his own success has depended on leaving his Spanish-speaking neighborhood behind. It is possible that young Vietnamese must similarly cast off their traditions and language to participate fully in American society. The question is whether the person who succeeds in leaving the poor ethnic community represents an aberration or a trend.

The ethnic context also serves as an important mechanism for social control. For this reason, we understand the concept of social capital as a version of one of the oldest sociological theories, Durkheim's theory of social integration. Durkheim (1951) maintained that individual behavior should be seen as the product of the degree of integration of individuals in their society; social integration involved not only participation, but also socialization into shared beliefs, values, and norms. Thus, the greater the integration of the individual into the social group, the greater the control of the group over the individual. In the context of immigrant adaptation, children who are more highly integrated into their ethnic group are likely to follow the forms of behavior prescribed by the group and to avoid the forms of behavior proscribed by the group. In any consideration of whether Vietnamese ethnicity should be seen as a source of social capital or as a disadvantage, then, it will be important to look at how integration into the Vietnamese community affects the adaptation of young people.

We see our work as describing how patterns of adaptation among young Vietnamese are shaped at a number of contextual levels that determine what opportunities are available to them and how they respond to those opportunities. Some of the shaping forces include the structure of opportunities, expectations created by the host society, and externally imposed racial and class constraints, as well as the adaptive controls and supports provided by ethnic groups or other social groups. Whether or not an immigrant group's social relations actually are adaptive depends on the structure of relations within the group and the fit between the group's sociocultural structure and that of the larger society. Although we are specifically concerned with the process of adaptation among Vietnamese children to American society, we believe that the analytical framework we have just described can be applied to members of other ethnic groups, immigrant or native, as an alternative way of understanding why ethnic groups show characteristic patterns of adaptation to school and to American society and why interethnic differences exist.

DATA AND METHODS

The Case Study of Versailles Village, New Orleans

This book relies mainly on a case study of Versailles Village, a low-income urban minority community in New Orleans and the second largest Vietnamese community (after the one in Houston) outside California. Chapter 3 provides a detailed description of the community. Our work in Versailles Village began in April 1993 and continued through the spring of 1995. During this time, we engaged in participant observation, undertook intensive interviews using open-ended questions, and administered two surveys of neighborhood high school students. One of the authors, Carl L. Bankston III stayed on the research site for the entire research period, serving as a volunteer in community-based youth programs and as a substitute teacher in one of the high schools being surveyed. Our in-depth interviews involved a snowball sample of one hundred young people, parents, grandparents, educators, counselors, community leaders, police officers, and refugee agency officials.

The two surveys elicited information from Vietnamese students in grades 9 to 12 attending public high schools in the study area. The Versailles Survey of 1993 focused only on Washington High School, a pseudonym we have given to the neighborhood high school located in Versailles Village and attended by over half the Vietnamese youths residing in the neighborhood. At the time of the survey, the school was a typical urban public school with a student body that was 77 percent black and 20 percent Vietnamese. We surveyed the entire Vietnamese student population who were present at school on the day of the survey in May 1993 ($N = 198$). For this survey, we used a questionnaire that included ninety-eight close-ended questions and one open-ended question, covering a wide array of demographic and socioeconomic characteristics of children and their parents, cultural values, identity, language proficiency in both English and Vietnamese, school grades, academic aspirations, future orientations, and mental health.

In the spring of 1994, we conducted a second survey of the Vietnamese students in Versailles Village, incorporating many of the items in the 1993 survey, refining the measures on language proficiency and school grades, and adding a set of new items on peer-group association, tastes and interests, deviant behavior, religious participation, and community involvement. The sample surveyed in 1994 contained 402 Vietnamese high school students from three public high schools in or near Versailles Village: 204 students from Washington High School where the 1993 survey was administered, 183 students from Jefferson High School, our pseudonym for another nearby public high school attended by the rest of the Vietnamese high school students residing in the Versailles enclave; and 15 students from a magnet high school attended by the best students in the New Orleans area.[2] The sample represented an estimated 75 percent of all Vietnamese high school students in Versailles Village. This 75 percent response rate thus refers not to a sample, but rather to three-quarters of the entire population under consideration.

Secondary Sources of Data

The Los Angeles Times *Poll of 1994*   Between March 29 and April 29, 1994, The *Los Angeles Times* conducted a poll that randomly surveyed 861 Vietnamese adult residents of Los Angeles, Orange, San Diego, Riverside, San Bernardino, and Ventura counties in California from a pool of Vietnamese surnames in telephone directories. The interviews were conducted by telephone in Vietnamese and in English by Vietnamese American interviewers. Vietnamese residents in Orange county were oversampled ($N = 502$) with the sampling error of plus or minus 5. The sampling error for residents in all other counties surveyed ($N = 359$) was plus or minus 7. The poll also acknowledged possible errors that might have been affected by factors such as question wording, the order in which questions were presented, and the omission of individuals with unlisted telephone numbers and those who did not have Vietnamese surnames (*Los Angeles Times* 1994).

The U.S. Census of Population and Housing, 1980 and 1990   Specifically, we used *The U.S. Census Public Use Microdata Sample (PUMS) Data of 1980 and 1990*. The PUMS data were used to identify national trends. In their raw form, these data were hierarchic, with households serving as the primary units of analysis. In order to build a file in which children served as the units of analysis, we used the SPSS INPUT PROGRAM to redefine PUMS. For this study, a child, who was under 18 years of age and still resided with his or her parent(s), was defined as the case of analysis. The SPSS INPUT PROGRAM cycled through the raw data and selected information from the housing unit record as well as information on the household head and spouse (if present). The file on which this study was based was built from a combination of up to four different types of records: the housing unit records, the household head record, the spouse record, and the child record. We identified two groups of Vietnamese children by using the nativity variable for children and their parents—foreign-born children who arrived at 5 years of old or over and U.S.-born children or foreign-born children who arrived at the age of 4 or under. We built a data file on the 1980 PUMS and a comparable file on the 1990 PUMS. A sample of young adults aged 18 to 24 was also drawn from the PUMS that included those living with their parents and those living by themselves.

Immigration and Naturalization Service Data   We compiled statistics from the Immigration and Naturalization Service (INS) statistical yearbooks from 1975 and 1995 to document the trend of refugee influx and the demographics of the Vietnamese admitted to the United States.

The Graduation Exit Examination of 1990 of the State of Louisiana   We used data from the Graduation Exit Exam (GEE) of Louisiana to examine the academic performance of young Vietnamese. Passing this standardized test is a requirement for graduation from Louisiana public high schools; therefore, this data source contained information on all public high school students in the state. Until 1991, the GEE collected information on the socioeconomic characteristics of parents of those who took the test. For this reason, we used the 1990 data to provide an external check on the validity of our survey findings on Vietnamese students in Versailles Village.

Archival Documents and Written Records   We supplemented our fieldwork with numerous government agency reports and newspaper reports on the Vietnam War and Vietnamese refugees, their families, their communities, and their adaptation experiences in the United States, dating back to 1975. These reports primarily came from the Bureau for Refugee Programs of the U.S. Department of State, the U.S. Department of Health, Education, and Welfare (USHEW) and later the U.S. Department of Health and Human Services (USHHS), and from major newspapers, such as the *Los Angeles Times*, the *New York Times*, the *Houston Chronicle*, and the *Times Picayune* (New Orleans), and other major magazines such as *Time* and *Migrant World*.

A Note on the Generalizability of Our Case Study

A case study makes it possible to examine continuity and change in the life patterns of a particular group and to make sense of the complexity of its social relations; it also makes it possible to take the social setting itself, on which these relations are based, as an object of study. Since individual behavior and mental states result from living in certain types of social settings, one cannot adequately interpret individual responses to survey or interview questions without understanding the setting and considering how a particular setting produces particular responses. In this study, we were especially interested in examining what gives Vietnamese children, whose families lack measurable human capital and economic resources and are trapped in poor neighborhoods, a competitive advantage to upward social mobility. We selected Versailles Village as our research site precisely because it is made up primarily of Vietnamese from agricultural backgrounds and low socioeconomic status. Thus, our case study has the advantage of providing us with built-in controls for the effect of social class.

Because of the unique refugee resettlement pattern, this community shares many characteristics with other Vietnamese communities dispersed throughout the United States; it is relatively homogeneous in socioeconomic backgrounds (characterized by low levels of educational attainment, high levels of poverty, and reliance on public assistance), its internal social structures are based on closely knit interpersonal ties and traditional organizations, and it is socially isolated from the American middle class. The similarities among Vietnamese communities ensure that our case study will shed light on the general process of Vietnamese adaptation to life in the United States.

We concede that Versailles Village differs from the much better known communities in Little Saigon (Orange County) and the community in San Jose, which are not only many times larger but also socioeconomically heterogeneous, containing a sizable ethnic middle class and a political elite. In recent years, many Vietnamese have moved to California through secondary migration, and most of them have perceived such a move as an upward step. Even so, striking similarities between Little Saigon and Versailles Village are evident in the development of ethnic institutions and patterns of intraethnic relationships, as revealed by the *Los Angeles Times* Poll of 1994 and a recent study of Vietnamese children in southern California (Rumbaut 1994a, 1995a, 1996).

The fact that Versailles Village is a predominantly Catholic community may be another differentiating factor. Will our findings apply to Buddhist or Cao Dai Vietnamese communities? We believe they will. Previous studies have treated Vietnamese Catholicism as a form of "Confucianized Christianity," because it has been deeply influenced by cultural traditions that are derived from centuries of Buddhist, Taoist, and Confucianist practices and that share a common cultural basis with many stylistic similarities (Nash 1992; Rutledge 1985). Moreover, while there are obviously major theological differences among these religions, our study has not been concerned with theology but rather with religion as a social institution that serves as a focal point for organizing relations and establishing identities among the Vietnamese. From our observations, Catholic churches and Buddhist pagodas share strikingly similar functions in refugee resettlement in both Versailles Village and Little Saigon.

Further, our study does not exclusively rely on the Versailles Village case. We have drawn on a variety of national data sources to identify the trends and issues and then used the case study to examine these trends and issues in depth. This multipronged approach, which links ethnographic case-study information with quantitative census data, survey data, and archival records, enables us to provide a unique perspective on Vietnamese American young people. Combining different types of data, as we have done, produces a mosaic in which the validity of any one piece of information may be checked by how it fits with all the other pieces, permitting us to gauge the degree to which our findings are representative of the broader population.

Values and Assumptions

All theoretical approaches to social issues make value judgments and reflect built-in assumptions. Our approach is no exception. We believe, however, that we can approach objectivity by making implicit values explicit and by carefully examining our underlying assumptions. As thinkers who attempt to be intellectually honest, we make an effort to look at the evidence, whether or not it accords with any ideological preferences we may hold. The fundamental value judgment of this book lies in our choice of "adaptation" as a research question. To some extent, this question involves taking mainstream American society, with all its injustices and inequalities, as given, and focusing on the factors that enable the children of Vietnamese refugees to advance in that society. In this respect, then, our research may seem to have an inherently conservative strand.

Given our choice of the research question, moreover, we conceptualize anything that appears to contribute to adaptation as having a positive effect. If, for example, adherence to Vietnamese cultural values is associated with superior school performance, we perceive these values, as manifested in particular ways, as facilitating rather hindering adaptation. At the same time, we recognize that traditionalism can have many negative consequences, such as an unquestioning acceptance of the status quo or stifled individualism.

In our theoretical framework, we emphasize the role of the ethnic community in promoting the adaptation of Vietnamese American young people. This emphasis does not stem from any desire on our part to glorify Vietnamese community life or to engage in ethnic boosterism. Neither of us is Vietnamese, and we have no commitment to promoting the intrinsic worth of Vietnamese communities. Rather, our observations and research have led us to believe that particular patterns of social relations embedded in the ethnic community can serve as sources of social capital and that these patterns may be the critical missing pieces in the puzzle of immigrant adaptation that begins at the margins of contemporary American society. Throughout the book, we attempt to present the key pieces of evidence from our case study as well as other sources of data that have led us to conclude that an ethnic social relations model, in which the ethnic community is the pivotal factor, interacting with other important factors, offers the best means of understanding the process of growing up American for socioeconomically disadvantaged immigrant children.

THE ORGANIZATION OF THE BOOK

Our study offers an in-depth examination of Vietnamese children growing to adulthood in the United States. Chapter 1 traces the historical process of Vietnamese resettlement in the United States, including the several waves of Vietnamese migration to the United States in the aftermath of the Vietnam War and the development of government programs of resettlement over the next two decades. It considers how the background of war, the organizational mechanisms of refugee resettlement, and popular opinion have continued to influence the lives of the Vietnamese and their children.

Chapter 2 offers a description of the demographic and socioeconomic characteristics of the Vietnamese population in the United States and the socioeconomic obstacles confronting this population. It provides a quali-

tative assessment of the effects of government policies and various resettlement programs on the settlement patterns, geographic distribution,
and population growth of this new ethnic minority group. It then discusses how the Vietnamese have recently made the transition from a
resettled refugee population to an integral part of the American mosaic,
describing some of the larger societal structures and internal structures of
the ethnic communities, such as household size and composition, residential concentration, occupation, inequality, and the rise of a new ethnic identity as a background against which young Vietnamese strive to
become American.

Chapter 3 provides concrete examples of how the ethnic community
and the family, as key institutions of an ethnic culture, can serve as
sources of social capital. Families are seen to impart a cultural heritage
and to adapt this heritage to new circumstances, and their traditionalism
is shown to be related to distinctive values regarding social relations.

Chapter 4 describes the patterns of social and kinship relations in the
ethnic social system in which Vietnamese families and their children are
contained. Integration into these patterns of social relations is directed
by the entire ethnic community and relies on the community's reinforce-
ment. The major dimensions of social relations among individuals, families, and the community that make possible the development of social
capital are examined, and it is argued that involvement in community
relationships, as a social context for young Vietnamese Americans, is an
important determinant of positive adaptation. Young people who function within the context of an ethnic community, rather than isolated
from it, experience social controls and encouragement that direct them
toward upward mobility.

Chapter 5 takes up the issue of parental native language and provides
an empirical account of the effects of advanced minority language abilities on the adaptation of young Vietnamese. Minority language skills
such as literacy are shown to enable young people to make greater use of
their ethnic social capital and can actually foster upward mobility in an
English-speaking society.

Chapter 6 begins with a general picture of school adaptation among
Vietnamese children, exploring the root causes of success or failure in
the American educational system. It discusses the questions of how the
school environment influences students' performance, what factors produce various orientations toward the school environment among Vietnamese students, and whether students connected with support systems
in the family and the community succeed in maintaining more positive

academic orientations than those who are alienated from ethnic families and communities.

Chapter 7 explains bicultural conflict and the issues of gender role changes and ethnic identification encountered by young Vietnamese. As the culture of origin is being reshaped into a specifically Vietnamese American culture, young people face many difficulties in balancing the demands of American culture with those of tradition-minded parents. The tensions between individual self-fulfillment and commitment to the ethnic community are considered with an emphasis on the impact of culture on the quality of life and on the psychological well-being of the young people.

Chapter 8 describes specific patterns of peer group association among Vietnamese children and examines how Vietnamese children may be affected by differential associations with peers of major American groups, with "Americanized" coethnic peers, and with the ethnic community. It examines the role of racial and bicultural conflicts and the effects of various levels of the social structures in encouraging the rise of delinquency and youth gangs. The concepts of being Vietnamese and being American are placed in the contexts of the different types of peer groups available to young people within the Vietnamese community and outside the ethnic community in the larger society. In keeping with the theme of the book, different types of peer group associations are seen to lead to variations in the meaning of "becoming American" for Vietnamese American young people.

Chapter 9 provides a summary of the main findings of the study and a discussion of the implications of these findings for young members of immigrant and native-born minority groups. Understanding the unequal positions of minority groups in American society depends on a consideration of both the social structures within the groups themselves and the opportunities provided or denied to them by the structure of the larger society. The American educational system can be among the most important of those opportunities. Therefore, a central issue in understanding and promoting the advancement of immigrant and other minorities is the fit between minority-group social structures and schools. The social structures of ethnic groups like the Vietnamese may change as young people move through the schools and into jobs and develop new views on becoming and being American. The success of immigrant or minority children in American schools and in the larger labor market depends not simply on the individual merits of these children or on the quality of schools they attend, but also on the social capital provided to these children by the communities surrounding them. To the extent that these young people succeed in the American educational system, they can move into new positions in the American job structure and become structurally assimilated. Consequently, young Vietnamese in the United States can be expected to become an increasingly integral part of American society. In the process, being Vietnamese will become yet another way of becoming American.

Chapter 1

The Scatterings of War

At the end of the Red River—do you know?—
In the land of my birth, is another river.
My heart weeps with nostalgia.

—Vietnamese Folk Song

Unlike their nostalgic parents, many of the children of Vietnamese refugees either were born in the United States or were too young at the time of flight from Vietnam to remember their native land. For them, the weeks in leaky boats and months in crowded refugee camps are only stories they have heard from their parents, relatives, and family friends. Yet they all carry the burden of war and exile. To understand the present-day experiences of the younger generation, it is important to look back to the recent past.

REFUGEES IN FLIGHT

In April 1975, Saigon, the capital of South Vietnam, fell to North Vietnamese troops. Vietnam was unified under the Hanoi government, and Saigon was renamed Ho Chi Minh City. The spring of 1975 saw panic-stricken efforts to leave the country, by sea, land, and air. From 1975 through the early 1990s, Vietnamese refugees poured into the United States in three significant stages (see figure 1.1). Exiles who fled at the end of the war made up most of the first group. Then came the "boat people," who entered the United States in two waves, one peaking in 1978 and the other in 1982. The influx of Vietnamese refugees then declined for several years, only to surge again between 1988 and 1992. Over six hundred thousand Vietnam-born people were resettled in the United States between 1975 and 1995, most of them as refugees. By the mid-1990s, the Vietnamese refugee crisis had eventually subsided. Subsequent arrivals are mainly immigrants rejoining their families already resettled in the United States.

The exiles who made up the first group of Vietnamese refugees were predominantly military personnel, professionals, the elite (former South

FIGURE 1.1   Vietnam-Born Persons Admitted into the United
States, 1975 to 1995

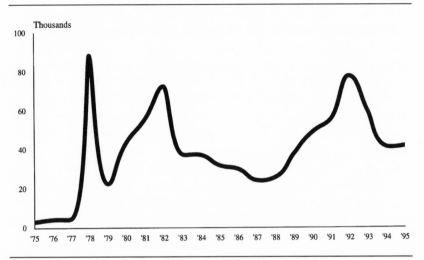

Source: Statistical Yearbook of the Immigration and Naturalization Service: 1975 to 1995.

Vietnamese government officials and wealthy business owners), and members of the Catholic Church. To some extent, the 1975 exodus of refugees from South Vietnam was an extension of an earlier exodus of Catholic refugees out of North Vietnam. In 1954, the division of Vietnam into the communist North and the anti-communist South had led about one million people to flee from the North to the South, with a smaller flow moving in the opposite direction. Most of those who fled south were Catholic, though non-Catholics with ties to the French colonial regime also had reason to fear reprisals from the anti-French Vietminh, the ruling force of the North, and thus to flee south. After the fall of Saigon, this same group took flight once again. Reporting on her research among the 1975 refugees at Fort Indiantown Gap in Pennsylvania, the professor of education Gail P. Kelly (1977) wrote, "I scarcely heard Vietnamese spoken without the distinct intonation and pronunciation patterns of the North. Of the sixty or more refugees we interviewed at length, fewer than ten spoke with southern or central Vietnamese accents" (p. 15).

If the flow of refugees out of Vietnam had ended in 1975, virtually all of today's Vietnamese children in the United States would have been U.S.-born. They would have had weaker ties to their ancestral country, and they would have been far fewer in number. In the years that followed, however, the harsh treatment of southern Vietnamese who had served the Americans or the defeated government of South Vietnam continued to produce an exodus of refugees.

Immediately after the fall of Saigon, former military officers were ordered to report to meeting places to engage in ten days of political education. Though told to bring only enough supplies for those ten days, they found themselves imprisoned for months, years, and even, in some cases, decades. Attempts to escape from reeducation camps were punishable by death. Those who were released from the camps faced pervasive discrimination. Unable to get jobs or to buy food and other necessities in government-owned stores, they struggled to survive by pedaling pedicabs or doing other kinds of menial labor. Their children were not allowed to enter colleges or universities.

Many southern Vietnamese who were not assigned to reeducation camps did not fare any better. They suffered instead from Hanoi's iron-fisted attempts to rebuild the war-torn country on a socialist basis. When the Hanoi government created agricultural collectives, known as New Economic Zones, in the ravaged rural areas, many southern Vietnamese were forced to settle in these zones, where life was especially difficult for people used to urban living. The damage to cultivatable land through years of bombing and the military use of herbicides was aggravated by natural disasters (a severe drought followed by floods in 1977), which exacerbated the food shortage and pushed thousands of people out of the country. "There was nothing there for us," a middle-aged former farmer now residing in the United States remarked. "You could try to get a boat and leave, or you could just stay there and wait for things to get worse. I talked to my wife and we decided that if we died trying to get out, we would be better off."

War with Cambodia and China further intensified the flight of refugees from Vietnam. On December 22, 1978, Vietnam responded to Cambodian attacks on Vietnamese villages along the border with a military offensive into Cambodia. In February 1979, China, wary of Vietnamese expansion into other areas in Indochina, formed an alliance with the Khmer Rouge and launched military raids on the northern provinces of Vietnam. Although China quickly withdrew from Vietnam, protracted wars with Cambodia combined with internal troubles—political repression and instability, natural disasters resulting in poor harvests, and a lack of capital investment—caused severe anxiety, fear, and the loss of livelihood for many. These conditions triggered the second exodus, which came to be known as the flight of the boat people.

Thousands of refugees used boats to flee Vietnam immediately after the fall of Saigon, but the phrase "boat people" came into common usage at the end of the 1970s and the beginning of the 1980s, when a flood of refugees cast off from Vietnam in overcrowded, leaky boats. By 1979, an estimated number of four hundred thousand refugees had escaped Vietnam in boats or on foot, headed for Hong Kong, Indonesia, Malaysia, the Philippines, Singapore, and Thailand. Many found themselves stranded in crowded refugee camps for months and even years, awaiting resettlement in a third country (Caplan, Whitmore, and Choy 1989; Starr and Roberts 1982; Tran 1991).

The mass exodus of boat people was made up of two ethnic groups: Sino-Vietnamese, who were pushed out after the war with China, and ethnic Vietnamese, who left in large numbers in the early 1980s. In 1978, over 85 percent of Vietnam's roughly 1.5 million Sino-Vietnamese lived in the South, where they dominated many business activities. For Hanoi, embroiled in tense relations with China, these ethnic Chinese were suspects by virtue of both their class status—they were members of the petit bourgeoisie—and their ethnicity. Believing that China was actively seeking to propagandize the ethnic Chinese in Vietnam in order to create a "fifth column" of secret sympathizers, Hanoi launched a series of campaigns against them (Duiker 1989). To escape persecution, the Sino-Vietnamese began to flee in 1978 on foot into southern China and by boat into the South China Sea. When war between Vietnam and China broke out, thousands poured out of the country. About 250,000 ethnic Chinese and those who were able to buy false papers to register themselves as Chinese headed for China (Hung 1985). Those who were forced to flee by boat in the South China Sea and picked up were placed in refugee camps in Hong Kong, Malaysia, and the Philippines.

The Vietnamese government did not actively seek to stop the flight of these perceived fifth columnists, and there was evidence that Vietnamese officials took bribes from the Sino-Vietnamese to allow them to leave the country. Since the ethnic Chinese had dominated much of the commerce of South Vietnam, they had access to boats that could leave along the old commercial routes. Ethnic Vietnamese followed suit as the surge of Sino-Vietnamese ebbed in the early 1980s. Some purchased papers identifying them as Chinese or simply paid larger bribes to officials than the Chinese did in order to get out of the country. Others managed to slip out on fishing craft, since the government could not prevent all ships in the country from leaving the harbor. Some refugees even used escape routes across Cambodia into Thailand that had been made possi-

ble by the disruptions of war. The militarization of Vietnam was continuing, and young men faced with conscription also joined this second
wave. "I was not afraid of being killed," said one young man interviewed
in a refugee camp in the Philippines. "I could have been killed when I
escaped. So, it was not fear of being killed that made me run away from
going into the army, but I would rather be killed than fight for the
Communists." It is difficult to know exactly how many ethnic Vietnamese fled during this period, since refugee agencies at this time generally kept records by nation of origin rather than by ethnicity.

Frequently the boats were made shaky and unseaworthy as a matter of
conscious strategy. "You had to get a boat that you thought would actually make it to some other country," one refugee explained, "but it had
to be a boat that looked like it wouldn't make it, so they [the Vietnamese officials] wouldn't be suspicious." Many of the overcrowded
boats capsized with all passengers lost at sea. And as more and more
defenseless refugees set out on the Gulf of Thailand and other nearby
waters, sometimes carrying gold and other small valuables, pirates began
to prey on the boats. According to some estimates, as many as 50 percent of all those who left Vietnam perished beneath the waves or at the
hands of pirates (Whitmore 1985). Those who survived often told hor-
rific stories. "We were in the boat for three weeks," reported one man.
"After two weeks, we started running out of water and rice. Running out
of water was the worst. We ran out of gas and we thought we would just
have to drift until we died. On the sixteenth day, it started to rain, heavy
rain, and we knew that it was dangerous for our little boat, but we were
glad of it because it meant fresh water. We filled our water cans with the
rain. Finally, we saw a tanker and it stopped and we knew we would
live."

Publicity given to the plight of the boat people, together with the
appalling stories told by Cambodian survivors of the Khmer Rouge era
who had fled into Thailand, and the growing desperation of the neighboring countries most affected by the continuous flow of refugees, awak-
ened the sympathies of the United States and other Western countries
and brought about a new willingness to receive refugees. In April 1979,
these countries resettled about 27,000 people fleeing from Vietnam; in
May, this number almost doubled, and in June, the number went up to
57,000 (Tollefson 1989). The international efforts to resettle refugees led
to the development of a system of overseas refugee camps and to the
emergence of a sizable Vietnamese ethnic group in the United States.

THE RESETTLEMENT CAMPS

Refugee Camps in the United States

By the middle of May 1975, the first wave of roughly 125,000 Vietnamese refugees had entered the United States. To manage this sudden influx, the U.S. government set up five reception centers at Camp Pendleton in California, Fort Indiantown Gap in Pennsylvania, Fort Chaffee in Arkansas, Eglin Air Force Base in Florida, and a military base in Guam. These reception centers served as places where refugees could be interviewed by voluntary agencies and then assigned to sponsors around the country.

U.S. government officials had not planned on a large Vietnamese influx, and most had no desire to create a new ethnic group in one or more ports of entry. According to the sociologist Rubén G. Rumbaut (1995b), the goal of resettlement through the reception centers was to disperse refugees to "avoid another Miami." Consequently, the initial resettlement efforts sought a wide geographic dispersal of Vietnamese families. U.S. policies also focused on a program of "Americanization." In addition to formal schooling for children, refugee camps operated classes for adults in the English language and on American life and culture. These adult classes attempted to provide Vietnamese refugees with basic survival skills such as shopping and budgeting, as well as instruction in how to interact with Americans socially and in the workplace.

If the Vietnamese had to learn to live in a radically new environment, American officials faced the opposite problem—learning how to meet the needs of a new and unexpected population. The appearance of the resettlement camps provoked the earliest studies of Vietnamese refugees in the United States by American scholars. Mental health and health care of refugees were the overriding concerns of these early studies (Kelly 1977; Liu, Lamanna, and Murata 1979; Rahe et al. 1978), which offer some of the most detailed descriptions of the backgrounds and situations of Vietnamese refugees in the mid-1970s.

Life in the forts that had been turned into refugee camps was spartan. The newcomers often lived in tents and slept on cots. In some of the camps, they had to wait in line to get their meals or to use the bathroom. Camp life was made more stressful for the refugees by the uncertainties about when and where they would be resettled and how they would organize their lives on their own in an unfamiliar environment, as well as by anxiety about how loved ones left behind in Vietnam were doing. Many of these early camp dwellers managed to cope successfully with their situation, however, by relying heavily on emotional support from their families and kin. Research found that those in multigenerational families, in particular, fared much better psychologically than those who had fled alone, and that young children or adolescents who had been separated from parents and other family members experienced more serious psychological problems than those in intact families or with relatives (Harding and Looney 1977).

Although set up for the purpose of dispersal and assimilation, the U.S. camps yielded an opposite effect. By bringing large numbers of Vietnamese people together in an American context, the camps served as places where refugees started to develop a conscious identity as "Vietnamese" and to organize their life in "Vietnamese Villages" (Liu, Lamanna, and Murata 1979). Many of the camp residents developed a strong sense of comradeship with other Vietnamese refugees despite socioeconomic differences. Intermediaries who knew English well assisted others in their dealings with the Americans. The first Vietnamese-language publications in the United States, such as Camp Pendleton's *Dat Lanh*, were produced. Some of the refugees even showed reluctance to leave these village-like Vietnamese environments when they were finally relocated with American sponsors, despite the hardships and strains of camp life (Liu, Lamanna, and Murata 1979). Between September and December of 1975, however, all the U.S. camps were closed, and most Americans expected that their closure marked the end of the Indo-Chinese refugee crisis.

Overseas Refugee Camps

When the large numbers of "boat people" created a new crisis, an international conference was convened in Geneva in July 1979 to address the problem, and the United States and other developed countries made pledges to increase their resettlement of Southeast Asian refugees. The Philippines agreed to provide a site on the Bataan Peninsula to serve as a processing center, a place where Indochinese approved for entry into the United States or another country could be held pending paperwork and location of sponsors. Two other refugee camps, at Galang in Indonesia and at Phanat Nikhom in Thailand, also became processing centers. Together, these three refugee camps became institutionalized transitional cities as well as educational institutions for the resettlement of Southeast Asian refugees.

Refugees in the overseas camps lived in "billets," single rooms in rows of long wooden houses. Each family was assigned a single billet, or several single adults might be housed together in a billet. Rice and other basic foods, as well as charcoal for cooking, were supplied to each refugee household. Camp residents had to carry their water in buckets from centrally located sources.

Like their counterparts in the earlier U.S. camps, Vietnamese refugees in these overseas camps suffered from extremely high levels of anxiety and emotional distress. In addition to their own hardships, they were grief-stricken and disoriented at the loss of family members and friends who had perished at sea or remained in Vietnam. Moreover, they were extremely anxious about which country would accept them and how long they would have to wait for relocation.

Most of the refugees held in overseas camps had little exposure to Western culture. They generally spoke little or no English and had few of the skills needed for competing in industrialized labor markets. In the spring of 1980, the U.S. State Department launched the Overseas Refugee Training Programs to address the needs of Indochinese refugees and to prepare them for resettlement in the United States. Some of these programs included English as a Second Language (ESL), Cultural Orientation (CO), and Work Orientation (WO). ESL put refugees into formal classes that helped them acquire or improve English language skills. CO was designed to familiarize refugees with American culture and way of life. It provided cross-cultural education that enabled refugees understand the differences in values, norms, and intercultural communications. It also dealt with many personal problems and issues, such as role changes, family planning, and spouse tension, that refugees often encountered during the resettlement process (Ancel and Hamilton 1987). WO was basically a job training program, designed to familiarize refugees with workplace rules and behavioral guidelines reflecting the cultural expectations of the workplace and the behavior and attitude expected of employees (Schumacher 1987). Child care centers were created to care for children while their parents were participating in these programs.

There were also programs specifically designed to help the children of refugees, including Preparing Refugees for Elementary Programs (PREP) and Preparation for American Secondary Schools (PASS). PREP targeted children aged 6 to 11½, helping them to develop language, academic, and social skills to ease their transition to new schools in the United States (Purdham et al. 1987). PASS prepared children and adolescents aged 11½ to 16 for entry into American high schools. While ESL was a main component of the PASS curriculum, the program also focused on how to behave in school and how to get along in an American-style school setting (Maciel 1987).

As in the earlier U.S. camps, family relations were important in enabling Vietnamese refugees to deal with transition and isolation. Since family members were often lost or left behind, the flight from Vietnam broke up many families. Moreover, family role changes occurred in the camps, often foretelling further changes in America. Children had to take on greater responsibility for household tasks and care of younger siblings than they had to in Vietnam. Overall, however, interviews with former refugees and observations in refugee camps have led to the conclusion that the camps, far from weakening Vietnamese families, actually strengthened them (Liu, Lamanna, and Murata 1979). Having lost their citizenship status and other forms of support, the refugees were driven to rely even more heavily on family members and friends who shared a similar culture and similar life experiences.

THE AMERICAN RECEPTION

The Impact of U.S. Refugee Admission Policies

Initially, the United States admitted Vietnamese refugees as a response to a special emergency, rather than as part of an ongoing process of resettlement. On April 18, 1975, President Gerald Ford authorized the entry into the United States of 130,000 refugees from the three countries of Indo-China (Vietnam, Cambodia, and Laos), 125,000 of whom were Vietnamese. At the time, the president's action was considered a one-time response to the victory of socialist forces in those countries. But the refugee exodus showed no sign of slowing down, and the crisis of 1979 and 1980 created pressure for a new refugee policy, which led to the passage of the Refugee Act of 1980. This act eliminated the old "seventh preference category" in the Hart-Celler Act of 1965, which had admitted refugees as a limited proportion of the total number of immigrants allowed into the United States. Instead, the 1980 Refugee Act provided for an annual number of admissions for refugees to be independent of the number of immigrants admitted and to be established each year by the president in consultation with Congress. This act involved the most comprehensive piece of refugee legislation in U.S. history, putting in place a policy of dealing with refugee resettlement as a continuing process rather than as reactions to emergency events.

Another important refugee policy is The Orderly Departure Program (ODP). The ODP was created in late May 1979 as the result of an agreement between the United Nations High Commission for Refugees and the Hanoi government, in response to the worldwide attention attracted by the boat people. The ODP mainly facilitated the departure of former South Vietnamese officers and soldiers, in prison or reeducation camps, and their families. It allowed persons interviewed and approved by U.S. officials in Vietnam for resettlement in America to leave by plane with their Vietnamese passports. By 1989, 165,000 Vietnamese had been admitted to the United States under the ODP, and by the mid-1990s this number had grown to over 200,000. When asked in Versailles Village, New Orleans, how they arrived in the United States, many Vietnamese said that they came as ODPs, and some Vietnamese children still identify their parents as such, although the youngsters may not know what the initials mean.

The Amerasian Homecoming Act of 1988

Amerasian children were the sons and daughters of Vietnamese women and American men who had been stationed in Vietnam during the war. In Vietnam, the physically distinct Amerasians lived as impoverished castaways, frequently targeted as objects of prejudice and discrimination by other Vietnamese and ostracized by a society that referred to them as *bui doi* (literally, children of the "dust of life"), the equivalent of "trash." In Vietnam, these Amerasians lived on the streets and survived by selling cigarettes or peanuts. Some never had a formal education, and a lot of them were orphans (DeBonis 1995; Schultz 1983). Throughout the decade and a half after the Americans left Vietnam, visitors to Ho Chi Minh City frequently remarked on the blue-eyed or black-skinned children (and, later, adolescents or young adults) seen begging or selling peanuts on the streets. All Amerasians suffered the taunts of their Vietnamese peers: "Amerasians no good. Go to America" (reported in the *Los Angeles Times,* April 13, 1989).

The United States government admitted Amerasians to the United

States as immigrants as early as 1975 but granted them eligibility for assistance benefits as refugees. Before the Amerasian Homecoming Act, about 6,000 Amerasians and 11,000 of their relatives left Vietnam legally under the ODP provisions. Just how many Amerasians were still left in Vietnam by the mid-1980s was difficult to pin down, because no official census was taken; U.S. estimates of the population were in the vicinity of 10,000, but Vietnamese officials thought that 16,000 was a more realistic number. In 1988, the U.S. Congress passed the Amerasian Homecoming Act, lifting quotas on Amerasian immigration and directing the U.S. government to bring as many of the Amerasian children to the United States as possible. Under the act, the United States cut the documentary requirement for an Amerasian to leave Vietnam to a minimum. "Essentially an Amerasian's face is his passport," said an U.S. official. "If you look like an Amerasian, we don't care if you have any documents at all. You don't have to have an identified father to move somebody out" (cited in the *Los Angeles Times,* April 13, 1989). After Amerasians and their families were allowed a special status under the Amerasian Homecoming Act in 1988, Amerasian children in Vietnam suddenly became "golden children," as many Vietnamese families claimed them in order to emigrate. By 1993, approximately 17,000 Amerasian children and young adults and about 65,000 of their accompanying family members had been resettled in the United States under this act.

The Humanitarian Operation Program of 1989

Political prisoners and their families have constituted the largest category of Vietnamese refugees admitted to the United States since 1990. Some former South Vietnamese civilian and military officials had been imprisoned in reeducation camps in Vietnam since 1975, and many of those who had been released from the camps were marginal members of a society that discriminated against them and their families in employment, housing, and education. In 1989, the United States and the Socialist Republic of Vietnam agreed that current and former detainees in reeducation camps would be allowed to leave for the United States.

Over 70,000 people have arrived in the United States under the Humanitarian Operation Program. Former political prisoners are often referred to in Vietnamese American communities as "HOs," and they have formed mutual assistance organizations with names such as the "HO Union." The HOs and their families have been arriving in the United

States in a context that is vastly different from that of the early Vietnamese refugees. Ethnic Vietnamese communities have been fully established in many parts of the United States, and the former political prisoners often have relatives in these communities who can provide support networks.

Government Resettlement Policy and Assistance

From the outset, U.S. refugee resettlement policy had two goals: minimizing the refugees' impact on the communities that would receive them and integrating them into American society as quickly as possible. The effort to minimize impact led initially to a policy of scattering Southeast Asians around the country. In later years, secondary migration and Vietnamese-sponsored resettlement resulted in the emergence of distinctive Vietnamese communities. Nonetheless, the early attempts at dispersion gave rise to Vietnamese communities in such places as New Orleans, Oklahoma City, Biloxi, Galveston, and Kansas City, that had previously received few immigrants from Asia.

Integration involved comprehensive preparation and support, beginning with the government-sponsored programs in the camps to help refugees prepare for resettlement described earlier in this chapter. The elaborate organizational structure developed to resettle Southeast Asian refugees in the United States operated under the Office of Refugee Resettlement of the U.S. Department of Health and Human Services. While a chief goal of resettlement was to help refugees achieve economic independence as quickly as possible, almost all Vietnamese refugees received generous government aid. Refugee status thus altered the encounter of the Vietnamese with America in ways that distinguished their experience from that of other immigrants.

Unlike most immigrants who arrive in the United States under the sponsorship of families or, less frequently, U.S. employers, the earliest contacts between Vietnamese refugees and Americans or American society involved voluntary agencies (VOLAGs). Most VOLAGs were private charitable organizations, the largest of which was the U.S. Catholic Conference. These organizations operated under contract to the United States government to be immediately responsible for resettlement. Before arriving in the United States, refugees in camps were assigned to specific VOLAGs, which then had the task of finding sponsors who would take financial and personal responsibility for refugee families for up to two years. Local VOLAGs and other organizations received funding from the government to provide a variety of services, including housing, English-language tutoring, job training and employment, and legal assistance (Lanphier 1983).

VOLAGs and individual or group sponsors played a crucial role in shaping the experience of the Vietnamese in the United States. Newly arrived refugees depended heavily on their sponsors. During the 1970s, a majority of sponsors were either VOLAGs or individual churches, but once the early refugees were settled, many of them quickly took over the sponsorship role for new arrivals. In 1984, for example, 37.4 percent of all Southeast Asian refugees, mostly Vietnamese, were sponsored by relatives who had arrived earlier, 33.7 percent by VOLAGs, 14.2 percent by churches, 7.8 percent by individual non–Indo-Chinese Americans, and 6.9 percent by Indo-Chinese nonrelatives (Tran 1991).

The voluntary agencies did more than find sponsors for refugees and places where they could live. During the newcomers' first month in the United States, these VOLAGs also provided the refugees with whatever support services they needed. Many voluntary agencies also offered assistance with job searches and English-language classes that extended well beyond that time. After the first month, the refugees became eligible for cash and medical assistance programs. The Vietnamese mainly used three types of cash assistance programs: Aid to Families with Dependent Children (AFDC), Supplemental Security Income (SSI), and Refugee Cash Assistance (RCA), the first two of which were forms of public assistance, or welfare, available to U.S. citizens and permanent residents from low-income families with children or the elderly or disabled poor. All refugees were generally eligible to receive RCA during their first six to eighteen months. They were also entitled to apply for food stamps. Despite this willingness to provide public assistance to refugees, the general policy of the American government was to encourage Vietnamese and other Southeast Asians to be economically self-sufficient and independent.

As the number of refugees soared, resettlement officials became concerned that the government was importing large numbers of permanent recipients of taxpayers' dollars. They therefore focused on employment training—both in overseas refugee camps and in local communities receiving refugees—and on programs that helped refugees make contact with employers. Some observers were critical of this type of job-oriented refugee training. These critics maintained that the U.S. refugee education program was characterized by condescension, official paranoia concerning "welfare dependency," and an eagerness to push refugees into minimum wage jobs (Tollefson 1989). These charges, however, over-looked the delicate political atmosphere created by the use of American tax dollars to fund the immigration of hundreds of thousands of people, many of whom threatened to become public charges upon arrival. Indeed, almost all Vietnamese refugees began on welfare, and some seemed trapped in welfare dependency. Whether they continued to drain tax dollars, however, was a matter of debate. In the chapters that follow, it will been seen that welfare dependency has steadily declined, that labor force participation has significantly increased, and that ethnic entrepreneurship has burgeoned.

Public Opinion

Official policy is only one of the forces shaping the reception that the Vietnamese encountered; another is public opinion. Since the end of the Vietnam War, the American public has had an ambivalent attitude toward receiving Vietnamese refugees. A Gallup poll taken in 1975, at the time of the initial entry of the Vietnamese, indicated that a majority of Americans would have preferred to keep the Vietnamese out of the United States (Kelly 1986). While publicity given to the boat people generated widespread public sympathy, Americans still had mixed feelings toward Vietnam and things Vietnamese. Many Americans felt that such culturally different people were simply too alien to be accepted. Senator S. I. Hayakawa of California remarked in 1979, "I get many letters from my home state saying that I should do everything in my power to keep the refugees from coming to the United States; that they bring with them mysterious diseases; that there is not enough room for them in America, or that they are Communist spies" (p. 3).

Americans sometimes also saw the Vietnamese as new economic competitors. Early research found that Americans of lower socioeconomic status—those most likely to have to compete with the new arrivals for jobs—were significantly more prejudiced against the Vietnamese than Americans of higher socioeconomic status (Cotter and Cotter 1979). The entry of Vietnamese people into the fishing industry along the Gulf Coast in the late 1970s and early 1980s provoked resentment from native-born fishermen concerned about competition (Bankston and Zhou 1996).

Prejudice against the Vietnamese occasionally led to violence. In 1983, for example, a group of white high school students attacked a Vietnamese high school student in Davis, California, and stabbed him to death. In 1989, in Raleigh, North Carolina, a Chinese American who was mistaken for Vietnamese was beaten to death by men who were angry over the Vietnam War. In 1990, in Houston, a young Vietnamese American was stomped to death by a racially motivated mob. These events were, of course, exceptional, but they provided the most extreme manifestations of the public disquiet over the arrival of the Vietnamese.

THE IMPACT OF RESETTLEMENT ON VIETNAMESE CHILDREN

The traumas of sudden exile have continued to haunt foreign-born Vietnamese children old enough to remember the flight and resettlement. The anthropologist Paul J. Rutledge (1992) recounted the stories of a young teen-aged girl raped by pirates at sea and a young man who, escaping from Vietnam across Cambodia at the age of nine, was captured and beaten by Vietnamese soldiers. Those who arrived under the auspices of the Orderly Departure Program or the Humanitarian Operation may be free of such awful memories, but they must still deal with concerns for loved ones left behind and the loss of the world of early childhood. Those who stayed in refugee camps experienced their families' extreme anxiety and insecurity, and those who were separated from their families fared even worse (Harding and Looney 1977). Many older children in refugee camps had to assume adult tasks and responsibilities. Almost all the children suffered from the general disruption of their lives (Williams 1990).

U.S.-born Vietnamese children and those who arrived in the United States as infants have no clear personal memory of life in Vietnam, nor of the flight from the ancestral land, or of life in the refugee camps. But the abruptness of the move from Vietnam to America has made life in Vietnam a continuing reality, even for the younger generation who have never been there. Parents often communicate to children with a strong sense of determination born of the struggle to survive. One 20-year-old female university student recounted the story of her own departure from Vietnam, as it had been told to her by her parents:

> When I was a baby, my mom and dad left Vietnam in a little boat crowded with other people. They were at sea for a long time, and I got sick. My mom said that I got real skinny and sick. There was a doctor in the boat who told her to throw me overboard, because I was going to die anyway and they needed to save on food. No matter how much the

people on the boat argued with her, she wouldn't let go of me. I guess it's just because she was so stubborn that I'm here now.

A 19-year-old male college student also had the story of family hardships impressed on him:

> My family left Vietnam because life was so hard under the Communists. We made it to Malaysia and we stayed in a refugee camp on an island there, Pulau Bidong. I only remember a little bit about it because I was only two when we got there and only three when we left. But my parents are always telling me how hard life was there. There wasn't much to eat and they had to carry their water back to these little shacks they lived in. They always tell me this story whenever I complain about anything and they say: "See, you have it pretty good now. Look what we all had to go through to get here."

The difficulties suffered in Vietnam and in the move from Vietnam to America have given adult Vietnamese a strong sense of their own identity, and the families have attempted to pass this ethnic identity on to their children. The traumas of repression and the pains of exile are not just individual biographical episodes but defining experiences for this whole group of people. While some of the children, whether born in the United States or overseas, may reject or resent their past, it remains an ever-present influence on their own lives.

Young Vietnamese, most of whom are in the group described as the 1.5 generation, must deal with their personal experience or their family history of traumatic exile. They face a unique set of challenges. At present, the most immediate dilemma derives from the social and economic marginality of the first generation. Members of the younger generation often perceive dependence on public assistance as a matter of shame and embarrassment. Even those whose families no longer receive public assistance know that their parents had to start their lives in America as public charges. The children not only admit to discomfort about welfare dependency but also feel uneasy about the relatively low-status jobs held by their parents. "I don't like it that my parents had to take welfare," remarked one young man. "I don't blame them, but I will never be on welfare." These children realize that their parents have very little chance of moving ahead in the labor market because of their limited human capital and English language skills.

But welfare is not just a matter of embarrassment; the young people also suffer real hardship. As will be discussed in greater detail in the next chapter, public assistance incomes are extremely limited, and poverty has slowed the adjustment of Vietnamese families to American society. These families can afford to provide their children with few economic resources and advantages, and they frequently live in low-income communities.

Economic and social marginality has put strains on parent-child relations and social relations with the group. For the younger generation, one of the greatest issues is whether to conform to their parents' cultural expectations or instead to rebel against them. Most children of immigrants face this same question, but for Vietnamese children, the fact that their parents are not simply immigrants but refugees adds a unique dimension since hardships in Vietnam and the sufferings of exile have created a shared family myth that shapes common understandings and behavior.

The sudden resettlement has created a power imbalance between Vietnamese parents and their children. The children usually have greater familiarity with American society than their parents do and must often act as translators and intermediaries between their families and the larger society. Not only do children see their parents as dependent on public assistance; the parents depend on the children themselves. This experience often undermines the children's respect for their parents and creates confusion regarding family roles.

There is also a gap in societal outlook between parents and children. Vietnamese parents are aware that their place in American society is tenuous and marginal, but they tend to attribute their position to their recent arrival not to an unfair class system. Consequently, the parents emphasize the opportunities offered in the United States rather than restrictions or discrimination found here. A 16-year-old girl reported:

> My mother is always telling me that she wanted to go to school in Vietnam and couldn't. So she says that I have to take advantage of the opportunity that I have here to get an education. She tells me that my dad and her are only refugees and they have to take whatever comes, but that if I don't accomplish everything they want for me there's no one to blame but myself.

The children feel that they are outsiders in America, however, and find it hard to accept their parents' optimistic view. Even members of the 1.5 or second generation who have had no personal experience of prejudice are aware of the somewhat tepid welcome extended to their group. "A lot of times I feel that Americans, I mean non-Asian Americans, don't really like us," remarked a 19-year-old college sophomore. "Sometimes I think they think of us as just these strange charity cases. I know that some of them don't like us, but I don't always know who thinks what. It makes me wonder what's going on inside of people's heads."

Life in low-income and minority-dominated neighborhoods can limit the chances for educational achievement. In underprivileged communities, the schools may provide poor learning environments and may be unsafe. Dominated by native-born American peers with little hope for the future, the schools are often permeated by a strong adversarial subculture that discourages learning, as will be described in detail in chapter 8. This confrontation with disruptive neighborhoods and poor public schools presents young Vietnamese with a forced-choice dilemma: Should they strive to meet their parents' expectations for academic achievement and as a result suffer ostracism as "uncool," "nerdy," or "acting white" by their American peers, most of whom are members of other racial minorities? Or should they submit to peer pressure and attempt to become "American" in the process, adopting the cultural ways, including the language and behavior, of the underclass?

In sum, growing up American can be a smooth acceptance or a traumatic confrontation, as the children of refugees are frequently caught in the conflictual demands from their families and on the street. Not only are there "generation gaps" between the first generation and the younger, or the American-born, generation, but there are also cultural gaps between the children who have spent most of their lives in the United States and the children who have arrived in late childhood or adolescence with regard to how to become American. The suddenness of the creation of the Vietnamese ethnic group has led to ethnic communities with fairly sharp lines of distinction between the "Vietnamese" Vietnamese and the "Americanized" Vietnamese. How that split has come about and the implications it holds for the adaptation are the subject of the remaining of this book. The chapters to come will provide a detailed look at the young people who have grown up in the wake of one of the largest government-sponsored programs of refugee resettlement in history. They will examine how coping with life in the new country has shaped Vietnamese ethnicity for the younger generation, how Vietnamese children have risen out of or been trapped in the unfavorable circumstances that receive their families, and how the second generation has continued to carry with them the history of their forebears as they form a new American ethnic group.

—— Chapter 2 ——

Resettlement

We want everybody to know that we do exist here, to share that we come
here for freedom, to show our gratitude, and that we are looking to the
future, which is our children.

—A Vietnamese American doctor

O n a mild spring day in 1994, in the heart of Little Saigon, a thriv-
ing Vietnamese community in Orange County, California, a press
briefing on "Project 20—Vietnamese Americans Twenty Years After
(1975 to 1995)" was held in a library room full of media representatives.
The project's administrator, also the editor-in-chief and publisher of a
Vietnamese newspaper, *Nguoi Viet Daily News*, announced a series of
forthcoming events to celebrate the identity of Vietnamese Americans,
their leadership, their lives here in freedom, and their gratitude to the
United States. Project 20 also included special programs for the children
of refugees, born or raised in America, to remind them of their heritage
and to help them understand what and who they are, what they will be,
and what they can do for their adopted homeland and for their land of
their ancestry (*Nguoi Viet Daily News*, May 12, 1990). As a Vietnamese
doctor pointed out in remarks to the group, which opened this chapter,
the children are their future.

Similar commemorative activities were organized in Vietnamese communities across the country. The Vietnamese, most of whom arrived as
refugees with fresh memories of protracted war and traumatic experiences of flight, have been struggling to rebuild their lives in America and
have rapidly become a visible component of the American ethnic mosaic. This chapter describes how Vietnamese refugees and their children
have fared in the process of resettlement and in the transition from
involuntary expatriates to permanent residents. First some general information is offered about the changes in demographic and socioeconomic
characteristics of this group over the past twenty years. It is followed by a
discussion of how group characteristics have interacted with contextual
forces to affect the adaptation of refugees and their children.

GENERAL DEMOGRAPHIC TRENDS

Up until 1975, only a small number of Vietnamese made their home in the United States. Because the U.S. Census Bureau did not begin to record this population specifically as Vietnamese until 1980, their exact numbers were unknown; the best estimates suggest that there were about 15,000 in the early 1970s. According to the Immigration and Naturalization Service, the United States admitted only 4,561 Vietnam-born persons between 1961 and 1970 (representing only 1.2 percent of the total immigration from Asia). Most of these Vietnamese were wives of U.S. servicemen, or students and trainees on nonimmigrant visas (Skinner 1980); almost none were children.

Only with the first evacuation of about 65,000 "high-risk" persons out of Vietnam by air and by sea in late April 1975 did the first large-scale contingent of Vietnamese arrive in the United States (U.S. Department of State 1975a). Between 1971 and 1980, the number of Vietnam-born arrivals climbed to 172,820 (making up 11 percent of Asian immigration), and 409,082 more Vietnamese gained entry to the United States between 1981 and 1994, with over three-quarters officially admitted as refugees (USINS 1996).

Table 2.1 shows the proportion of new arrivals by type of admission in selected years between 1978 and 1994. Most contemporary immigrants from the rest of Asia and other parts of the world came to the United States under the sponsorship of close family members; by contrast, the great bulk of the Vietnamese came as refugees, who were admitted under emergency Southeast Asian refugee programs and were thus exempt from numerical limitations under the 1965 Hart-Celler Act. The end of the Vietnam War made Vietnam the latest source country of refugees resettled in the United States. During the 1980s, according to the Office of Refugee Resettlement, Vietnamese refugees represented almost a third of total refugee admissions into the United States (USHHS 1993).

The passage of the 1988 Amerasian Homecoming Act further swelled the flow; the number of Amerasians and their families arriving in the United States increased from 213 in 1987 to about 13,000 in 1990 and to about 17,300 in 1993. Since then, although Vietnamese refugees have continued to arrive in substantial numbers, their proportion of the total refugee flow has steadily decreased. Over time, the proportion of family-sponsored immigrants is likely to increase as the earlier arrivals get settled and become naturalized U.S. citizens.

TABLE 2.1 Vietnam-Born Persons Admitted into the United States, by Selected Types of Admission, Selected Fiscal Years

	1978	1980	1982	1987	1990	1992	1993	1994
Subject to numerical limitations (%)	2.56	9.56	3.08	14.07	17.83	15.79	9.75	9.84
Exempt from numerical limitations								
Parents, spouses, or children of U.S. citizens (%)	.53	.07	1.00	6.05	13.15	14.54	10.46	11.69
Refugee and asylee adjustment (%)	96.89	90.31	95.82	79.79	42.09	41.36	50.74	66.07
Special immigrants or IRCA legalization (%)	.03	.06	.08	.08	.30	.02	.00	.00
Amerasian provision (%)	.00	.00	.01	.01	26.62	28.28	29.04	12.40
Number admitted	88,543	43,483	72,553	29,993	48,792	77,735	59,614	41,345

Source: Statistical Yearbook of the Immigration and Naturalization Service, 1978 to 1995.
Note: Totals may not always equal to 100 because of rounding.

Geographic Distribution

Unlike immigrants from elsewhere in Asia, Vietnamese refugees initially lacked preexisting ethnic community networks to assist them; moreover, the U.S. government and the voluntary agencies working mainly under government contracts oversaw their resettlement and in most cases decided their destinations. As has already been noted, U.S. refugee policy has aimed at residential dispersion. Vietnamese refugees have indeed been dispersed all over the United States, as table 2.2 shows, establishing a presence even in those midwestern and mountain states least populated by recent immigrants.

But only some have scattered; most have regrouped to form large concentrations at the state, metropolitan, and neighborhood levels, reproducing settlement patterns characteristic of most other contemporary immigrants. One could notice the tendency toward concentration as early as 1978, when 27 percent of all Vietnamese refugees in the United States lived in California alone and another 35 percent were concentrated in just nine other states. Geographic concentration became steadily more visible in the 1980s and 1990s. In 1980, over a third of the Vietnamese lived in California, and another 36 percent concentrated in nine other states. By 1990, almost half the Vietnamese had settled or resettled in the state of California alone, and about a third lived in the other nine states on the top-ten list. Figure 2.1 illustrates the concentration.

This tendency toward convergence in a handful of places results from two trends: secondary internal migration and subsequent international migration. We have limited information on the magnitude of internal migration among the Vietnamese, but we do know that the secondary migration occurred within a short period of time. A 1984 survey found that almost a third of the Vietnamese refugees in Orange County, California, were secondary migrants from other states, who moved because of climate, better job opportunities, and the existence of an established ethnic community (Baldwin 1984). More information comes from the 1990 census, which contains a question on place of residence five years prior to the census. Between 1985 and 1990, as figure 2.2 shows, internal migration shifted the Vietnamese population westward and southward. The Midwest lost Vietnamese residents to the Northeast and the South; the Northeast lost to the South; and the West gained from all other regions. As the most likely destination for westbound migrations, California experienced the highest net gains, while Texas and Louisiana were the most likely destinations for southbound migrants.

TABLE 2.2 Distribution of Vietnamese Americans in the United States, by State, 1978, 1980, and 1990

	1978		1980		1990		Growth % 1980 to 1990
	N^a	% Vietnamese in U.S.	N	% Vietnamese in U.S.	N	% Vietnamese in U.S.	
Top 10 States in 1990							
California	46,637	27.46	89,601	34.23	280,223	45.60	212.75
Texas	15,894	9.36	29,112	11.12	69,634	11.33	139.19
Virginia	6,791	4.00	10,000	3.82	20,693	3.37	106.93
Washington	6,104	3.59	9,838	3.76	18,696	3.04	90.04
Louisiana	7,237	4.26	10,884	4.16	17,598	2.86	61.69
Florida	5,454	3.21	7,600	2.90	16,346	2.66	115.08
Pennsylvania	7,642	4.50	9,257	3.54	15,887	2.59	71.62
New York	4,596	2.71	6,644	2.54	15,555	2.53	134.12
Massachusetts	1,582	.93	3,172	1.12	15,449	2.51	387.04
Illinois	5,210	3.07	7,034	2.69	10,309	1.68	46.56
Other States							
Alabama	1,227	.72	1,333	.51	2,274	.37	70.59
Alaska	229	.13	383	.15	582	.09	51.96
Arizona	1,224	.72	1,932	.74	5,239	.85	171.17
Arkansas	1,739	1.02	2,051	.78	2,348	.38	14.48
Colorado	3,464	2.04	4,026	1.54	7,210	1.17	79.09
Connecticut	1,642	.97	1,825	.70	4,085	.66	123.84
Delaware	193	.11	205	.08	348	.06	69.76
District of Columbia	705	.42	505	.19	747	.12	47.92
Georgia	1,607	.95	2,294	.88	7,801	1.27	240.06
Hawaii	2,724	1.60	3,463	1.32	5,468	.89	57.90
Idaho	417	.25	429	.16	600	.10	39.86
Indiana	1,900	1.12	2,338	.89	2,467	.40	5.52
Iowa	3,055	1.80	2,476	.95	2,882	.47	16.40
Kansas	2,185	1.29	3,690	1.41	6,577	1.07	78.24
Kentucky	1,021	.60	1,090	.42	1,506	.25	38.17

Maine	284	.17	465	.18	642	.10	38.06
Maryland	2,856	1.68	4,131	1.58	8,862	1.44	114.52
Michigan	2,916	1.72	4,209	1.61	6,117	1.00	45.33
Minnesota	4,160	2.45	5,866	2.24	9,387	1.53	60.02
Mississippi	776	.46	1,281	.49	3,815	.62	197.81
Missouri	3,006	1.77	3,179	1.21	4,380	.71	37.78
Montana	438	.26	275	.11	159	.03	−42.18
Nebraska	1,456	.86	1,438	.55	1,806	.29	25.59
Nevada	782	.46	1,124	.43	1,934	.31	72.06
New Hampshire	156	.09	209	.08	553	.09	164.59
New Jersey	1,872	1.10	2,884	1.10	7,330	1.19	154.16
New Mexico	735	.43	1,043	.40	1,485	.24	42.38
North Carolina	1,277	.75	2,391	.91	5,211	.85	117.94
North Dakota	275	.16	283	.11	281	.05	−.71
Ohio	2,994	1.76	3,905	1.34	4,964	.81	41.46
Oklahoma	3,518	2.07	4,671	1.78	7,320	1.19	56.71
Oregon	4,114	2.42	5,564	2.13	9,088	1.48	63.34
Rhode Island	749	.44	314	.12	772	.13	145.86
South Carolina	888	.52	1,072	.41	1,752	.29	63.43
South Dakota	448	.26	386	.15	268	.04	−30.57
Tennessee	1,386	.82	1,391	.53	2,062	.34	48.24
Utah	1,275	.75	2,108	.81	2,797	.46	32.69
Vermont	52	.03	85	.03	236	.04	177.65
West Virginia	154	.09	253	.10	184	.03	−27.27
Wisconsin	2,645	1.56	2,249	.86	2,494	.41	10.89
Wyoming	96	.06	167	.06	124	.02	−25.75
Total	169,823	100.00	262,125	100.00	614,547	100.00	134.80

Source: U.S. Census of Population and Housing, 1980 and 1990; Darrel Montero, *Vietnamese Americans: Patterns of Resettlement and Socioeconomic Adaptation in the United States* (Boulder, Col.: Westview Press, 1979), 8, table 1.2.

Note: Totals may not always equal 100 because of rounding.

[a] Vietnamese refugees only.

FIGURE 2.1   Distribution of Vietnamese in the United States, by
State, 1990

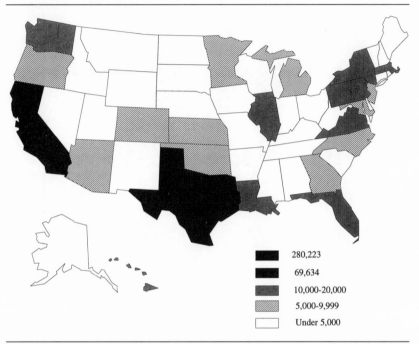

■	280,223
■	69,634
▨	10,000-20,000
▨	5,000-9,999
□	Under 5,000

Source: U.S. Census of Population and Housing, 1990.

Within states, the Vietnamese have also clustered in just a few metropolitan areas. As of 1990, over three-quarters of California's Vietnamese
population lived in four metropolitan areas—Orange County, Los Angeles, San Diego, and San Jose. In other states, the Vietnamese were
likely to converge in a single metropolitan area. In Texas, for example,
44 percent of the Vietnamese resided in Houston; in the metropolitan
area around Washington, D. C., that includes Maryland and Virginia,
76 percent of the Vietnamese lived in Washington, D.C.; in Washington
State, 71 percent of the Vietnamese lived in Seattle; and in Louisiana,
close to two-thirds of the Vietnamese lived in New Orleans. Moreover,
this same tendency to cluster occurred within metropolitan areas, so that
the Vietnamese often found themselves living in neighborhoods that had
large proportions of coethnics. Thus, despite government policies aimed
at dispersion, geographically centered Vietnamese communities have
been formed, drawing in growing numbers of compatriots through word
of mouth and through extensive kinship and family networks.

FIGURE 2.2   Migration Trends of Vietnamese in the United
States, 1985 to 1990

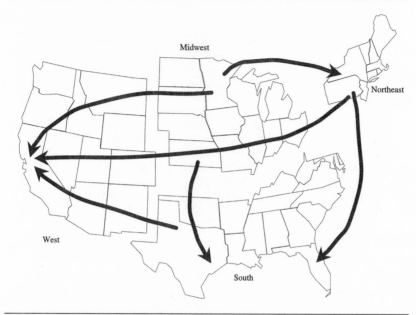

Source: U.S. Census of Population and Housing, 1990.

Sex Ratio, Age Structure, and Generational Distributions

The process of flight and resettlement has affected the demographic profile of the Vietnamese in the United States. As of 1990, the sex ratio was distinctly skewed, with many more males than females (about 113 males per 100 females, compared with 95 males per 100 females in the U.S. population overall). In general, refugee groups have often exhibited a skewed sex ratio, because men have been more successful than women in escaping. Comprised with the typical refugee pattern, the male/female ratio among the Vietnamese is actually more nearly balanced, reflecting the fact that Vietnamese fled in family groups rather than as individuals (Liu, Lamanna, and Murata 1979).

Other demographic characteristics are probably more important; the Vietnamese are much younger than the general American population, and they experience a much higher fertility rate. As of 1990, a substantial age gap separated the Vietnamese from the general U.S. population, as shown in figure 2.3, where the two age-sex pyramids offer sharp con-

FIGURE 2.3   Age-Sex Structures of U.S. Population and U.S.
Vietnamese Population, 1990

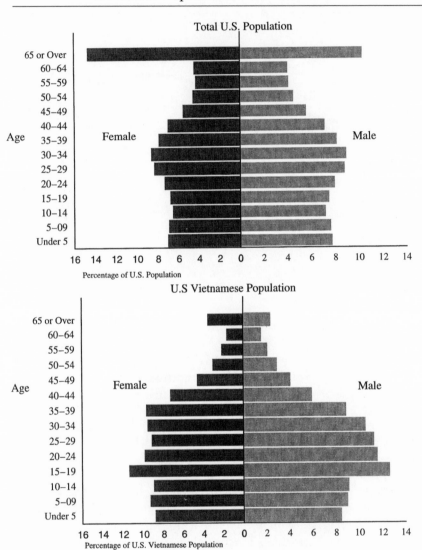

Source: U.S. Census of Population and Housing, 1990.

trasts both at the top and at the bottom. Overall, half the Vietnamese were
under 25 years of age, and only 3 percent were 65 or older, compared with
36 percent and 13 percent, respectively, for the U.S. population.

The unusually wide base of the Vietnamese pyramid is its most notable feature, attesting to the atypical flight pattern in which refugees made considerable effort to bring family members, particularly young children (Barringer, Gardner, and Levin 1993). The presence of a large number of children distinguished the Vietnamese flight from other refugee flights. A 1978 Department of Health, Education, and Welfare report found that 43 percent of the 1975 entrants were under 18 years of age, 37 percent between 18 and 34, and only 5 percent 65 or over. In 1980, the median age of the Vietnamese was only 21 years. Though it increased slightly to 25 years by 1990, the median age remained eight years lower than that of the U.S. population overall.

High fertility rates carried over from Vietnam also account for this skewed age structure (Rumbaut and Weeks 1986). While high fertility manifests itself in a high child/woman ratio (CWR)—396 children aged 0 to 4 per 1,000 Vietnam-born women aged 15 to 44, compared with 309 per 1,000 women in the overall population—it entails an important sociological consequence, the rapid expansion of the second generation. Although the overwhelming majority of the U.S. Vietnamese in 1990 were foreign-born, the U.S.-born component had increased from 9 percent in 1980 to 18 percent in 1990. More important for the future is the composition of the cohort under 25 years of age, which already made up half of the group; here the proportion born in the United States was one in three as of 1990 and has grown rapidly since then.

Table 2.3 displays the generational distribution for children and young adults under 25 years of age using the 5-percent Public Use Microdata Samples (PUMS) of the 1990 U.S. census. For comparison, non-Vietnamese Southeast Asians (Cambodians, Laotians, and Hmongs combined) and one established immigrant group (Chinese) are also shown. Two age groups are examined: children under 17 (most of whom live with at least one of their parents) and young adults between 18 and 24 (many of whom may have left their parents' homes to live by themselves). With these age groups, three foreign-born groups are categorized by age on arrival: those arriving before their fifth birthdays, those arriving between ages 5 and 12, and those arriving at adolescence. Because foreign-born children who arrived as preschoolers share many psychological and developmental traits with their U.S.-born counterparts and are thus almost fully part of the "new" world, they are included in the second generation. Those who arrived in adolescence are defined as the first generation, since they will have spent more years in the "old" world when they reach adulthood. Finally, those who arrived between the ages of 5 and 12 are defined as the 1.5 generation, a term coined by Rubén

TABLE 2.3   Generation by Age, Selected Ethnicities, 1990

	Vietnamese	Other Southeast Asian	Chinese
Aged 18 to 24[a]			
First generation (%)	45.0	51.2	39.0
1.5 generation (%)	47.7	46.3	23.3
Second generation (%)	7.3	2.5	37.7
Total (%)	100.0	100.0	100.0
N	4,271	2,222	8,726
Aged 0 to 17[b]			
First generation (%)	3.9	2.7	3.3
1.5 generation (%)	17.0	17.5	12.7
Second generation (%)	79.1	79.8	84.0
Total (%)	100.0	100.0	100.0
N	8,634	8,451	17,350

Source: U.S. Census of Population and Housing, 1990, 5-percent PUMS.
[a] Sample includes all persons aged 18 to 24. About 14 percent of Vietnamese, 9 percent of other Southeast Asian, and 7 percent of Chinese in this age group still lived with their parents.
[b] Sample included only children under 18 years of age who lived in family households containing at least one child of the household head or of the spouse of the household head.

G. Rumbaut to distinguish those who are in many ways "marginal to both the old and the new worlds, and are fully part of neither of them" (1991, 61).[1]

The top panel of table 2.3 shows that the 1.5 generation considerably overshadows the second generation (48 percent versus 7 percent) among the cohort of young adults aged 18 to 24. But the lower panel shows that the pattern is reversed among the 0 to 17 cohort (17 percent versus 79 percent). In both age cohorts, the Vietnamese and the other Southeast Asians show a similar generational pattern. The Vietnamese differ from the Chinese only in the older cohort, where Chinese young adults are more than five times as likely to be members of the second generation. In general, the refugee and immigrant groups included in table 2.3 all have experienced a rapid growth of the second generation.

Household Size and Family Structure

Large, extended households, which included minor children, unmarried grown children, married children, grandchildren, other relatives, and even nonrelatives, were the norm among the Vietnamese upon their arrival in the United States. A 1975 study of the initial refugee group found that approximately two-thirds of the refugees arrived in family units (which included nonrelatives who claimed to be family members for the sake of resettlement); the other third were single people. Among those fleeing with their families, half belonged to families of five to ten people, 7 percent to families of more than ten people, and the rest to families of four or fewer people (USHEW 1975a, 1975b). A slightly later study found that almost 40 percent of the Vietnamese households contained six people or more (Montero 1979).

Vietnamese households steadily decreased in size following resettlement; nonetheless, they remained larger than those of the general American population. In 1990, Vietnamese households averaged four persons per household and six persons per family household with children. By contrast, the same household types in the U.S. population were three and four persons, respectively. In general, the respondents in our Versailles Village study came from large households; the average respondent was the fifth-born child in the household. One respondent actually reported being the fourteenth-born child, and only a handful had grown up as only children (Bankston and Zhou 1995b).

Family size can influence children's lives and future in contradictory ways. Prior research summarized by the demographer Donald J. Hernandez (1986, 1993), has shown that large families can be both beneficial and disadvantageous for American children. Children with many siblings may enjoy greater opportunities for caring sibling companionship, for lasting love and friendship with siblings, and for experience in caring for younger siblings. But siblings can also compete for parental time and attention and for family resources, and that competition may have adverse consequences later in life. Large family size has little effect on the psychological well-being of children during adulthood, but children with many siblings appear to live in families with less marital and parental satisfaction, to complete fewer years of education, and to enter lower-status occupations with lower incomes when they reach adulthood than those with fewer siblings.

For the Vietnamese, however, large family size offers certain adaptive advantages. It allows for the pooling of household incomes and economies in household expenses such as housing, utilities, and transportation, as well as the provision of child care. Large family size also yields an environment conducive to learning, as the anthropologist Nathan Caplan and his associates found: "After dinner, the table is cleared, and homework begins. The older children, both male and female, help their younger siblings. Indeed, they seem to learn as much from teaching as from being taught" (Caplan, Choy, and Whitmore 1992, 39–40).

Family size is not all that counts; just as important is family structure. In the United States, the dominant family structure has been two-parent families. As of 1990, almost 80 percent of American families were married-couple families, and 72 percent of all American children under 18 lived in these married-couple families. Recent research has suggested that immigrant children from two-parent (especially two-natural-parent) families consistently display better psychological health, higher levels of academic achievement, and stronger educational aspirations than those in single-parent families (Rumbaut 1994b, 1996). There are ethnic and racial variations in household structures, however. Table 2.4 compares Vietnamese children with children of two other Asian categories and with children of two native-born groups—non-Latino blacks and whites—using the 5-percent PUMS. Four types of family households are considered: traditional breadwinner-homemaker families, in which male household heads worked full-time and their spouses stayed out of the labor force); other married-couple families; female-headed single-parent families; and male-headed single-parent families.

Among all groups, traditional breadwinner-homemaker families were no longer the norm. Over 80 percent of the children lived in married-couple families, except for black children, who disproportionately lived in single-parent households. The Vietnamese displayed proportions of family types similar to those of whites; they differed significantly from other Southeast Asians only in the proportion of traditional breadwinner-homemaker families and from the Chinese in single-parent families. For the Vietnamese, as well as for other Southeast Asians, single-parent families were primarily attributable to refugee flight, rather than to voluntary single-parenthood. Those missing immediate family members showed a strong tendency to live in family households with other related individuals. If two-parent families contribute to positive adaptation outcomes, all Asian immigrant children have a clear advantage over black children.

It has been suggested that the support of unbroken married-couple families, especially the traditional breadwinner-homemaker type, contributes to social and psychological well-being and to the school performance of children (Coleman et al. 1966). By contrast, our research to be reported later in this chapter indicates that the structure of social relations in which families are embedded is more important than family type per se. Strong and stable social relations within communities can

TABLE 2.4 Household Composition for School-Aged Children in the United States, Selected Ethnicities, 1990

	Vietnamese	Other Southeast Asian	Chinese	Black	White
Traditional married-couple families (%)[a]	20.0	11.7	25.4	7.8	25.4
Other married-couple families (%)[b]	61.5	72.5	66.6	38.8	59.4
Female-headed, single-parent families (%)	13.8	12.9	5.8	48.8	11.9
Male-headed, single-parent families (%)	4.7	2.9	2.2	4.6	3.3
N	8,634	9,424	17,350	110,801	72,956

Source: U.S. Census of Population and Housing, 1990, 5-percent PUMS.
Note: Sample includes children under 18 years of age who lived in family households containing at least one child of the household head or of the spouse of the household head. The ethnicities of black and white were undersampled.
[a] Includes married-couple families with a male full-time breadwinner and a female homemaker.
[b] Includes all other married-couple families (with two wage earners or with female breadwinner and male homemaker).

facilitate the formation and growth of social capital in single-parent as well as two-parent families. This form of social capital can, in turn, provide an essential adaptive mechanism for survival and a means of maintaining consistent standards, establishing role models, and ensuring parental authority and effective social control over children. Truncated social networks, on the other hand, can seriously weaken the ability of individual families to control the direction and the outcomes of their children's adaptation. If the presence of both parents at home is considered a source of social capital, the loss, or truncation, of the family system can reduce the access to social resources available to children (Fernández-Kelly 1995; Rumbaut 1996).

Most immigrant households in the United States are nuclear rather than extended families. While migration extends social and familial ties across national borders—ties that facilitate further migratory flows—it simultaneously disrupts the traditional family system and the social network of which the family is a part (Landale 1996). In some cases, family disruption and the resulting isolation from the ongoing networks of kinship relations in the homeland can cause serious problems for children's upbringing in the American context. The so-called "relayed migration" or "serial migration," a process under which members of an immigrant family arrive (either intentionally or involuntarily) at different times, can strain parent-child and sibling relationships (Sung 1987; Waters 1996). The truncation of family networks, when routine interactions among kins and former neighbors or friends are broken, can weaken traditional mechanisms of control and support.

SOCIOECONOMIC PROFILES

The initial group of Vietnamese refugees came from South Vietnam's privileged segment: generals, policemen, military officers, government ministers and civil servants, teachers, businessmen, employees of American agencies and corporations, and members of the elite class; these were people whose lives were most threatened by the new communist government (Baldwin 1982; Skinner 1980). Though many had relatively high levels of educational attainment, good occupational skills, knowledge of English, considerable exposure to Western cultures, and urban experiences, they did not constitute a homogeneous group. Their ranks included fervent anti-Communists, religious conservatives, liberal intellectuals, as well as apolitical professionals (Skinner 1980); over half were Catholics and over a quarter were Buddhists (Montero 1979; Caplan, Whitmore, and Choy 1989). But because of South Vietnam's sudden collapse and the need to flee almost immediately, most shared a common experience: leaving property and belongings behind and arriving as penniless as the less-privileged counterparts who came later.

Most members of this initial group came on the airlift, however, and were thus spared lengthy hardships while in flight. Later arrivals had it much worse. The second and third waves of Vietnamese refugees had to endure prolonged periods of extreme difficulty in overseas refugee camps before resettlement. In comparison with the initial group, later arrivals were also less skilled and were less likely to have had any urban experience. Their background made the adjustment to America hard but even so, members of the second and third waves managed to move ahead.

The Socioeconomic Characteristics of the Vietnamese: 1980 and 1990

The past two decades have seen great improvement in the overall socioeconomic profile of the Vietnamese in the United States, as can be seen in table 2.5. In 1980, over 90 percent of the Vietnamese were new arrivals; many spoke English with difficulty or not at all, and few were

TABLE 2.5 Socioeconomic Profile of Vietnamese in the United States, 1980 and 1990

	1980 Vietnamese	1990 Vietnamese	1990 All Americans
Immigrant Status[a]			
Length of U.S. residency			
five years or less (%)	90.3	24.5	24.7
Does not speak English "very well" (aged 5 and over) (%)	42.4	33.8	47.0
Not a U.S. citizen (%)	89.7	57.3	59.5
Schooling			
College graduate (aged 25 and over) (%)	12.9	17.4	20.3
High school dropout (aged 16 to 19) (%)	14.6	8.9	11.2
Labor Force Status (aged 16 and over)			
In the labor force (%)	57.3	64.5	65.3
Employed full-time-year-round (%)	48.7	53.4	55.0
Self-employed (%)	2.8	6.5	7.0
Professional occupations (%)	13.4	17.6	26.4
Unemployed (%)	8.2	8.4	6.3
Family Economic Status			
Median household income ($)	12,545	29,772	30,056
Home ownership (%)	27.2	49.8	64.2
Poverty (%)	35.1	23.8	10.0
Public assistance (%)	28.1	24.5	7.5
N	245,025	614,547	248,709,873

Source: U.S. Census of Population and Housing, 1980 and 1990.
[a] For the foreign-born only.

citizens. Ten years later, new arrivals accounted for only a quarter of the population; their self-reported English proficiency exceeded the level attained by the U.S. foreign-born population overall, and close to a majority had gained citizenship.

Resettlement brought progress on other fronts. Among adults, the proportion of college graduates grew while the high school dropout rate among the 16 to 19 age cohort declined. Although still lagging behind other Americans in educational attainment, Vietnamese adolescents were more likely than other Americans to remain in school—a trend that, if it continues, foreshadows a catch-up and eventual surpassing of the U.S. educational norm.

Changes in economic indicators point in the same direction. In the early stages of resettlement, Vietnamese refugees displayed particularly high rates of labor force nonparticipation and unemployment. Three months after landing in the United States, for example, 32 percent of the 1975 Vietnamese refugees were still unemployed; that rate dropped to 18 percent after seven months; and then to 14 percent after fifteen months, a level considerably above the U.S. average (Stein 1979). In Orange County, California, the unemployment rate hovered close to the 40 percent mark among Indochinese refugees in 1980 (Baldwin 1982). Those refugees lucky enough to find jobs often experienced severe downward mobility; whereas more than 30 percent of the 1975 arrivals had had professional occupations in Vietnam, only about 7 percent were in similar occupations within the first twenty-seven months after arrival (Stein 1979).

However dismal this early picture was, the 1990 Census showed a considerably brighter one. After a decade or so of adjustment, the labor force status of the Vietnamese had improved in terms of labor force participation in general and the proportions of year-round workers, self-employed workers, and professional workers. While Vietnamese workers were making progress and catching up with other Americans in the labor market, however, their occupational status remained significantly lower than that of the average American worker. For instance, in the early 1980s most Vietnamese workers in California were employed in electronics, pharmaceutical, and computer industries as assembly line workers, technicians, machine operators, and office workers; and most of these industries became consolidated ethnic niches by 1990 (Baldwin 1984; Waldinger 1996). In New Orleans, Vietnamese were concentrated in a few jobs such as cashier, waiter or waitress, cook, fisherman, and textile sewing machine operator (Zhou and Bankston 1994). Moreover, the unemployment rate for Vietnamese workers remained higher than that for American workers (8.4 percent versus 6.3 percent in 1990). The persistently high unemployment was probably caused by a disproportionate number of new arrivals and by a lack of human capital. Figure 2.4 indicates clearly that the Vietnamese unemployment rate has decreased with longer U.S. residence and with higher levels of educational attainment.

FIGURE 2.4 Unemployment by Length of U.S. Residency and Education, Vietnamese Workers Aged 16+, 1990

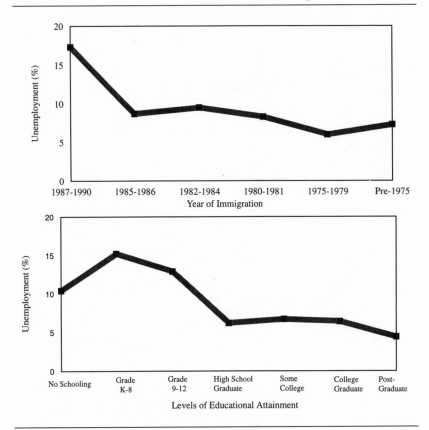

Source: U.S. Census of Population and Housing, 1990.

As the occupations of the Vietnamese steadily improved, so too did their economic well-being; by 1990, their median household income stood roughly on a par with the average for all American households. Home ownership rates, though still well below the U.S. average, were also up, reflecting the gradual climbing up the economic ladder. Poverty rates had dropped significantly, but they were still more than twice the U.S. average; and the Vietnamese continued to remain highly dependent on public assistance—three times as much as average Americans. The extent of their advancement needs to be assessed in light of the economic circumstances under which the Vietnamese began their life in America. As refugees, almost all of them began on welfare (Caplan, Whitmore, and Bui 1985).

FIGURE 2.5   Vietnamese Public Assistance Utilization by Length of
U.S. Residency and Education, 1990

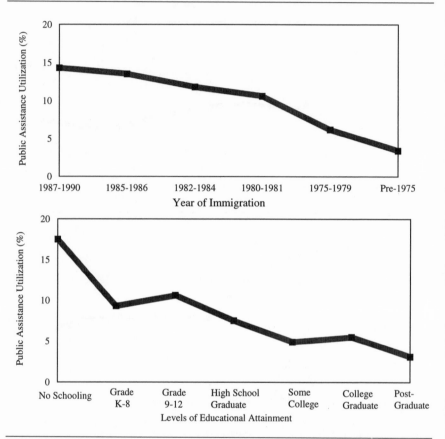

Source: U.S. Census of Population and Housing, 1990.

Although reliance on public assistance was relatively high among the
new arrivals, it decreased with longer U.S. residence and higher educational attainment. Figure 2.5 shows the relationships between public assistance utilization and length of U.S. residence (upper chart) and between public assistance utilization and educational attainment (lower
chart). The high rate of reliance on public assistance among the Vietnamese was due mainly to the relatively short time since their arrival and
to a lack of education. These trends are consistent with findings from
prior studies on Vietnamese refugees, which challenge the perception of
refugees as "social-service parasites" (Baldwin 1982; Caplan, Whitmore,
and Bui 1985; Gardner, Robey, and Smith 1985; Gordon 1989; Rut-

ledge 1992). As one Vietnamese parent put it, "We come to America in search of work, in search of freedom, and in search of family. I've worked hard, and I want to pass it to my children that it is a shame to be on welfare." Thus, it would be misleading to read the overall statistics without regard to the fact that a disproportionate number of Vietnamese were recent arrivals of relatively low socioeconomic status.

Young Adults: Characteristics and Progress

In 1980, most Vietnamese young adults (aged 18 to 24) were not just foreign-born, but "fresh off the boat," suffering from many of the problems confronted by other refugees in flight from a poor country like Vietnam: poor English language abilities, limited literacy, and high rate of poverty. Ten years later, however, significant progress could be detected. A sizable 1.5 generation (47.7 percent) and a small second generation (7.3 percent) had now emerged. As is shown in table 2.6, the profile of the first generation now looked much stronger, and the 1.5ers seemed to be faring relatively well. Given the very low starting point, this progress was substantial. True, major problem areas were noticeable in persistently high rates of unemployment and poverty; but the latter had dropped by almost half in ten years' time.

School-Aged Children: Characteristics and Progress

Notwithstanding their improvement, Vietnamese children (aged under 18) still lagged behind their American peers. Table 2.7 shows variations in children's socioeconomic circumstances by generation. Again, the Vietnamese were compared with four other ethnic groups—other southeast Asians, Chinese, non-Latino blacks, and non-Latino whites. Among the Asians, first-generation children were in more disadvantaged family circumstances than 1.5- and second-generation children; their parents had lower human capital and labor force positions, their family economic status was more disadvantaged, they had more problems with English, and they had higher dropout rates. Both first-generation and 1.5-generation Vietnamese children, as well as their other southeast Asian counterparts, were in much worse socioeconomic circumstances than those confronting children of the most underprivileged native group, with the exception of family structure. Except for the Chinese second generation, all Asian children generally lagged substantially behind native white children on all indicators.

TABLE 2.6 Socioeconomic Profile of Vietnamese Young Adults in the United States, 1980 and 1990

	1980	1990		
	All Young Adults	1st Generation	1.5 Generation	2nd Generation
Immigrant Status				
Does not speak English				
"very well" (%)	35.4	30.1	3.3	4.2
Not a U.S. citizen (%)	90.7	77.7	40.1	11.5
Schooling				
Currently enrolled				
in school (%)	51.4	59.4	75.9	61.9
Enrolled in college (%)	21.2	43.5	29.8	39.7
Currently not enrolled				
in school (%)	48.6	40.6	24.1	38.2
High school dropout (%)	42.9	51.4	24.7	26.2
High school graduate (%)	39.6	27.9	34.6	46.2
Some college	14.1	15.8	28.3	21.8
College graduate (%)	3.4	4.9	12.4	5.8
Labor Force Status				
In the labor force (%)	52.6	55.6	55.6	64.1
Employed full-time,				
year-round (%)	23.4	31.3	21.5	27.6
Self-employed (%)	1.3	3.3	2.9	1.6
Professional				
occupation (%)	9.1	9.0	14.7	10.1
Unemployed (%)	10.3	13.0	10.5	11.9
Family Economic Status				
Median household				
income ($)	14,345	30,000	35,400	29,882
Home ownership (%)	26.7	32.4	55.0	53.7
Poverty (%)	62.3	32.1	21.3	20.8
N	1,981	1,950	2,009	312

Source: U.S. Census of Population and Housing, 1980 and 1990, 5-percent PUMS.
Note: Sample includes all persons aged 18 to 24.

TABLE 2.7 Socioeconomic Profile of School-Aged Children in the United States, Selected Ethnicities, 1990

	Vietnamese			Other Southeast Asian			Chinese			Black[a]	White[a]
	1st Generation	1.5 Generation	2nd Generation	1st Generation	1.5 Generation	2nd Generation	1st Generation	1.5 Generation	2nd Generation		
Household Head's Characteristics											
Does not speak English "very well" (%)	58.9	56.7	32.9	77.3	68.0	55.9	58.1	52.9	20.4	—	—
College graduate (%)	8.0	9.9	18.1	5.5	5.3	8.4	24.9	30.0	50.4	9.4	25.7
Professional occupation (%)	6.3	8.0	15.7	3.1	3.4	5.9	21.0	24.1	42.6	12.6	27.1
Self-employed (%)	2.1	2.9	3.6	1.3	.6	.7	6.3	6.4	7.8	1.4	6.2
In labor force (%)	61.0	64.1	78.0	29.3	39.5	47.6	77.7	82.5	92.0	63.4	92.6
Unemployed (%)	12.2	9.3	6.4	7.6	11.8	11.3	5.6	4.8	2.5	12.6	3.7
Family Economic Status											
Median household income ($)	20,000	20,444	32,000	16,234	18,200	19,943	23,750	28,960	49,274	19,500	37,725
Home Ownership (%)	18.2	28.5	52.7	8.0	16.3	21.1	42.3	54.0	75.7	38.7	74.1
Female-headed (%)	28.6	23.7	17.5	24.4	24.5	19.4	18.8	14.3	9.7	54.6	16.7
Poverty (%)	47.6	45.0	28.7	35.6	44.8	49.3	32.2	23.9	10.8	40.6	10.8
Children's Characteristics											
Does not speak English "very well" (%)	48.2	19.3	8.2	40.9	26.3	18.3	29.7	16.2	4.8	—	—
Currently enrolled in school (%)	90.8	95.5	81.1	90.7	94.5	75.9	95.0	96.6	86.9	84.8	84.2
Dropout (aged 16 +) (%)	10.3	4.1	1.9	5.8	8.8	6.0	1.8	4.5	2.3	7.9	6.2
N	336	1,470	6,828	225	1,479	6,747	575	2,203	14,572	110,801	72,956

Source: U.S. Census of Population and Housing, 1990, 5-percent PUMS.
Note: Sample includes children under 18 years of age who lived in family households containing at least one child of the household head or of the spouse of the household head.
[a] Undersampled (1 percent of non-Latino black children and .4 percent of non-Latino white children belong to the first or 1.5 generation).

The general trend for Asian children suggests consistent improvements in parental socioeconomic characteristics and in family economic status and steady decreases in children's English language difficulties and dropout rates with each succeeding generation. The socioeconomic circumstances in which most Vietnamese children find themselves are still greatly disadvantaged, however, comparable only to those encountered by children of the most underprivileged native group. If Vietnamese children are to succeed in school and later in society, they cannot depend on the human capital and economic resources of their families, since these resources are so limited. They and their families may have to find other sources of support to overcome such limitations; these will be discussed in subsequent chapters.

FROM TEMPORARY EXPATRIATES TO PERMANENT RESIDENTS

"Hoai Huong" versus "Mary": Generational Differences in Orientation

Names send messages, and by giving their U.S.-born children such names as *Hoai Huong* (looking homeward), many Vietnamese have sought to express their nostalgia for the lost homeland. The flight to America guaranteed them self-preservation when they were driven from their homes, but at the price of a dispiriting, humiliating, and traumatic ordeal. From the moment of their arrival in the United States, many refugees have looked toward a return to Vietnam. They have been attentive to events in their native land and become involved in homeland politics. The refugee politics of the Vietnamese resembles the experience of Cuban Americans. As have Cuban Americans, the Vietnamese have frequently issued calls for armed struggle to overthrow the Communist government of Vietnam.

In the 1980s, Southern California was home to approximately 140 Vietnamese political organizations, most of which were dominated by anti-Communist hard-liners with little tolerance for any formal contact with Vietnam. Political paranoia haunted Little Saigon, where few Vietnamese dared to take a public stand in favor of lifting the U.S. trade embargo against Vietnam or normalization of U.S.-Vietnam relations, positions considered pro-Communist, disloyal, and traitorous. Those who advocated lifting the trade embargo found themselves threatened and their businesses burned. In rare instances they were assassinated, were kidnapped, or mysteriously disappeared. The *Los Angeles Times* (December 7, 1992) reported that between 1980 and 1992, there were at least a dozen such disappearances, mostly in California. The editor of a Vietnamese entertainment weekly died in 1987 in a firebomb attack on his Garden Grove office after he published advertisements for companies that did business with the Hanoi government (*Los Angeles Times*, June 13, 1994). Liberal Vietnamese community leaders found themselves forced to wear bulletproof vests, hire armed bodyguards, and ignore the insults and curses shouted by demonstrators outside their offices. Some had to take out full-page advertisements in Vietnamese-language newspapers denying rumors that they were Communist sympathizers.

But the politics of exile and violence left many other Vietnamese refugees untouched. Whatever their initial orientations, they settled down to building new lives in the United States rather than trying to reclaim the lives lost in Vietnam. Since the 1990s, a more conciliatory approach has gained ground, despite resistance from adherents of the exile politics of the older generation. Some Vietnamese have called for the United States to soften its stance toward Vietnam, believing that normalizing relations between the United States and Vietnam is inevitable and that the lifting of economic sanctions against Vietnam could be used as a lever to extract democratic reforms and human rights improvement. In an article on December 7, 1992, the *Los Angeles Times* reported on the changing political orientation of the Vietnamese community. Nguyen Cao Ky, former South Vietnamese premier and vice president, was quoted as saying, "It is time to heal—time to let bygones be bygones." Another refugee changed his position on normalization while remaining concerned with Hanoi's dismal human rights record, saying, "We cannot just sit and demand that Vietnam become a perfect place before we normalize relations. We can push more with diplomatic leverage."

Members of the 1.5 generation and the second generation, now grown into adulthood and preferring to speak English and to be called by Western names, have been still more flexible. The *Times* article noted that at a 1992 conference convened by the Vietnamese Student Association at University of California, Irvine, to discuss political issues on the home front, the organization's 24-year-old president, whose family had split on how to approach Vietnamese politics, advocated a change in the tactics used in dealing with the Communists and urged those attending the conference to take a more realistic stand. A young machinist from Little Saigon echoed, "In reality there has been no nation that has successfully beaten Communism. Communism, we have seen, destroys itself. So why not normalize relations with Communist Vietnam and help people inside fight against Communism?"

Many young Vietnamese see normalization as a way to enable them to visit relatives and friends freely, resume contact with their ancestral land, and gain a sense of wholeness. They also believe that normalization can generate emotional and spiritual benefits for the American society at large, not just for the Vietnamese in the United States. A Vietnamese student from Harvard was quoted in the *Times* article as saying, "The American people could come back to Vietnam now as moral victors and do the healing work with the Vietnamese. By doing the healing work in Vietnam, they heal themselves. They can now say: 'We went to Vietnam for a good cause. Now we return to do a good job again.'"

A poll conducted by the *Los Angeles Times* in 1994 provided evidence that the Vietnamese community was making peace with the past and looking to the future. The poll showed that over half (54 percent) of Vietnamese in Southern California approved President Clinton's lifting of the nineteen-year-old trade embargo against Vietnam in February 1994, and a similar percentage wanted to push even further to support full diplomatic relations. But while 20 percent voiced opposition to such moves, another fifth of the people did not respond to either question, because of the lingering fear of being called "traitors" by their extremist coethnics (*Los Angeles Times*, June 12, 1994).

It has taken twenty years for Vietnamese refugees to temper their contempt for Communism with support for renewed ties with Vietnam. In the process of softening their homeward politics and reorienting themselves politically, the Vietnamese, especially the growing second generation, are more likely than before to turn away from the obsession of returning and to concentrate on adapting to their host country as other immigrants have done.

Naturalization and Political Participation

Naturalization is often used as a measure of a long-term commitment and loyalty to the host society (Liang 1994; Portes and Mozo 1985). By law, an immigrant is eligible to apply for U.S. citizenship if he or she has been in this country for at least five years (or three years for the spouse of a U.S. citizen), has obtained some knowledge of basic American history and the U.S. political system, and has acquired some proficiency in English.

Immigrants have routinely sought to become naturalized, but those from Asia and Latin America are relatively slow to pursue naturalization, compared with their European counterparts. The reasons that many non-European immigrants do not try to become naturalized citizens are varied, ranging from allegiance to their home countries and transnationalism to their fear of the required standardized citizenship exam and INS interviews. An Indochinese cultural center in Houston reported that most of the Vietnamese who took the oath of citizenship in 1992 had to study there every day for at least one year and some for several years before attempting the exam (*Houston Chronicle*, September 17, 1992).

Although many contemporary immigrants have relatively low naturalization rates, the Vietnamese constitute an exception. In the 1980s, the INS reported that Vietnamese refugees were, on average, eight times more likely than immigrants from Canada to become naturalized. The 1990 Census found that 41 percent of the Vietnamese who arrived between 1975 and 1985 had become naturalized, compared with only 29 percent of the immigrants from China during the same period. The 1994 *Los Angeles Times* poll cited earlier showed that half of those Vietnamese surveyed had become naturalized U.S. citizens, and over 80 percent of noncitizen Vietnamese expected to become citizens in the next few years.

Varied motivations promote naturalization. Some Vietnamese, especially the former officials of the old South Vietnamese regime and members of the elite, who remain fiercely anti-Communist, have a desire to participate in the political process. Enjoying close ties to the State Department, they tend to be staunch Republicans, and many still revere President Nixon for his escalation of the Vietnam War. "They have been driven out by the Communists, and they tend to think that Republicans are anti-Communists who have a lot to do with gaining their country back," according to a member of the Vietnamese Voters' Association in Little Saigon (*The Economist*, April 4, 1992, 28). In the 1988 presidential election, 80 percent of all Vietnamese voters were registered Republicans.

Other Vietnamese refugees are less involved politically. For them, the right to political participation and involvement does not seem to be the chief motive for naturalization. Even among those who have become naturalized citizens, many feel that as newcomers they are "guests" and should remain silent out of gratitude to their hosts. They also tend to have a strong aversion to domestic politics, a tendency also shared by other immigrants from Asia who have experienced despotic regimes and wars. In the United States, many Vietnamese still tremble when they hear the word politics. They view the government with fear, disdain, or, at best, indifference because of their experience with a dictatorial political system in Vietnam and with an uncompromising and sometimes violent bent in exile politics. "Back in Vietnam, people did not want to engage in any political participation because it would mean death or jail. The tradition of shying away from politics continues in the United States," explained a community organizer in New Orleans.

Moreover, many Vietnamese are too busy making a living and educating their children to focus on public affairs. In traditional Vietnam, the welfare of the family is often the chief priority, and civic duties are secondary in importance. Therefore, it appears that for the majority of this refugee group, the right to make a living is a more important motive for naturalization than the right to vote or participate in politics. Noncitizens do not have access to certain jobs, such as the police force and the civil service, and they may unintentionally violate rules and regulations just by trying to make a living and doing what other Americans do.

The case of Vietnamese fishermen (described in the *San Francisco Chronicle*, November 1, 1990) offers an example. In the late 1970s and the 1980s, many Vietnamese were engaged in the fishing industry along the Pacific Coast and the Gulf of Mexico. They drew a precarious living from the sea, hoping to better their lives through hard work. But they found themselves laboring under the threat of a two-hundred-year-old federal law prohibiting noncitizens from operating large commercial fishing vessels. Many Vietnamese fishermen had to squeeze their meager incomes to hire "paper captains," citizens who were paid about $200 a week to sit on board and read magazines. Some were fined and threatened with the confiscation of their boats. John Lam, a former soldier in the South Vietnamese Army who escaped in the early 1980s, was stopped at sea by the Coast Guard ten times and was fined more than $1,000 in 1988. He was told by the Coast Guard that he had to be a citizen to fish. Those like Lam, whose livelihoods were directly affected by noncitizen status, were highly motivated to become naturalized as soon as their residence requirement was met, and they were motivated to act politically only when their means of making a living was threatened. In 1989, the Vietnamese Fishermen Association filed suit in San Francisco against the U.S. Coast Guard, arguing that the law banning noncitizens from operating fishing vessels larger than five tons was discriminatory, and in the following year Congress repealed the law. By then,

John Lam had become a naturalized citizen. When he talked to the media, however, he expressed his gratitude instead of agonizing over his past experience with the law: "I want to thank all Americans, the U.S. government, and Congress for accepting the Vietnamese refugees here and give them the opportunity to make their living." Lam's feeling reflects the guest mentality that has been a general attitude of many working Vietnamese, the first generation in particular, toward their host society.

The propensity among Vietnamese to become naturalized is also attributed, to a great extent, to their refugee status. As refugees, they cannot return to their homeland; they do not have a recognized national identification card, such as a passport, that would allow them to travel freely to countries other than the one of exile; and many suffer from a sense of loss of a national identity. Refugees who wish to return to their homeland for visits are the ones most likely to become citizens. "What's good about becoming a citizen? For me, I can make safe trips to and from home," said a naturalized Vietnamese in Versailles Village, reflecting the views of many Vietnamese refugees who still consider Vietnam their home and are nostalgic for their old country.

Despite widespread political apathy, Vietnamese communities have seen a growing political awareness throughout the 1990s. The Vietnamese, especially the young people, have begun to realize that they have the right to get into politics and that they should get involved to assert their right. The *Los Angeles Times* poll of 1994 showed that close to 70 percent of those surveyed considered participating in American politics as "very important." Also, political participation has been taken as a way to contribute to the country. Tony Lam, the mayor of the City of Westminster (the heart of Little Saigon in Orange County) elected in 1992 primarily by non-Vietnamese voters and believed to be the first and the only Vietnamese refugee ever elected to office in the United States, has repeatedly appealed to his coethnics to take part in the political process. "I feel I am opening up the door to my children, paving the way," he has said. "I will always be grateful. I consider this country has been our sheltering tree, and we have to pay back what has been given to us" (*New York Times,* November 16, 1992).

While a certain reluctance to become involved in American politics still lingers on in Vietnamese communities across the country, political participation is expected to become a major concern among those in the second generation, as pointed out by a Vietnamese elder: "For our young ones who were born here or raised here, the U.S. is their first country.

Second is the country of Vietnam. So now, they have to go out and vote. As Americans, they still have a fatherland, and if they want to improve the fatherland there they've got to work right here" (*Los Angeles Times*, June 13, 1994). As the older generation gradually turns away from inflexible, home-oriented exile politics and begins to develop greater interest in the civic life of the host country, Vietnamese American political leaders are expected to emerge, in time, from the second generation.

In sum, many first-generation Vietnamese may still have a guest mentality toward their new country, and their political and civic lives may continue to be dominated by thoughts of the lost homeland. They seem to have become more settled in their host country, however, and to be more eager to become citizens. Their attitudes toward Vietnam are less bitter and more flexible than before. These reorientations, particularly noticeable among younger Vietnamese, are helping to increase the identification of the second generation with America.

—————Chapter 3—————

The Reconstruction of the Ethnic Community and the Refugee Family

Overnight, my family became smaller [his extended family was broken into two parts to be received by two sponsoring families in different towns] and was dropped in some place that did not seem to lead to anywhere. My wife and I were very worried. I didn't know much English, had no job, didn't know anybody or anything, and had four kids to feed. I had no idea what was ahead of us. My host family helped us in every way possible, and for that, I couldn't be more grateful. But just imagine how trashy you would feel when you found yourself suddenly without hands or legs and had to depend on others for even small things like buying food.

—A Vietnamese refugee man

For many immigrants, adaptation is as much a function of social groups as it is of individuals, and for the Vietnamese refugees, the ethnic community is central to the process (Haines 1985). When asked about ways in which refugees help each other within the family context, one Vietnamese refugee woman responded, "Not just the family, but the whole Vietnamese community." As a Vietnamese social worker explained, "The community is the major, or the most desired, source of practical and emotional support for the refugees" (Rose 1981, 314–15). This chapter examines how Vietnamese refugees have rebuilt their communities and how these immediate ethnic contexts serve as the locus of support for children's adaptation.

THE COMMUNITY: THE CENTER OF ETHNIC TIES

The Need for a Community of Their Own

The federal government's refugee resettlement policy of residential dispersion was sharply criticized by social workers and scholars, who faulted it for disregarding the historical value of communities and hindering the development of ethnic organizations and networks conducive to the maintenance of traditions and psychological well-being (Skinner and Henricks 1979). In New Orleans, as elsewhere in the United States, federal authorities pressured local resettlement agencies to scatter the Vietnamese throughout the city. But Elise Cerniglia, then the local Director of Resettlement and Immigration Services for Associated Catholic Charities in New Orleans, did just the opposite when she tried to find housing for the new arrivals. Having previously overseen the resettlement of Cuban refugees, Cerniglia believed that refugees should live alongside one another for mutual support. Interviewed in March 1994, she commented, "I said, 'No, they need one another.' So, I started to resettle them in communities. That's why I looked for housing that could take large numbers of people." Thanks to Cerniglia's belief in the importance of communities and the effort of many other like-minded sponsors, New Orleans' distinctive Vietnamese communities were formed.

The literature on the Vietnamese experience has shown that Cerniglia was right; Vietnamese refugees dispersed in isolated neighborhoods recovered more slowly from the trauma of war and defeat and were more likely to feel homeless, displaced, and unwelcome than those who were resettled as groups (Finnan and Cooperstein 1983; Hagerty 1980; Starr and Jones 1985). Feeling overwhelmed and disoriented when they left the camps, the refugees needed contact with their compatriots; the enthusiasm and generosity of the receiving communities and sponsoring families did not suffice to reduce their sense of loss (Nhu 1976). Mr. Vu,* whose story opens this chapter, is a businessman in Baton Rouge, Louisiana, whose family was initially resettled in a small town in Ohio in 1979 but moved south after nineteen months. Interviewed in June 1993, he went on to say, "When you are in a foreign culture and asked to adapt, it is very difficult. First, you are afraid because of the unknown. You then become quiet because you don't have enough English to express yourself or you don't think people would understand you. When you don't talk much, people assume that you should be okay. And then you are on your own. In the end, you become more isolated and ill-adjusted and start to have problems. Then people would wonder, 'What's wrong with you?'"

There were numerous programs to help resettle the refugees, but language difficulties and cultural barriers made it hard for the Vietnamese to learn which resources were available and how to tap into them. Spon-

*Denotes the use of a psuedonym.

sors tried to help the refugees regain their independence, expecting that newcomers would be on their own once they had gotten settled, learned their way around, acquired some English, and found a job. But many sponsors had little knowledge either of the refugees' culture or of the complexity of involuntary uprooting; they were often frustrated when things did not work out as they expected. One benefactor quoted in the *New York Times* (June 10, 1978) complained, "The winter was disappointing. We wanted Hanh [the mother] to begin doing her marketing herself. She wouldn't. When we stopped taking her, she asked others; when they stopped, she found a third set of benefactors. Partly out of conviction, and partly out of anger, I let her drift."

The refugees had complex needs rooted in religion, customs, diet, and traditional ways of coping with crisis, and these were the requirements that many American sponsors probably could not grasp. What the refugees required was communities. Mrs. Tsan, a Sino-Vietnamese woman, had to travel all the way from Rhode Island to Orange County at least once a year just to worship a particular goddess at a Buddhist temple. One of her children, interviewed by telephone in 1994, said, "Mother was a very quiet and somewhat depressed woman, but whenever she got back from California, she talked a lot at the dinner table, and that made everybody happy. My brothers and I have just started our jobs here. Otherwise we would have wanted to move to California just so mother would have been close to that temple."

The Formation of Ethnic Communities

The need for community has shaped the geography of Vietnamese America. As studies conducted by the Office of Refugee Resettlement have found, community formation among the Vietnamese has occurred in three phases (USHHS 1993). First came the initial wave of war exiles, mostly from middle-class backgrounds. They were placed in various localities across the United States, but from the beginning, a process of spatial regrouping could be observed. The refugees began to develop small communities in California, Texas, and Louisiana, where the climate resembled that of Vietnam and where occupational niches could be found—in manufacturing in California or fishing in Texas and Louisiana along the Gulf of Mexico. At the end of this phase, secondary migration, mostly from the Midwest and the North (as is shown in figure 2.2), expanded these initial refugee concentrations as the newcomers rebuilt their networks. The second phase lasted from 1979 to 1982, when two major groups of refugees—the Sino-Vietnamese, who were predominantly members of the petit bourgeoisie, and the rural poor, who had extremely low socioeconomic status—arrived in large numbers. Though they were scattered by resettlement agencies, secondary migration led these newcomers to the newly established communities. The third phase was community-oriented. Since the 1980s, Vietnamese communities had taken deeper roots, ethnic businesses had begun to flourish, and informal and civic organizations and other community social structures were taking shape to provide both tangible and intangible support to newcomers and their families (Finnan and Cooperstein 1983).

With clustering came distinctive Vietnamese ethnic communities. Sizable Vietnamese enclaves can now be found in several metropolitan areas in California, Texas, Virginia, Washington, and Louisiana. The best known is Little Saigon in Orange County, California, which is the largest Vietnamese community in the United States and has the largest concentration of Vietnamese outside Vietnam. Other ethnic enclaves, such as Versailles Village in New Orleans, have also been visible, though their developments have been on a much smaller scale.

Like other immigrant concentrations, Vietnamese communities started with the need for people to band together for mutual support in a reconstructed cultural environment that resembled the homeland. In the process of ethnic concentration, economic, cultural, and social institutions were all established. Little Saigon started when about 2,500 refugee families were resettled in southern California in 1975. As an ethnic commercial area emerged in the cities of Garden Grove, Westminster, and Santa Ana in Orange County, it exercised a gravitational pull. In just fifteen years, the size of the Vietnamese population in the Little Saigon community grew to over 70,000; by 1990, according to Census Bureau figures, the Vietnamese made up 12 percent of the population of Orange County, which had been almost exclusively white in 1970. Local Vietnamese leaders maintained that their share of the population was actually much greater, that the census had undercounted the Vietnamese in the area by half. While not all of the area's Vietnamese live in Little Saigon, many live in areas that provide easy access to the ethnic community. "We are survivors, grasping each other for support," noted a Vietnamese social worker. "A place like Little Saigon provided that support" (Gropp 1992, 28). In recent years, the Vietnamese American population in areas within easy driving distance of Little Saigon has grown rapidly not only through immigration from abroad but also through secondary migration from other states.

Why does Little Saigon thrive? Commerce has provided a crucial spur. The ethnic economy grew rapidly from just a handful of businesses in 1979 to almost 2,000 in 1994. Its diverse establishments now include pagoda-style mini-malls, glittering jewelry booths, trendy fashion boutiques, fabric stores, hair salons, fancy restaurants, noodle shops and cafes, bakeries, supermarkets, laser-karaoke outlets, music stores, and night clubs—all reminiscent of the fallen capital of the former South Vietnam. On weekends, these Vietnamese-owned businesses draw as many as 50,000 coethnic shoppers, not only from neighboring communities but also from northern California (reported in the *Los Angeles Times*, June 14, 1994). Vietnamese-operated minibuses offer easy transit from San Jose to Orange County during weekends.

The desire to cluster in a familiar cultural environment has provided further stimulus to the community's growth. As it expanded, Little Saigon is no longer little, nor is it a mere commercial center. Instead, it has become a cultural mecca, a place for all things Vietnamese, from the food they eat to the sundries they need, a site where the refugees can mingle with others who speak their language and share a common heritage. "I don't come to buy things," said an elderly Vietnamese, a frequent visitor to the community. "I come to see people, strangers mostly, who come to do ordinary, everyday things, but in an environment where, because of the familiarity of faces and language, we never feel out of place" (quoted in the *Los Angeles Times*, June 14, 1994).

Institutional development has provided yet another source of attraction. The Vietnamese have brought many of their own institutions with them, turning them into American-style social organizations. With a chamber of commerce of some 2,000 members, Little Saigon has become home to dozens of service organizations run by refugees themselves. Religious institutions also proliferate. Buddhists, nearly 80 percent of Little Saigon's residents, have built their temples and worship regularly; the other 20 percent are Catholics and active in their own ethnic churches. The community has also established a network of thirty-five schools that children attend every Sunday to learn to speak, read, and write Vietnamese. Annual *Tet* celebrations feature the songs, dance, poetry, literature, and food of Vietnam. The ethnic media maintain an active presence, serving the community with forty-two newspapers and magazines and two small television studios producing Vietnamese language programs (*Los Angeles Times*, May 3, 1990).

The *Los Angeles Times* poll of 1994 found that almost half the Vietnamese in southern California considered Little Saigon their community's "most important" business, cultural, and social center, while another 23 percent rated it "important." Little Saigon was found to transcend the generation gap; almost half the young Vietnamese thought of the community as their most important cultural asset, as did 55 percent of those aged 65 years and over. "This is where my roots are, where I can practice my Vietnamese, where I can get authentic Vietnamese food," said a 21-year-old college student (reported in the *Los Angeles Times*, June 14, 1994).

While it is the capital of Vietnamese America, Little Saigon is in some ways unlike other Vietnamese communities in the United States. It has emerged in an area formerly serving a white middle-class population. Its Vietnamese residents, many of whom came in the first wave of Vietnamese resettlement in the United States, are socioeconomically heterogeneous, and a disproportionately large percentage of them come from the former Vietnamese elite and the well-educated middle class. Elsewhere the Vietnamese communities were established mostly by refugees from the second and third waves. They are located in inner cities or poor suburbs, and their residents come from rural backgrounds and are less well educated. These are the people who have settled in Versailles Village, and the story of that community's formation will be described in the following pages.

Versailles Village of New Orleans

Unlike earlier immigrant communities, which were usually established in central cities with high immigrant concentration, the Vietnamese community in New Orleans was formed on the eastern fringe of a city that in the past had attracted few immigrants and fewer still from Asia. According to Rhonda Cooperstein, coauthor of a federal report on refugee communities (personal interview, June 1993), New Orleans did not rank high on all the factors—a good economy, an existing Vietnamese community, higher welfare benefits, and warm weather—that generally influenced agencies' decisions on where to resettle the Vietnamese. New Orleans' economy was on the decline, and its welfare programs were not particularly good in the late 1970s. But the city did offer proximity to fishing opportunities, a strong Catholic organization funded for resettlement and social services, and a Catholic cultural ambience, as well as a climate similar to that in Vietnam (New Orleans Indochinese Resettlement Task Force 1979).

In one sense, the Associated Catholic Charities selected the locations where the Vietnamese would resettle in New Orleans. But in fact these neighborhoods were "seeded by chance," as a *Times Picayune* reporter wrote April 1, 1985, at the time Associated Catholic Charities began seeking housing for the refugees on the basis of the availability of rental housing. The entry point was in the Versailles Arms Apartments, a 405-unit U.S. Housing and Urban Development–subsidized apartment complex that made up one-third of the Versailles neighborhood (Airriess and Clawson 1991). These apartments were vacant because of a cutback in a local facility of the National Aeronautics and Space Administration (NASA). The vacant complex was considered undesirable by many New Orleanians, because it was far from the city center and inadequately served by public transportation. As a result, Catholic Charities was suddenly able to secure entire blocks of apartments for the Vietnamese.

The Versailles neighborhood was also experiencing "white flight" that contributed to the decline of the area. Over a relatively short period, the neighborhood was transformed from a predominantly white middle-class community to a poor racial minority community. The change stemmed from a variety of sources: a decline in employment at the local NASA facility, the area's most important employer; an influx of black families seeking a suburban way of life; and an accelerated outflow of the remaining whites who were unwilling to live in a minority neighborhood. By the early 1980s, housing construction had shifted from single family homes to rental units, bringing in a more transient and a poorer black population.

In 1975, about a thousand refugees from Vietnam were resettled in the Versailles Arms Apartments. This initial group provided the first link in a chain migration. In the following year, another two thousand Vietnamese arrived on their own. While Associated Catholic Charities continued to resettle refugees in this neighborhood, many more residents were drawn to the area by ties to friends or relatives from the same towns or villages in Vietnam. According to Sister Ann Devaney, head of refugee social services for Associated Catholic Charities, three-fifths of those who had settled in the community were secondary migrants from other states. The experience of Mr. Nguyen,* a resident of Versailles Village, is a case in point. The refugee resettlement agencies initially settled Nguyen and his family in Minnesota. Uncomfortable in the cold

*Denotes the use of a psuedonym.

weather, Nguyen contacted friends and relatives in warmer climates and moved to New Orleans' Versailles neighborhood because his wife's brothers were already living in the area.

By the early 1980s, when settled Vietnamese had themselves become sponsors for secondary migrants and newly arrived refugees, replacing the organizational sponsorship of the first years, new arrivals increasingly came directly from Vietnam to New Orleans. By 1990, the Vietnamese population had grown to 4,600 in New Orleans East—the area designated as Census Tract 17.29—shown in figure 3.1, though community leaders maintained that the actual number was over 6,000.

Tract 17.29 represented the larger Versailles neighborhood. In 1980, this neighborhood was shared equally by Vietnamese, blacks, and whites. By 1990, it had become almost evenly divided between Vietnamese (43 percent) and blacks (46 percent). These two groups were not evenly distributed on every street, however. The Vietnamese were heavily concentrated in only a few streets branching out from the initial site of resettlement, the Versailles Arms apartment complex on the eastern edge of the neighborhood (A in figure 3.1). These streets encompassed the area of what the Census Bureau designated Block Group 3 on the upper right corner of figure 3.1. In the mid-1980s, over half the population of the apartment complex residents was still Vietnamese, but the complex no longer served as the first residence for most new arrivals. Many of its remaining Vietnamese residents were older people who preferred to stay when their children and grandchildren moved out to freestanding housing nearby (F in figure 3.1).

Because newcomers were drawn by extended family ties, they either moved in initially with relatives or were settled in their own homes by their relatives in the surrounding area west of the apartment complex. Consequently, the Vietnamese community grew up in a triangle with the initial center to the east, the Vietnamese Catholic church to the west (B in figure 3.1), and the business center to the south (C in figure 3.1). Bilingual street signs in this area increased the visibility of this newly established immigrant community.

In 1980, Versailles Village had all the signs of a rapidly deteriorating working-class suburb. In almost all aspects, the residents of the neighborhood fared poorly in comparison with others living in the larger local area, the city, or the state, as can be seen in table 3.1. Block Group 3, the core of the Vietnamese community in Versailles, had a population that was 49 percent Vietnamese and 42 percent black. Over 95 percent

FIGURE 3.1   Versailles Village, New Orleans East

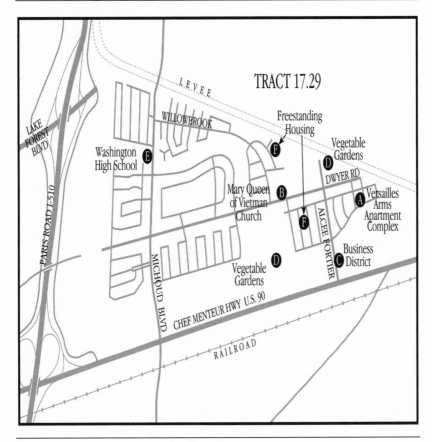

Source: U.S. Census of Population and Housing, 1990, Census Tracts.
Note: New Orleans East is covered in census tract 17.29.

of the Asians in Block Group 3 or in Tract 17.29 were Vietnamese. The Vietnamese in the New Orleans community had low levels of schooling; in Block Group 3, less than a third had finished high school, compared with 75 percent of blacks and 67 percent of whites. Our Versailles Village Survey of 1993 underscored the pattern of limited educational attainment reflected in the U.S. Census. Among those Vietnamese students surveyed who responded to the questions on their parents' highest level of education, 80 percent of the fathers and 81 percent of the mothers had not completed high school. The Vietnamese also ranked

TABLE 3.1   Comparison of Selected Characteristics of Block
Group 3, New Orleans East (Tract 17.29), Orleans
Parish, and Louisiana, 1990

	Block Group 3	New Orleans East Tract 17.29	Orleans Parish	State
Total population	6,399	10,607	496,938	4,219,973
Vietnamese (%)	49.3	43.0	1.3	0.4
Black (%)	42.0	45.8	62.1	30.8
White (%)	7.0	10.0	34.7	67.3
Other (%)	1.7	1.2	1.9	1.5
High school graduates (%)	50.6	60.0	68.1	68.3
Asian (%)	28.5	36.5	59.3	68.1
Black (%)	74.6	76.2	58.4	53.1
White (%)	67.3	73.5	81.4	74.2
Median household income ($)	12,790	17,044	18,477	21,949
On public assistance (%)	23.0	18.0	15.0	12.0
Below poverty level (%)	48.6	37.1	31.6	23.6
Female-headed households (%)	31.7	25.5	24.1	20.9
Asian (%)	6.8	6.0	10.6	10.1
Black (%)	55.3	41.8	50.9	45.2
White (%)	18.3	17.3	15.7	11.5

Source: U.S. Census of Population and Housing, 1990 Census Tract.

low in occupational status, since most of the Vietnamese came from
villages. A 1979 New Orleans Indochinese Resettlement Task Force ap-
pointed by the Mayor of New Orleans described them as "agricultural-
ists and fishermen" in their native country.

Many of the Vietnamese in this neighborhood were struggling economically. In Block Group 3, the median household income was only
$12,790, much lower than the levels for Tract 17.29, the parish, or the
state. These household incomes were severely strained, since the Vietnamese had more persons per household than either blacks or whites.
About 23 percent of the households in Block Group 3 depended on
public assistance, contrasted with 18 percent in the tract as a whole, 15
percent in the parish, and 12 percent in the state. Nearly half the house-

holds fell below the poverty level, much higher than in other areas. Though very poor, the Vietnamese displayed one characteristic not usually associated with poverty: the overwhelming majority (81 percent) of families in Versailles Village were married-couple families. Female-headed families accounted for only 6 percent of the Vietnamese family households, compared with 55 percent of black families and 18 percent of white families.

In sum, the Vietnamese of Versailles Village were low-income and low-skilled residents concentrated in the poorest part of a poor area in a poor city in a poor state, a situation that might seem hopeless. Obviously, if Vietnamese children of this community were to advance in this society, they could not do so on the basis of the human capital or the financial capital of their families since these are so limited. They might, however, be able to overcome these limitations with the social capital formed in their intact families and their ethnic community.

As in Little Saigon, the structures of Versailles Village became more formally institutionalized over time. In the beginning, the community was largely maintained by the informal networks of families and friends. As time went on, existing formal organizations were consolidated and new organizations were established. The Catholic church was the most important of the various formal organizations. Eighty percent of the Vietnamese in this community were Catholics (compared with about 20 percent in Little Saigon). Geographically, the Catholic church shifted the religious life of the community from its eastern edge, at the Versailles Arms apartment complex, to the west (A in figure 3.1). Located within close walking distance of its parishioners, the newly built Mary Queen of Vietnam Church (B in figure 3.1) to the northwest of the neighborhood became a focal point of the community, reflecting the social centrality of the religious institution. The importance of religion could also be seen in the homes; statues of the Virgin Mary were placed in many of the front yards, and inside each home, at least one room (usually the living room) contained a shrine: statues of Mary and Jesus, with flowers and candles in front and a religious painting behind. Though the objects were different, the Catholic shrines resembled those found in the homes of Buddhist Vietnamese.

The ethnic economy also grew and took on a more structured character. The Vietnamese who arrived in Versailles Village moved into a neighborhood that was economically depressed and had few business activities. Once settled, these newcomers began to pursue entrepreneurial projects by pooling resources from the family and kinship networks. By the 1990s, Versailles had become a miniature Little Saigon. An ethnic commercial strip, located right in the center of the Vietnamese enclave (C in figure 3.1), included over fifty permanent businesses ranging from restaurants, grocery stores, beauty salons, night clubs, and music stores to service-oriented offices such as insurance, law, and medical clinics. Every Saturday, the strip was home to a farmers' market offering fresh vegetables, fruits, and meat that catered to Vietnamese tastes. The ethnic economy provided an array of goods and services for Vietnamese residents in the enclave and many others who lived outside of it.

The neighborhood also contained a highly visible system of ethnic gardens (D in figure 3.1). Elderly Vietnamese residents intensively cultivated plots in their backyards and behind a nearby levee, producing foodstuffs for the open farmers' market, and also perpetuating traditional folkways and culture (Airriess and Clawson 1991, 1994). Some of the gardeners were on public assistance, and none of them paid taxes on earnings from their products, so it was difficult to measure the scale of their contribution to the economic life of the community. When asked about earnings, gardeners invariably claimed to be growing primarily for their own use. But while much of the produce was indeed consumed by growers, given away to extended family and neighbors, or bartered, gardening apparently became one important means of bringing capital into the community. During our field research between 1993 and 1994, we observed large produce trucks in the neighborhood every two weeks, loading produce to be distributed to other Vietnamese communities and to be sold to Vietnamese restaurants across the United States.

As some members of the community achieved material success and as self-employment grew from less than one percent in 1980 to over 8 percent in 1990, self-help and service-oriented social organizations and a group of secular community leaders also emerged. Successful fishermen and owners of small businesses furnished the ranks of community leaders. These leaders, in turn, formed and financed a system of formal civic organizations, the most important of which were the Vietnamese-American Voters' Association, the Vietnamese Educational Association, and the Vietnamese Parent-Teacher Association. The various formal organizations, as well as the existing networks of families and friends, furnished coethnic members with both intangible (emotional, cultural, and spiritual) support and tangible support in the form of jobs, education, and housing.

In sum, the ethnic community has come to provide manifold benefits for its members. Practically, it meets the basic demands of coethnic members by providing goods and services unavailable or not easily accessible in the larger society. Socially, it offers several levels of social support, establishes goals, reinforces community standards, and shields group members from outside influences in their underprivileged community (see detailed discussion in the following chapter).

Culturally, it preserves the status quo within the community and recreates a symbolic homeland, where traditional values and a sense of ethnic identity may be nurtured. These community-generated benefits foster the development of social capital that enables individuals and their families to surmount structural barriers, to minimize the effects of living in socially isolated and disadvantaged neighborhoods and to develop the habits and skills for socioeconomic advancement. This is precisely what an ethnic community can do for the resettlement of Vietnamese refugees that a socially isolated local community cannot.

THE RECONSTRUCTED FAMILY

The Vietnamese family in Vietnam is the chief source of social identity for the old and the young and has served as the only way of life for the Vietnamese. For the Vietnamese, the family is the strongest motivating force in life, stronger than religion and nationality. "Anything a man does, he does out of family consideration rather than for himself as an individual. Each person in the family, in fact, must come second to the family as a whole" (Hanh 1979, 77). Uprooted from their place of birth, however, Vietnamese families have confronted challenges in reestablishing themselves in the New World.

The Traditional Family

The traditional Vietnamese family system bears the lasting imprint of the centuries of Chinese domination that began in 111 B.C. and ended in 939 A.D. Long after independence from China, Confucianism was deeply rooted in Vietnamese society and its family system (Shaker and Brown 1973). Unlike Buddhism, the other dominant religion in Southeast Asia offering precepts that focus on the individual, Confucianism prescribes communal salvation and emphasizes ancestor worship, respect for authority, the belief in consensus, a willingness to put society's or the family's interests before individual interest, a high regard for education as a means of mobility, clear rules of conduct, constant self-cultivation, and the importance of face-saving.

The refugees came from a tradition in which the family generally consisted not only of the living—father as head of the family, grand-parents, the mother and children, the sons- and daughters-in-law—but also of all the spirits of the dead, as well as those not yet born (Hanh 1979, 77). The patriarchal order defined the status and role of each family member. The father, the authority figure of the family, made all important family decisions; the mother was expected to take care of her husband, her parents-in-law, and her children. In a departure from her role in many other East Asian cultures, however, the mother also managed the family finances and was known as *noi-tuong* or the "home minister." In this respect, Vietnamese women had a larger share of power in their families than did most other East and Southeast Asian women. Children were expected to be loyal and show respect not only to their parents but to all elders. Families preferred sons over daughters because sons would stay in the family to provide lifelong support and to continue the family name, while daughters would marry out. Boys were thus viewed as the future of the family and were often pushed to attain their highest achievements at school, while girls were raised to be house-wives. Older children were also responsible for the welfare and behavior of their younger siblings.

The extended family functioned as an economic unit—"one fire one lamp," as the Vietnamese put it (Hanh 1979). While the middle genera-tion worked outside the home, the elders stayed home to take care of the young. The extended family served as the center for all social activities, linking individual members to the community and the larger society. Overall, the traditional family valued harmony, filial piety, mutual obli-gation, hard work, obedience, and discipline. Although modernization (though at a very slow pace), incessant warfare, and Western influences had drastically changed many family traditions in contemporary Viet-nam even before the Vietnam War, the traditional family values had remained strong.

The Uprooted Family

Vietnamese families often arrived in the United States in fragments of nuclear or extended families. Fragmentation was a common strategy of flight; large extended families were divided into multiple nuclear units, and smaller units were also broken up, with spouses, younger children, and grandparents left behind and brought over after the core unit had been resettled. Thus, what appeared to be a nuclear family was often an incomplete unit from which children or grandparents were missing. Similarly, a single-parent Vietnamese household might actually be part of a married-couple family with the spouse still languishing in a refugee camp, or worse, in Vietnam.

Resettlement in pieces complicated the process of adaptation and exposed refugee families to many risks. For the incomplete families, reunification proceeded slowly; loss of contact—whether because of the war, imprisonment in Vietnam, or the flight to a safe haven—aggravated the wait (Allen and Hiller 1985; Palmer 1981). Consider the case of one Vietnamese family. The mother left Vietnam in 1975 with her two older children, leaving her husband and a two-year-old son behind. The husband, a former South Vietnamese soldier, escaped Vietnam on a fishing boat two years later, leaving the son with his grandparents. In 1990, the son, nearly 20 years old then, received permission to leave Vietnam via the Orderly Departure Program. He arrived in the United States, only to reconnect with parents who had become strangers and to discover two younger siblings who were born after his separation.

Family reunification in stages such as these forced families to make continual adjustments to internal changes, such as the sudden arrival of a parent, a relative, or an older sibling, which reopened the wounds of exile. Family members already settled and those who were fresh off the boat had to adapt to each other in a new family situation. Crowded housing, financial strains, and cultural gaps created high levels of anxiety and stress among both adults and children, the settled and the newly arrived. These encounters occasionally produced tragic results. The young man whose case was just described came into constant conflict with his long-lost parents and ended up leaving home and drifting with a group of alienated Vietnamese gang members. In 1995, he shot and killed a young man in a barroom argument; he was convicted of murder and sent to prison.

Resettlement was often accompanied by role reversals between husband and wife, between parents and children, and between children and other adult family members. These shifts led to further strain. Lacking education, job skills, and proficiency in English, Vietnamese men frequently found themselves unable to act as providers and depended instead on help from their wives and, to a lesser extent, their children, as well as public assistance. Wives frequently assumed primary economic responsibility (Allmen 1987; Kibria 1993). Working outside the home gave women a measure of independence and a degree of separate identity, but these working women were expected to retain their traditional roles in child-rearing, cooking, and other domestic chores. These developments created tension in spousal relations; role reversal confronted husbands with a loss in function and a threat to their authority, and women had to carry heavy workloads both outside and inside their homes. When both parents worked, parents and children spent less time together, and the likelihood grew that the generations would diverge and clash with each other. Chapter 7 will consider this point in greater detail.

Many parents, unable to speak English, were forced to rely on their children as interpreters and translators in such matters as reading report cards and notes from school, filling in forms to obtain public assistance benefits or other social services, paying utility bills, and answering phone calls. The heavy dependence on children in many cases weakened the parents' direct control over children. Loss of parental authority accompanied the changes that affected grandparents as well. The grandparents' dependence on other family members and their isolation from the outside world eroded the respect in which they had historically been held.

The Adjusted Family

Despite all the risks, many Vietnamese families have adjusted to life in America remarkably well. The path to adjustment has involved incorporating traditional values, communal solidarities, and refugee experiences into a lifestyle adapted to American ways (Caplan, Whitmore, and Choy 1989; Gold 1992; Rutledge 1992). For example, family boundaries have frequently been redefined by new family circles that bring friends and distant relatives who had been marginal members of the family in Vietnam into the active circle of kin relations in the United States. This reconstructed family pattern, based on kinship or fictive kinship, yields extended families that appear to be traditional but actually contain distantly related or even unrelated members of different generations (Hein 1995; Kibria 1993). One study provides the following illustrative case. A couple expanded their family first by taking in a young man who became a fictive sibling and uncle to the couple's children, and later by adopting a second young man. Both men contributed as full members of the household, which in its new configuration included fourteen people (Hanh 1979). But one need not rely on anecdotes. The 1990 census shows that 9 percent of Vietnamese households with school-aged children included nonrelative members, as compared with 4 percent among Chinese families and 5 percent among white families.

In reconstructed families, members shared common experiences of flight and developed a sense of collective strength in coping, giving rise to new mechanisms in reestablishing social ties and networks of support, such as cooperative kinship-based economic practices (Hitchcox 1988; Kibria 1993). As a result, family networks in refugee resettlement communities became even more extended than in the homeland and provided a basis for community formation.

The changes in family relations also created conditions of greater equality between men and women and between the young and the old as family members became more and more adapted to their new environments (Kibria 1993). In the best-adjusted families, members began to practice a new form of family collectivism that combined the traditional belief in mutual protection and support and with the American ideal of equality in family relations. Although at times the greater equality among family members led to weakened power of men over women and of parents over children, it did not always cause men or women to reject the traditional Vietnamese family system. Instead, the struggle to adjust to the new environment frequently produced attempts to preserve and adapt images of traditional families (Kibria 1993). Even the young people who seemed most dissatisfied with the hierarchy in traditional Vietnamese family life generally took pride in the cooperative nature of their families. Young people who were well adjusted in school and in the workplace often perceived the pursuit of educational goals or career as "form" and the family as "substance" and "a key to life" (Rumbaut and Ima 1988). As will be discussed in chapters 7 and 8, the attempts to balance traditional Vietnamese family values and the American lifestyle have not been without pain and contradiction for the younger generation, nor have they always been successful.

Family Values: An Example from Versailles Village

In well-adjusted Vietnamese families, the basic principle is that the family always comes first. In Versailles Village, we observed that elders placed high value on respect, cooperation, and harmony within the family and emphasized mutual obligations that bound members of a household not only to each other but also to the larger kinship network. But are these values of the ethnic community and elders passed on successfully to the younger generation growing up in America? The results from our Versailles Survey of 1993 suggest that the answer is yes.

Our 1993 survey included a number of items assessing the degree to which Vietnamese youth retained a traditional outlook. From our field interviews in Versailles Village, we found that both students and their parents consistently identified obedience, industriousness, and helping others as traditional Vietnamese family values. They also consistently characterized independent thinking and concern with individual social prestige as American or "Americanized" family values. Accordingly, we listed five value statements in our questionnaire: three invoking traditional values—"to obey," "to work hard," and "to help others"—and two invoking values of a more individualistic kind—"to think for himself or herself," and "to be popular." In each case, we characterized the value as one that the family considered to be one of the most important things a child must learn to prepare for life. We then asked students to report their degree of agreement with the statements, using a four-item scale in which responses ranged from "strongly agree" to "strongly disagree."

As table 3.2 shows, an overwhelming majority of Vietnamese high school students strongly agreed that obedience and working hard were the most important values in their families. Girls were somewhat more likely than boys to agree strongly, but only a small proportion of either gender voiced strong disagreement. Students did not respond to the perceived importance of helping others with the same level of emphatic agreement, but the pattern remained the same; 43 percent of the boys and 51 percent of the girls strongly agreed on the importance of helping others, while fewer than 9 percent registered disagreement. Once again, girls were more likely than boys to agree strongly—a likely indication of greater traditionalism—but girls were as likely as boys to indicate disagreement.

When students were asked about mainstream American values, a different pattern emerged. Fewer than half our respondents strongly agreed that their families valued independent thinking, and only about a third strongly agreed that their families placed importance on popularity. The proportions of disagreement to both items increased to almost a third, many times higher than the negative responses to the first two items. This reversed pattern of the last two items indicated that independent thinking and popularity, generally considered to be highly valued by American peers, were deemphasized by the families of Vietnamese students.

TABLE 3.2   Family Values as Perceived by Vietnamese Youths, by Gender

	Strongly Agree (%)	Agree a Little (%)	Disagree or Strongly Disagree (%)
To obey	72.3	22.9	4.8
Male	67.7	26.9	5.4
Female	76.8	18.9	4.3
To work or study hard	70.8	25.5	3.7
Male	64.1	31.5	4.4
Female	77.1	19.8	3.1
To help others whenever they need help	47.0	44.8	8.2
Male	43.0	49.5	7.5
Female	51.1	40.0	8.9
To think for oneself	44.1	24.6	31.3
Male	38.6	28.4	33.0
Female	49.5	20.8	29.7
To be popular	33.5	30.8	35.7
Male	36.6	30.1	33.3
Female	30.3	31.5	38.2

Source: The Versailles Village Survey of 1993.
Note: Respondents were Vietnamese high school students in Versailles Village, New Orleans (*N* = 198).

It is one thing to see that traditional values persist and another to know how these values affect the behavior of the Vietnamese youth of Versailles Village. To explore this area, we asked three questions about work habits, one pertaining to housework ("How often do you help with housework—always, often, sometimes, or rarely?"), the second to homework ("How many hours do you usually spend on your homework or on reading and writing when you come home from school each day—over two hours, one to two hours, half an hour to an hour, less than thirty minutes, or never do homework?"), and the third to leisure time ("How many hours do you usually watch TV at home each day—over two hours, one to two hours, half an hour to an hour, less than thirty minutes, or never watch TV?").

As is shown in table 3.3, over half the students reported that they

TABLE 3.3   Work Habits Among Vietnamese Youth, by Gender

	Always %	Often %	Sometimes %	Rarely %
Help with				
housework	31.1	22.3	37.3	9.3
Male	16.0	19.1	52.1	12.8
Female	45.5	25.3	23.2	6.0

	Over 2 Hours %	1 to 2 Hours %	½ to 1 Hour %	Less Than ½ Hour[a] %
Time spent on				
home-work	26.0	28.8	18.6	26.6
Male	26.4	28.7	11.5	33.4
Female	25.6	28.9	25.5	20.0

	Over 2 Hours %	1 to 2 Hours %	½ to 1 Hour %	Less Than ½ Hour[b] %
Time spent				
watching TV	37.7	26.5	17.6	18.2
Male	39.5	27.2	19.8	13.6
Female	36.0	25.8	15.7	22.5

Source: The Versailles Village Survey of 1993.
Note: Respondents were Vietnamese high school students in Versailles Village, New Orleans (*N*=198).
[a] Includes those who answered "I did not do homework" (10.2 percent of the total).
[b] Includes those who answered "I did not watch TV" (4.1 percent of the total).

always or often helped with housework, and only 9 percent reported that they rarely did. Girls were significantly more likely than boys to report that they always or often helped with housework, but this gap narrowed when the students were asked about time spent on homework daily. More than half the boys and girls reported that they spent at least an hour each day on homework, although about a third of the boys and a fifth of the girls spent less than thirty minutes or did not do homework at all. With regard to television time, a prominent pastime of American young people, fewer than 40 percent reported watching more than two hours daily. Girls seemed to watch less television than boys, possibly because they were expected to spend more time doing housework.[1]

But are these work habits related to the values of the students' families? The answer emerges from a correlation matrix between these two sets of variables. As is shown in table 3.4, the three traditional values are

TABLE 3.4 Correlations Between Family Values and Work Habits Among Vietnamese Youths

	1	2	3	4	5	6	7	8
1. Obedience	1.00							
2. Industriousness	.34**	1.00						
3. Helping others	.32**	.46**	1.00					
4. Independent thinking	−.17*	−.27**	−.20**	1.00				
5. Popularity	−.15*	−.14	−.17*	.46**	1.00			
6. Time on housework	.24**	.20**	.20**	−.11	−.04	1.00		
7. Time on homework	.24**	−.02	.09	−.08	−.22**	.27**	1.00	
8. Time on television	−.12	−.02	.07	.01	.16*	−.10	−.31**	1.00

Source: The Versailles Village Survey of 1993.
Note: Respondents were Vietnamese high school students in Versailles Village, New Orleans (*N*=198).
* *p* < .05; **p* < .01 (two-tailed).

positively correlated with one another, bearing strong and statistically significant relationships (the *r*'s range from .32 to .46). In contrast, these traditional values stand quite distinct from the two highly correlated nontraditional values (*r* = .46). Moreover, obedience, industriousness, and helping others are significantly and positively related to time spent on housework, while popularity is negatively related to time spent on homework but positively related to time spent watching television. The matrix provides strong evidence that those Vietnamese youth in Versailles Village with stronger traditional family values tended to display more industrious work habits.

These results indicate that the family continues to play a central role in the lives of the Vietnamese and their children. In Versailles Village, Vietnamese families emphasize obedience, industriousness, and helping others and discourage the nontraditional values of independent thinking and popularity, which are most commonly associated with contemporary American society. Moreover, as will be discussed in Chapter 8, Vietnamese children are pressured to avoid associating too much with non-Vietnamese children in the neighborhood, not to date non-Vietnamese, and not to become too "American." Conformity to the values and behavioral standards prescribed by the family affects both the extent to which these children adapt to American ways and the mechanisms by which that adaptation takes place.

The book, so far, has focused on how the communities have developed and how the Vietnamese have reconstructed their families in order to adapt to life in their new surroundings in spite of their socioeconomic disadvantages. Vietnamese families continue to be the backbone of the life of the Vietnamese in the United States, and the attitudes toward the family are related to attitudes toward self, others, and work. Vietnamese families do not function in isolation, however; many of them have to depend on their ethnic communities for support. By connecting families and providing formal and informal mechanisms of cooperation, the ethnic community helps to transform the traditions and aspirations of individual families into effective means of social control and encouragement for the younger generation. The chapter that follows describes how family-based, interknit, multileveled social ties within the ethnic community integrate individual members and families to facilitate adaptation.

————— Chapter 4 —————

Networks of Social Relations:
Support and Control

Elizabeth Nguyen, 16, was born in Versailles Village in New Orleans two years after her parents arrived in the United States from Vietnam. Her father is a former South Vietnamese military officer who now works as a fisherman. She is a straight A student, as are her two older sisters. She meets every day after school with a study group of four friends. "My parents know pretty much all the kids in the neighborhood," she says, "because we all go to the same church. Everybody here knows everybody else. It's hard to get away with much."

For most American children, families and the social relations built around them within a community are the means of transmitting cultural norms and values and shaping social contacts and future opportunities. For immigrant and refugee children, however, families alone are not enough. As illustrated in chapter 3, one reason is that the traditional bonds and practices and values that hold families and communities together have been disrupted. Another reason is that the social environments in which many immigrant or refugee families live are socially isolated and lack meaningful connections to mainstream institutions. A third reason is that many immigrant or refugee parents lack adequate human capital—education and skills—and economic resources. Thus, the kinds of resources afforded by individual families, such as loyalty and mutual assistance, may be sufficient to enable children to cope with daily survival but not to help the children get ahead in American society.

For adult refugees, community and family are important in easing the tensions caused by uprooting and facilitating the adjustment. For children, the story is unlikely to play out in quite the same way. The youngsters, never as deeply rooted in Vietnam as their parents, do not carry as much cultural baggage. They are also apt to change more quickly, being more eager to embrace American ways, enjoying more opportunities to mingle with other American children, and finding it easier to learn a new style of life. How is it possible to ensure that immigrants and their

93

offspring maintain their values and work habits and learn the skills for socioeconomic advancement? An answer to this question requires something more than a check-list of kinship ties or socioeconomic characteristics of individual families. In this chapter, the Versailles Village case is used to illustrate what makes Vietnamese young people adhere to the values and norms prescribed by their families and how networks of social relations serve as a chief mechanism of support and control. The chapter focuses on three identifiable characteristics crucial to the maintenance of networks of social relations: respect as an affirmation of social relations, complexity of ethnic involvement, and integration as a mechanism of control.

RESPECT: FOUNDATION OF VIETNAMESE SOCIAL RELATIONS

Respect—for elders, for authority, for peers, and for the self—is a fundamental Vietnamese cultural value that has been carried from the homeland and transplanted on American soil. Linguistic practices embody the respect shown to elders and authority. Vietnamese routinely uses "status pronouns" to establish the relative positions of the speaker and the person addressed (Bankston 1997). The most important word used as a status pronoun may be *thay* (teacher or master). It is usually used together with a noun *thay giao* or *thay hoc*, both meaning "teacher." When it is used alone, *thay* serves as a form of address that conveys the respect a student must show to a male teacher.[1] Moreover, first-, second-, and third-person pronouns vary according to status to indicate respect, formality, and a degree of social distance.

Greetings are the mostly commonly mentioned examples of the verbal demonstration of the expected respect for elders. A man in his 50s remarked, "When they [young people] pass me on the street or see me in a shop, they should say *Chao Ong* ['Good Day, Sir']. They shouldn't just walk past and act like I'm not there." Another middle-aged man, a father of six children, said, "Sometimes my children bring home friends from school. When they come into my house, they must come and talk to me first to be polite. If they just walk by, I'd not like it, and I tell my children not to bring those friends to my house."

Respect for authority stands in close relation to respect for elders, since old age, which serves as a symbol of wisdom, and parenthood are sources from which authority derives. Although age and parenthood establish authority, it is the social persona of the individual within the system of social relations that is more important. For example, the pastor of the Catholic church in Versailles Village receives a great deal of respect in recognition of his key position in the system. A 15-year-old high school sophomore explained, "We respect our pastor, of course. We like him, too, but that doesn't have anything to do with it. It's who he is and who we are that's the important thing."

Failure to show respect is a failure to acknowledge one's social identity and to affirm one's relationship to the family and the community. When children demonstrate respect for authority, they show that they accept the norms prescribed by the community and that they remain under their parents' effective control. When we conducted an interview at the home of Mr. Ngoc Thanh Nguyen, for example, all three of his children, aged from 7 to 13, came into the living room to greet us, and each served us a cup of hot tea. In so doing, the children complied with the way of welcoming guests generally expected in Vietnamese families. Although the children did not initiate the action, but were prompted to do so by their parents, the act itself indicated that children conformed to their parents' expectations.

Thus, respect for elders and authority, as a set of collectively held ideas about desirable and undesirable forms of behavior, translates into actions that mark one's position in a hierarchy of social relations. Clearly some aspects of traditional social relations have been transplanted without change from Vietnam to the United States while others have developed in the process of resettlement; nonetheless, the Vietnamese in Versailles Village and elsewhere in the United States see respect for elders and authority as defining what it means to be Vietnamese. The anthropologist Jesse W. Nash (1992) found respect for persons in positions of authority a defining characteristic of the Vietnamese social order. Nash observed, "Vietnamese children, when asked to draw pictures of people they admire, drew their parents, priests, policemen, and community leaders. A similar, American group of children initially refused my request, saying it was 'silly.' When they finally did respond to the request, they drew rock stars and rich socialites" (p. 43).

Respect for peers and for the self also has a defining character. One high school student from Versailles Village, who recently graduated at the top of his class and received a college scholarship, considered young people who showed no respect for their friends or for themselves too "Americanized." When asked how he could recognize these "over-Americanized" youth, he explained, "It's in the way that they act. They're loud when they talk to their friends and act in ways that look rude. I guess the best way that I can explain it is that they don't look like they think the people around them are important."

Vietnamese children who are disrespectful are often considered "bad kids" by the Vietnamese in the community and are rejected as "outsiders" to the system of ethnic relations. A 30-year-old man remarked, "The bad ones are the ones that hang out on Alcee Fortier [one of the main streets in the Versailles neighborhood, see figure 3.1]. Even though they're in public, you can see them just sitting down on the sidewalk, drinking and smoking cigarettes. The good ones behave properly; they go home instead of acting like the street is their living room."

The culture connects respect for others with the respect for the self, implying that the self takes on meaning within an established set of social relations. The following remark by a young man echoed the view of many Vietnamese in Versailles Village:

> Some of the Vietnamese kids who were brought up in this country act like they don't respect themselves. They are messy in the way that they dress and the way that they behave. If they don't respect themselves they can't respect other people. They don't realize that they are Vietnamese and have to act in ways that are appropriate for Vietnamese people.

Respect therefore provides an affirmation of an identifiable set of social relations. By demonstrating respect, young people show that they recognize, accept, and place themselves in a set of roles (age, authority, gender, family, and peer roles) that are explicitly seen as Vietnamese. Therefore, respect involves more than just a value, but it also functions as a concrete expression of the forms of behavior between individuals holding different positions in the network of social relations, and engagement in that network provides entrance into the ethnic group as a whole, access to the group's resources, and exposure to the norms prescribed by the group.

THE COMPLEXITY OF ETHNIC INVOLVEMENT

Vietnamese communities across the United States are characterized by multiple levels of ethnic involvement. In one way or another, the common refugee experience and cultural heritage have brought almost all Vietnamese refugees and most of their offspring into a dense social system made up not merely of family and friendship ties but also of connections of ethnic religious and work organizations. These networks help

Vietnamese gain access to material support as well as to intangible support and thus actively engage both adult and young members of the community. Over time, these connections become increasingly closed and complex in form.

Family and Kinship Networks

The Vietnamese community of Versailles Village has developed through chain migration, newest arrivals having been drawn by relatives and friends from the same towns or villages. The Reverend Michael Viet-Anh, a priest in the Versailles area, was quoted in the *Times Picayune* (April 1, 1985) as estimating that "about 60 percent of the Vietnamese in the Versailles community once lived in Bui Chi province in North Vietnam and later moved to Vung Tau (a coastal town in former South Vietnam)." Another 30 percent of the residents came from two other northern villages that moved south en masse in the 1954 division of Vietnam. But, as was seen in the last chapter, this reconstruction of Vietnamese villages on the banks of the bayous resulted from ethnic networking, rather than from official resettlement policy.

Almost all our interviewees in Versailles Village reported that they had been attracted to New Orleans by some sort of family or kinship connection. They told us they came "because my brother was here," "because my uncle was here," or "because some other relatives were already here." In other cases, migrants moved for occupational and climate reasons: "I heard there were jobs for fishermen" or "I heard the weather was like the weather in Vietnam." But here too we saw the effect of family networks, since information about New Orleans was conveyed through family connections: "My wife's uncle, who was already here, told us about it in a letter" or "I heard about it from my cousin." Migration through networks thus created a transplanted village; in this setting, the migrants succeeded in retaining their traditional ways and adapting their homeland practices to American life at a more gradual pace. Because they shared connections, they were also likely to share a high degree of consensus on community goals, norms, and standards as well as on the issue of change.

Religious Participation

Religious participation provides yet another form of ethnic involvement. Buddhism and Catholicism are the most important religions among

Vietnamese refugees in the United States, and for both Buddhists and Catholics, the religious institution is much more than a house of worship; it is a place where they can share feelings and emotions, engage collectively in the struggle to reestablish their lives, and transmit the ancestral language and culture to the younger generation. Thich Thien Chi, the chief monk of Phap Hoa Temple in a small Vietnamese community in New York City, said to us, "The point of this temple is to have people come together and teach them how to be a good person. To guide them out of their suffering."

The temples and churches are sites for regular worship and other formal religious practices; they also function as social service organizations, operating a wide range of programs such as after-school programs for children, youth programs, summer camps, festival celebrations, and family counseling. One Buddhist center in Little Saigon, for example, conducts courses for Vietnamese children on Sunday mornings, when roughly two hundred children aged 7 to 18 are taught Vietnamese and hear talks on Vietnamese culture. Similar programs for both children and adults can be found in the Catholic church.

Versailles Village is heavily Catholic, and the Catholic church is the single most important ethnic institution. Of the Vietnamese high school students we surveyed, 87 percent told us that they were Catholic; 10 percent were Buddhists, and the rest fell into a range of other denominations, such as Baptists and *Cao Dai* (an indigenous Vietnamese religion). There were no Vietnamese Buddhist temples in the immediate vicinity of Versailles Village, but there was a Vietnamese temple in New Orleans, easily reached by car. The neighborhood contained two Vietnamese churches: a small Baptist church, with a tiny but almost exclusively Vietnamese congregation, and a large Catholic church, Mary Queen of Vietnam Church, whose location at the geographical center of the neighborhood reflected its institutional centrality to the community, as all the Catholics were parishioners of that church. The pastor of the Catholic church maintained close contact with monks at the nearby Buddhist temple, and the religious leaders often coordinated activities that concern all the Vietnamese in New Orleans. Despite the theological differences between the Catholics and the small number of Buddhists, we observed little difference in the social functions of Vietnamese Catholic churches and Vietnamese Buddhist temples in New Orleans, which corresponded to the anthropologist Paul J. Rutledge's findings of a Vietnamese community in Oklahoma City (1985).

Like the religious institutions in Little Saigon, Mary Queen of Vietnam Church in Versailles Village ran after-school classes for young people. While these classes were organized by religious personnel, such as Brother John Nhon, the volunteer teachers were frequently Vietnamese public school teachers or assistant teachers. The church concerned itself not just with religious teachings but with broader educational issues as well. For instance, when leaders in the Vietnamese community attempted to initiate the teaching of Vietnamese as an elective in a public high school in 1991, and when Vietnamese educators and concerned citizens were protesting the elimination of the Office of ESL–Bilingual Education in 1992, community leaders met with an official of the Orleans Parish ESL–Bilingual Education Section in Monsignor Luong's office at the church (personal communications with Jesse Nash, Sept. 1, 1993, and Charlotte Stever, Sept. 23, 1993).

Given its centrality, the church serves as a primary mechanism for integrating young people into the community's system of ethnic relations. Theoretically, we thus argue that the involvement with ethnic religious institutions can strengthen ethnic identification while also reaffirming ethnic affiliation. To validate this theoretical argument, we asked in our 1994 survey whether young people who participated more often in Vietnamese religious organizations were more likely than others to describe themselves unequivocally as "Vietnamese" rather than as "Vietnamese American" or "American." Since most young people in this community showed some level of religious participation, we looked at differences among those who attend their church or temple once a month or less, about once a week, and more than once a week.

It should be noted that religious participation appears to be extremely intense. As is shown in table 4.1, about 43 percent of the Vietnamese high school students whom we surveyed went to church or temple more than once a week; another 38 percent went to church or temple about once a week, and only 20 percent of them were infrequent churchgoers or nonparticipants in ethnic religious institutions. Those who went once a week or more than once a week were more likely to describe themselves as "Vietnamese" than the infrequent churchgoers or nonparticipants. None of those who attended more than once a week chose "American" as a self-description. By contrast, over 10 percent of the infrequent churchgoers or nonparticipants preferred "American" as a self-description.

Self-description, of course, is only one aspect of involvement with an ethnic group: one can describe oneself as belonging to a group and yet maintain no day-to-day contact with coethnic members. Moreover, our

TABLE 4.1 Ethnic Self-Identification of Vietnamese Youths, by Frequency of Church or Temple Attendance

	Church or Temple Attendance			
	Once a Month or Less	About Once a Week	More Than Once a Week	Row Total (N)
American (%)	10.3	3.4	0.0	3.3 (13)
Vietnamese American (%)	38.5	29.5	33.9	33.2 (131)
Vietnamese (%)	51.3	67.1	66.1	63.5 (251)
Column total (%)	19.7	37.7	42.5	100.0
(N)	(78)	(149)	(168)	(395)

Source: The Versailles Village Survey of 1994.
Chi-Square = 20.63; $p < .01$

argument establishes a linkage between religious involvement and ethnic affiliations. We measured ethnic affiliations by ethnic preferences for co-ethnic friendship and marital partners. One can judge the extent to which individuals find themselves enmeshed in an ethnic network by the degree to which ethnicity defines their friendship circles. To explore this issue, we looked at the relationship between church or temple attendance and the proportion of the respondents' friends who were coethnic (see table 4.2). Here there was a linear relationship, with striking differences between frequent and infrequent religious participants. Nearly 70 percent of the students who attended church or temple more than weekly responded that either all or almost all of their friends were Vietnamese, and only 4 percent of them reported that they had some or very few Vietnamese friends. In contrast, only 42 percent of those who showed little or no participation in ethnic religious institutions said most of their friends were Vietnamese, while well over a fifth (22 percent) of them reported that they had some or very few Vietnamese friends.

We then asked about preference for marital partners. As table 4.3 shows, young Vietnamese who attended a religious institution often were more likely to prefer a Vietnamese spouse. Of the two groups of respondents who attended once a week or more, almost two-thirds said that they would "prefer" or "definitely want" to marry someone who was Vietnamese. Marrying within the group was widely desired and widely expected. Those who attended church or temple infrequently or not at

TABLE 4.2 Proportion of Coethnic Friends Among Vietnamese Youths, by Frequency of Church or Temple Attendance

	Church or Temple Attendance			
	Once a Month or Less	About Once a Week	More Than Once a Week	Row Total (*N*)
None (%)	3.8	1.3	0.0	1.3 (5)
Very few (%)	7.7	5.4	2.4	4.6 (18)
Some (%)	10.3	3.4	1.8	4.1 (16)
About half (%)	15.4	8.1	9.5	10.1 (40)
Most (%)	20.5	34.2	17.8	24.6 (97)
Almost all or all (%)	42.3	47.6	68.5	55.3 (219)
Column Total (%)	19.8	37.7	42.5	100.0
(*N*)	(78)	(149)	(168)	(395)

Source: The Versailles Village Survey of 1994.
Chi-square = 40.88; $p < .01$

all, however, were more likely to say that they did not care whether they married a Vietnamese person or not (46 percent, compared with 38 percent for weekly participants and 28 percent for those who attended more than weekly), or even that they definitely did not want or preferred not to marry someone who was Vietnamese (9 percent, compared with 2 percent of those who attended weekly and less than 1 percent—one individual—of those who attended more than weekly). Moreover, commitment to endogamy is not simply associated with participation in ethnic religious institutions. The relationship is linear: the greater the participation, the greater the commitment to marrying within the group. Of course, the theoretical choice of a marriage partner is highly speculative, and the actual choice may be limited by the lack of contact. For example, one of the young Vietnamese men that we interviewed remarked, "I don't have anything against other (non-Vietnamese) girls. I just don't think they would completely understand what I have to say, even if I say it in English." Nonetheless, endogamy indicates intense ethnic involvement.

TABLE 4.3 Commitment to Endogamy Among Vietnamese
Youths, by Frequency of Church or Temple
Attendance

	Church or Temple Attendance			
	Once a Month or Less	About Once a Week	More Than Once a Week	Row Total (N)
Definitely do not want Vietnamese spouse (%)	5.1	1.3	0.6	1.8 (7)
Prefer non-Vietnamese spouse (%)	3.8	0.7	0.0	1.0 (4)
Do not care (%)	46.2	37.6	28.0	35.2 (139)
Prefer Vietnamese spouse (%)	28.2	40.9	41.6	38.7 (153)
Definitely want Vietnamese spouse (%)	16.7	19.5	29.8	23.3 (92)
Column Total (%)	19.8	37.7	42.5	100.0
(N)	(78)	(149)	(168)	(395)

Source: The Versailles Village Survey of 1994.
Chi-square = 28.09; $p < .01$

Community-Based Organizations

Closely connected to the religious institutions are various secular social
organizations. In Versailles Village, for example, the formalized, well-
established, and influential organizations include the Vietnamese-American Voters' Association, the Political Prisoner Veterans Union, the Versailles Neighborhood Association, the *Dung Lac* (a youth program), and
the Vietnamese Educational Association. The most important organization affecting young people directly is the Vietnamese Educational Association. This association runs two major projects—after-school classes at
the Child Development Center and an annual awards ceremony in
honor of Vietnamese students who have excelled in the public school
system. Although both projects are held on the grounds of the Catholic
church, the educational association is not an exclusively Catholic organization. A Buddhist monk sits on its board of directors, and Buddhist as
well as Catholic children may participate in after-school classes and receive awards at the annual ceremony. The after-school classes, offered on

a voluntary basis to elementary and high school students, emphasize language instruction in both English and Vietnamese, although other academic subjects are also offered from time to time. The English language classes serve the needs of relatively new arrivals and others whose English skills are weak; the Vietnamese language classes serve the native-born and those who have lived in the United States since early childhood. The Vietnamese language classes, which are taught by a Vietnamese priest attached to the church, place a heavy emphasis on reading and writing skills, since many young people who learn to speak their parental language in the home have never had an opportunity to develop literacy.

Vietnamese social workers run the *Dung Lac* (named after a Vietnamese religious martyr), which was set up by a Vietnamese priest in 1991 to cope with the growing problems of troubled youths. This organization, which features weekend retreats, evening sports events, and service projects such as cleaning up the neighborhood, seeks to involve troubled youths in productive activities and eventually get them into "life planning" courses that provide counseling and access to jobs.

Virtually all community organizations and activities have a church connection. For example, the local Vietnamese Voters Association, which helps to prepare eligible community members for the test for U.S. citizenship, holds all its meetings on the grounds of the church, and a priest serves as its advisor. The church also provides the site for community meetings at irregular intervals to discuss problems and goals. Every Saturday morning, the church grounds become an open-air market, where all Vietnamese in the Versailles neighborhood can sell their goods. The entire church parish divides itself into zones, each of which has a "zone leader," an influential person, who represents zone residents at meetings held at the church to decide both secular and religious activities and policies. All these continuing church-centered activities provide ample opportunities for ethnic interaction and thus help strengthen ties among members while also reinforcing the leadership roles of religious institutions and community-based organizations.

Participation in Ethnic Economies

Various economic activities within the Vietnamese community add yet another dimension to the complexity of ethnic involvements. In Versailles Village, informal ethnic resources—loans, labor, and protected markets—facilitate the birth and growth of immigrant businesses. As many studies have found, ethnic entrepreneurship provides group members with an alternative path to upward social mobility (see for example, Aldrich and Waldinger 1990; Light 1972; Light and Bonacich 1988; Portes and Zhou 1992; Zhou 1992). Though its economic benefits have been widely acknowledged, the social effects of economic entrepreneurship have been less frequently recognized. This is an important gap, for in the Vietnamese community, as in many other immigrant communities, ethnic economies have intensified ethnic attachment in many ways.

Once again, the gardens of Versailles Village provide a useful example. Gardening not only fulfills an economic function but affects the process of adaptation through its impact on family relations. Gardening preserves traditional dietary patterns and tastes by supplying ethnic produce to the open-market and to restaurants and thus enhances ethnic identification (Airriess and Clawson 1994). At the same time, it helps to maintain the authority of the older generation and restore the respect that is weakened by the elderly's economic dependence. Most of the gardeners are elderly and have had difficulty in finding a place in the larger American labor market, but they have found a protected niche in gardening. A 62-year-old woman told us, "I do not know what else I could do. I don't know any English, and I'm too old to get a job. I like to garden, and it is the only thing for me." Gardening also provides a way for the older generation to contribute to the welfare of the family, and that in turn helps the gardeners regain some level of independence, sustaining their role as a valued source of direction and tradition.

The economic activities in the Vietnamese community not only enable families to be self-sufficient but also help finance community-based organizations and keep capital within the ethnic network of social relations. For example, contributions from Vietnamese around the New Orleans area furnished the funds needed to build the churches and temples. Similarly, Vietnamese shopkeepers and fishing-boat owners played key roles in endowing the Child Development Center and the annual awards ceremony of the Vietnamese Educational Association. Whatever the cause, the names of the contributors and the amounts of their contributions become public information. "If they don't give enough," one informant observed, "everyone knows and they will lose face. But if they give a lot of money, everyone will look up to them."

In sum, the resources generated through intact families and cooperative community-based organizations provide important, albeit partial, compensation for the low socioeconomic status of the Vietnamese. Intertwined as they are, the various community-oriented activities operated by the religious institutions and by the formal or informal secular organizations have created multiple memberships for the Vietnamese. While the membership of a particular organization changes somewhat from year to year, the same group of people tends to provide members for each of those interlocking community organizations. Our 1994 survey found that not only did over 80 percent of the Vietnamese students participate in religious activities once a week or more, but over a third of their parents belonged to at least one ethnic organization (Bankston and Zhou 1995b). Such a "dense set of associations," to borrow a phrase from James S. Coleman (1990b), gives Versailles Villagers a particularly strong network of social relations in the ethnic community.

INTEGRATION AS A MECHANISM OF SOCIAL CONTROL

Integration into the ethnic community involves the acceptance of beliefs, values, and norms shared by the members. As has been discussed, the members of the Vietnamese community have access to both tangible and intangible supports. However, they are also subject to social control in the community. Social control in the Vietnamese community takes two contrasting forms: sanctions and affirmation. Sanctions are mainly imposed through the informal channels of the "Vietnamese microscope" (Nash 1992). People in Versailles Village know one another well. They enjoy connections to one another through family and friendship networks, and they meet often at such places as the church, restaurants, and the market place. Funerals and wedding ceremonies are not simply big family events but also community events, often involving as many as four to five hundred people. These occasions provide opportunities to socialize with others, to show off recent familial accomplishments, to compare with others, and to exchange gossip and rumors. All these connections and interactions yield a small-town effect; people are aware of what is going on around them, which family is doing what, who has just opened up a store, who has bought a new house, who is getting married, who has died, whose child has won a scholarship, and whose child has been involved in a gang or in shameful activities.

Observation and judgment are thus pervasive. The community is watchful and ever-vigilant, and there is consensus about norms. Violation of the rules is to be punished, especially when the rule breakers are children. In Versailles Village, the old Vietnamese proverb that, "parents may be far away, but neighbors are always near," lives on (Nash 1992).

Violation of the norm—when a child flunks out or drops out of school, when a boy gets involved in a gang, or when an unmarried girl becomes pregnant—brings shame not only on the individual violator but on the family as well. Expressing a common attitude, a father with four daughters and one son told us, "When my children do well, everyone knows, and they think I have done well. When my children do something bad, everyone knows that too, and I have to take the blame." A 17-year-old high school student gave us a similar account, albeit with a slightly different angle: "The Vietnamese people here, they're always minding everyone else's business, so you really can't get away with anything. Anything I do, everybody knows, and there's so much gossip that you have to watch your step all the time."

If community sanctions are strict, affirmation of expected behavior is equally forceful. When a child makes good grades or wins awards in school, the community honors both the child and his or her family. As one parent remarked, "My children know that if they become doctor or become engineer, I share it with them, and our friends and neighbors share it. But if they fail, we all fail." An 18-year-old man acknowledged, "If you graduate at the top of your class and it looks like you're going to become a doctor or engineer, you're like a hero to everyone." The entire Versailles community recognizes academic achievement each spring in an awards ceremony to honor young people who have done exceptionally well in school. The ceremony, attended by most of the neighborhood's residents, serves as a strong formal affirmation of accomplishment.

By American standards, Versailles Village seems to have all the constraints and inhibitions of small-town life and all the qualities that make that life irksome for youth. "In the Versailles neighborhood, I don't feel I am in America," said a U.S.-born, 16-year-old high school student. "Here even if you help out at home, do well in school, conform to rules, you always feel you haven't done enough. My parents don't know much English, and they work days, nights, and weekends. They are so busy that there is no time for family communication or conference with the teacher. But I always feel they know how I am doing. I really can't feel free to do things I like." But are such tight controls necessarily suffocating? "I'd have to say no," replied the same student. "Young people can easily get lost in a maze of confusing values and norms in America. I think the control is necessary and good for you after all."

Thus the community and family networks of Versailles Village create a distinctive set of social relations based on "respect" according to social roles, surround young people with a complex system of ethnic involvements including economic, religious, and psychological elements, and hold young people to a system of norms and values directing them toward constructive patterns of behavior. Paradoxically, intense ethnic involvement increases rather than decreases the probability that young people will gain entry into the world beyond the ethnic community. In emphasizing the benefits of family and of the ethnic community, however, we have described only one side of the story. In the social relations of family, neighborhood, and ethnic community, the residents of Versailles Village have established an island of social harmony that smooths out many of the difficulties in refugee adjustment, as will be discussed in the next two chapters. However, the ethnic community cannot possibly solve all the problems, and indeed, it may become the source of new tensions. Chapter 7 will discuss some of the ways in which the social pressures of this tightly knit ethnic community produce tensions as well as achievements, especially when these achievements come at some cost to the individual. And Chapter 8 will consider some of the ways in which the high level of integration characteristic of the Versailles enclave simultaneously aggravates the difficulties of the youth who rebel or otherwise refuse to conform.

—— Chapter 5 ——

Language and Adaptation

> The meaning of my name is sad autumn
> I'm 16 years old and I'm always sad,
> I often write poems
> Now I have many poems, but they are all in Vietnamese.
> I cannot change it to English
> Cause my English is very bad,
> Oh, my story is very sad!
> —a teenager at the Philippine Refugee Processing Center
> (Kuntz 1986, 55)

In the eyes of the American public, proficiency in English is the first step to successful immigrant adaptation to American society and an important part of "becoming American." House speaker Newt Gingrich made it clear, "If we want to ensure that all our children have the same opportunity in life, alternative language education should stop and English should be acknowledged once and for all as the official language in the United States" (*Los Angeles Times*, October 31, 1995). In order to understand fully the process of adaptation of Vietnamese refugees and their children, it is necessary to consider the role of language—both proficiency in English and literacy in their native tongue. Does the lack of English skills hinder the assimilation of Vietnamese children into American society? Does the maintenance of their parents' native tongue necessarily lead to unfavorable outcomes as these children adapt to school and grow into adulthood? This chapter first examines some of the main factors involved in the abandonment or maintenance of the parental language. Next, it considers the socioeconomic correlates of language use. Finally, it addresses the issue of how use of the Vietnamese language in communicating with coethnics may affect children's adaptation to school.

LINGUISTIC ADAPTATION
The Language Barrier

Learning the ropes involves learning English. For most contemporary immigrants from non-English-speaking countries in the Americas and Asia, that goal often poses a real challenge. For the Vietnamese, English-language difficulties are particularly severe; in 1990, when half of all immigrants reported to the census takers that they did not speak English very well, as many as three-quarters of the Vietnamese characterized their English this way.

The majority of Vietnamese children begin with less than a full command of English, and most of their parents speak very little English. In 1992, for example, San Diego classified over 40 percent of its Vietnamese students as Limited English Proficient (LEP), compared with 16 percent of the children of other Asian immigrants (Rumbaut 1995a). In the two New Orleans public schools that we studied, at least a third of the Vietnamese high school students experienced at least some difficulty in English; close to 70 percent of the Vietnamese students at Washington High School who took the Louisiana Graduation Exit Examination were classified as LEPs, while about a third at Jefferson High School fell into that category. Almost all of Versailles Village's Vietnamese students spoke Vietnamese at home.

Linguistic isolation aggravates problems of English proficiency. In 1990, a quarter of all immigrants in the United States lived in linguistically isolated neighborhoods, but over half (53 percent) the Vietnamese lived in such neighborhoods. Many Vietnamese children were attending schools where their peers overwhelmingly spoke either foreign languages or nonstandard English. Public schools in Little Saigon received Latinos and other foreign-born students along with a disproportionately large Vietnamese population. In New Orleans, where there are relatively few immigrants, most Vietnamese children lived in linguistically isolated neighborhoods with other coethnics and attending public schools in which the large majority of students are black.

Linguistic isolation makes English acquisition extremely difficult. Children living in isolated neighborhoods do not have much contact with people who speak standard English. Moreover, they generally come from families with limited or no English, and since these families usually operate at a disadvantage in the marketplace, the children with weak English-language skills also tend to have few financial and other resources. Nonetheless, these children constantly face pressure, both from their schools and from parents, to become proficient in English.

The language barrier creates academic and social stresses that often impede children's adaptation to the American school system. A Vietnamese college student who arrived as a teenager in Versailles Village recalled the anxiety she suffered on her first day of high school:

> I kept my mouth shut all the time. In class, I was sitting there like a dummy. I didn't know what the teacher was saying, what my fellow students were doing, and what I was supposed to be doing. I wished to be able to speak English, but was afraid to try. The class periods seemed unbearably long. I sat still, but I was restless inside. When the bell rang I rushed to my [Vietnamese] friends just to say something, anything [in Vietnamese].

Another Vietnamese college student, who also arrived in New Orleans as a teenager, echoed these feelings:

> I told my parents to buy me a watch after I got off the first day of school. I had to have a watch to be wearing to school. I just couldn't stand sitting there waiting mindlessly for the bell to ring. All I wanted was for class to be over. The watch really helped, because I at least knew how many minutes away from the next time when I was able to speak with friends.

Even when students gained limited proficiency, they still had to struggle to increase their vocabulary; and the ability to use English to express more complex thoughts remained elusive. A Vietnamese high school student who had learned some English in a refugee camp in Hong Kong before arriving in New Orleans explained:

> I understood just a few English words on my first day of school. The only class that seemed to make some sense to me was the math class, because I was sort of able to guess what the teacher was saying by looking at the symbols she wrote on the board. Actually, math became my favorite subject; it was quite easy and straightforward. What I was frustrated at most was that I wasn't able to express myself or raise my hand in class when I had a question or when I knew the answer to a question. But in social science or language and arts, I was hopeless. Now things are getting much better, but I still can't imagine myself making A's in language and arts.

Many urban schools in immigrant cities have sought to help English-deficient students. From our observations in the New Orleans public schools, bilingual education (BE) and English as a Second Language (ESL) classes, specially designed for Vietnamese students, were their most effective tools. Although the schools we studied had extremely limited resources, the available BE and ESL programs served as vital means of introducing newly arrived Vietnamese students to the American school system. Not only did these classes help students achieve the necessary command of English, but they also served to mediate between the larger English-speaking environment of the schools and the small circle of Vietnamese students. Washington High School employed one ESL teacher and a Vietnamese assistant teacher. Because of the close connection to the Vietnamese, the ESL teacher was also in charge of the *Tet* (Vietnamese New Year) celebrations, the Asian Club, and virtually all the other activities oriented toward the Vietnamese that took place at the school.

One student who had just completed the ESL program remarked:

> I certainly think these programs have helped me. In ESL classes, I remembered, the course work I had trouble understanding would suddenly make sense to me with the help of teachers who spoke Vietnamese and were specially sensitive to our feelings. Plus, I didn't have to be afraid to ask a question when I had one, because I was able to use my own language. Here I wasn't feeling totally alone and nervous. It was a different room atmosphere and made me feel like I was in school. I think the ESL classes were not just helping us to learn English, they helped us overcome the uneasiness of being nobody.

Along similar lines, a teacher observed, "I can't say whether these Vietnamese kids would have learned English faster in their homeroom than through the ESL program, since most went through ESL. But ESL programs at least help them regain self-esteem and the sense of being in school and eventually meld their broken English into their required course work."

School programs like ESL and bilingual education, however, are only catch-up programs for those operating under linguistic handicaps. Their goal is to move students toward facility in English. In Versailles Village, both Vietnamese children and their parents agree that English ability is a necessity for success in school. But many disagree that English acquisition should necessarily be at the expense of Vietnamese language skills.

In fact, the dominant language-use pattern among Vietnamese children, as well as among other children of non-English-speaking immigrants, is fluent bilingualism rather than English monolingualism.

The Shift Toward English

Despite the recency of immigration, Vietnamese children have rapidly shifted their primary language use toward English, as have other immigrant children from non-English-speaking countries. Based on the 1990 census, table 5.1 illustrates the main language-use patterns—fully bilingual, limited bilingual, and English monolingual—among immigrant children aged 5 to 17 years. The Vietnamese are compared with the Chinese and other Southeast Asians and also with black children and white children who were living with least one foreign-born parent. "Limited bilingual" refers to those who speak English less than "very well" and speak a non-English language at home, "fully bilingual" to those who report speaking English "very well" and also speak another language at home, and "English monolingual" to those who speak only English (Lopez 1996).

As table 5.1 shows, the children of all Asian groups were less likely to be English monolinguals than either the black or the white children of immigrant parentage. Vietnamese and other Southeast Asian refugee children, however, were more likely than Chinese children to fall into the category of "limited bilingual," and thus to have greater language difficulties, perhaps because of their more recent arrival. In the 1990 census, foreign-born persons made up 80 percent of all Vietnamese, 76 percent of other Southeast Asians, and 69 percent of all Chinese. Among the foreign-born, 62 percent of the Vietnamese, 82 percent of other Southeast Asians, 57 percent of the Chinese have entered the United States after 1980.

Controlling for immigrant generations changes the pattern, producing a general shift toward English, as can be seen in table 5.2. On the one hand, the proportion of those who were limited bilinguals dropped substantially from the first to the second generations for all groups. On the other hand, for Asian children, regardless of nationality groups, the dominant mode of linguistic adaptation was to become "fluent bilinguals" rather than "English monolinguals," whereas the children of black or white immigrants were more likely to become English monolinguals by the second generation.

For Asian children, then, the shift toward English does not result in

TABLE 5.1 Children's Language Abilities, Selected Ethnicities, 1990

	Limited Bilingual[a]	Fluent Bilingual	English Monolingual
Vietnamese (%)	44.1	46.2	9.7
(N)	(2,897)	(3,034)	(642)
Other Southeast Asian (%)	60.7	34.9	4.4
(N)	(3,572)	(2,057)	(259)
Chinese (%)	30.8	45.9	23.3
(N)	(3,810)	(5,696)	(2,892)
Black (%)[b]	9.1	15.6	75.3
(N)	(482)	(831)	(4,012)
White (%)[b]	6.4	24.0	69.6
(N)	(205)	(772)	(2,242)

Source: U.S. Census of Population and Housing, 1990, 5-percent PUMS.
Note: Sample included children aged 5 to 17 living in family households.
[a] Includes a small percentage (under 2 percent) of children who did not speak English at all.
[b] Undersampled; respondents had at least one foreign-born parent.

rapid abandonment of their parents' native tongues. Three interconnected factors may account for native language retention. First, continuing high rates of immigration from Asia and family reunification keep the second generation in immediate contact with new arrivals from their parents' native countries. Second, the parents' lack of English proficiency, commonly the case in Asian families, requires children to speak their parents' native tongue at home. Third, living in an area inhabited by coethnics, as Asian children are more likely than others to do, tends to slow the shift toward English monolingualism.

What accounts for the distinctive Asian pattern? Language environments at home, for both Chinese and other Southeast Asian children, provide a crucial contributing factor. Though children shift to English more rapidly than their parents, parental linguistic ability strongly influences the rate of change, as can be seen in table 5.3. In the 1990 census, limited-bilingual children were most likely to live with parents who spoke no English; fluent-bilingual children were most likely to live with parents who were also fluent bilingual; and a very high percentage (80 percent) of English- monolingual children lived with parents who also spoke only English. Place of residence yields an additional effect; living in neighborhoods characterized by high Vietnamese density delays the shift toward English monolingualism.[1] Density slows but does not halt the pattern, however, even in ethnically concentrated neighborhoods, almost half the children were fluent bilinguals.

TABLE 5.2   Children's Language Abilities by Generation,
Selected Ethnicities, 1990

	Limited Bilingual (%)	Fluent Bilingual (%)	English Monolingual (%)
Vietnamese			
1st generation	84.7	14.1	1.2
1.5 generation	54.0	43.0	3.0
2nd generation	37.0	50.4	12.6
Other Southeast Asian			
1st generation	79.7	17.5	2.8
1.5 generation	64.6	33.3	2.1
2nd generation	36.4	58.3	5.3
Chinese			
1st generation	71.2	26.5	2.3
1.5 generation	49.9	45.5	4.6
2nd generation	23.9	46.6	29.5
Black[a]			
1st generation	17.9	16.8	65.3
1.5 generation	14.3	16.9	68.8
2nd generation	7.8	15.3	76.9
White[a]			
1st generation	29.4	41.2	29.4
1.5 generation	19.8	48.1	32.1
2nd generation	5.1	22.2	72.7

Source: U.S. Census of Population and Housing, 1990, 5-percent PUMS.
Note: Sample included children aged 5 to 17 living in family households.
[a] Undersampled; respondents had at least one foreign-born parent.
Includes a small percentage (under 2 percent) of children who did not speak English at all.

Family socioeconomic status exercises yet another influence on children's language abilities, as can been seen in table 5.4, which presents data on second-generation children only, in order to isolate children with little homeland exposure to Vietnamese. As one might expect, limited bilingualism declines as parental social standing increases, whether parental education or occupation serves as the indicator. In other words, second-generation Vietnamese children who are further along on the shift to English tend to come from households whose heads are better educated and hold managerial and professional occupations. Clearly, there are advantages associated with the shift toward English for Vietnamese children; English predominates in socioeconomically privileged families and nonsegregated neighborhoods. Nevertheless, fluent bilingualism, rather than English monolingualism, remains the most com-

TABLE 5.3   Influences of Parents' Language Abilities and
Residential Concentration on Vietnamese Children's
Language Abilities

	Limited Bilingual (%)	Fluent Bilingual (%)	English Monolingual (%)
Parents' language abilities			
No English	73.6	23.9	2.5
Limited bilingual	49.7	45.3	5.0
Fluent bilingual	26.3	64.7	9.0
English monolingual	7.2	12.3	80.5
Residential concentration			
Coethnically concentrated neighborhoods	45.9	47.1	7.0
Other neighborhoods	38.1	43.6	18.3

Source: U.S. Census of Population and Housing, 1990, 5-percent PUMS.
Note: Sample included children aged 5 to 17 living in family households.

mon mode of second-generation children's language use; advantageous parental socioeconomic status accelerates the shift to English but does not sever the tie to Vietnamese.

SKILLS IN THE PARENTAL NATIVE LANGUAGE AND ADAPTATION

Language shift itself serves as an indicator of assimilation, but one would also expect it to affect other aspects of adaptation, most importantly, children's performance in school. The conventional view is that English-dominant Vietnamese children will do better in school than their Vietnamese-dominant peers. Analyses of our findings, however, suggest a different relationship.

The Model of Parental Native Language and School Adaptation

The use of a parental native language can inhibit the development of English proficiency, in which case the parental native language may be a liability. The impact of parents' linguistic patterns, however, is mediated by the social context in which language shift occurs. If the social contacts within an ethnic group contribute less to an individual's advance-

TABLE 5.4   Language Abilities of U.S.-Born Vietnamese
Children, by Family Socioeconomic Status

	Limited Bilingual %	Fluent Bilingual %	English Monolingual %
Household head's education			
Less than high school	46.2	46.4	7.4
High school graduate	38.1	48.6	13.3
At least some college	30.5	53.0	16.5
Household head's occupations[a]			
Managerial/professional	24.0	54.4	21.6
Technical	32.7	53.3	14.0
Sales/service	36.0	52.6	11.4
Laborer	38.3	49.5	12.2

Source: U.S. Census of Population and Housing, 1990, 5-percent PUMS.
Note: Sample included children aged 5 to 17 living in family households.
[a] Including only those reporting occupations.

ment than the social contacts outside of the group, then the use of the
ethnic language will be less advantageous than English. If, however, non-
English-speaking parents consciously push children to do well in school
and if social contacts within the ethnic group promote academic achievement as a means to upward social mobility, then continued facility in the
parental native language can contribute to adaptive scholastic outcomes. In
this case, advanced skills in the parental native language may act as a
conduit for social capital, solidifying children's ties to the ethnic community and maintaining their exposure to the norms it embraces and the
measures it uses to enforce those norms (Bankston and Zhou 1995a).

It is this model of the relationship between skills in the parental native language and school adaptation that is now assessed in the remaining of this chapter. On the basis of our 1994 survey in Versailles Village,
our model examines two dimensions of adaptation: present-day scholastic accomplishment and future educational aspirations. Present-day performance is measured in terms of reported grades. A composite measure
of future educational aspirations is constructed from answers to a survey
question asking "How important is going to college for you?" Respondents could answer "I definitely do not want to attend college," "It's not
very important," "Going to college is fairly important for me," or
"Going to college is very important for me."

One of the main independent variables is Vietnamese literacy, which was taken from students' own evaluations of their reading and writing abilities in responses to two questions: "How well do you read Vietnamese?" and "How well do you write Vietnamese?" Possible responses to both of these questions were "not at all," "a little," "fairly well," and "very well." Although there might be some individual variation in understanding what constitutes reading and writing a language well, in the aggregate these variations should not affect the reliability of the measure. Responses to these two items were extremely highly correlated ($r = .944$), indicating that such reporting reflects consistency.[2] Although there may be some question about the ability of these students to evaluate their own language skills according to the standards of a trained linguist, our purpose was to compare the students with higher literacy skills with those with lower literacy skills, and therefore what mattered was whether these students showed a consistent pattern of reporting the skills, not whether an individual student's reporting was accurate. As will be seen in the discussion that follows, the self-assessments among respondents are associated with other variables in readily comprehensible patterns.

Another important independent variable is ethnic identification. Identification with the ethnic group is the most complex and abstract of the variables included here. In essence, this variable addresses the issue of the extent to which the students feel their own identities to be tied to the identity of their ethnic group. We therefore consider the five worldwide characteristics of ethnicity suggested by the anthropologists Charles Wagley and Marvin Harris (1964): unequal treatment as an ethnic minority group member, easily identifiable by physical or cultural characteristics, a sense of peoplehood, ascribed membership, and the practice of endogamy. Three of these characteristics (unequal treatment, identifiable traits, and ascribed membership) are involuntary and externally imposed; two (sense of peoplehood and endogamy) are voluntary and indicate the extent to which ethnic group members include themselves in the ethnic group, rather than having group membership imposed upon them. As chapter 4 described, questions in our survey measured both of these voluntary aspects of ethnic group membership (see tables 4.1 and 4.3). The items on self-identification and commitment to endogamy were combined to create a scale of ethnic identification ranging from 0 (self-identification as "American" combined with a definite intent to marry outside the group) to 6 (self-identification as "Vietnamese" combined with a definite intent to marry in the group).

In any study of academic achievement, it is important to consider the part played by the students' own efforts. Our respondents were asked "How much time do you usually spend on homework each day?" They could answer "I don't do homework," "less than thirty minutes," "half an hour to an hour," "one to two hours," or "over two hours." Another important control variable is the socioeconomic background of the family. We used the father's education as a reasonable proxy for the socioeconomic background of the students' families in Vietnam, since the current economic status of their families in the community under study did not differ substantially. The father's education varied from less than high school to completion of a graduate degree.

Table 5.5 shows the percentage distributions of the variables included in this analysis. Because so few students were at the lowest grade levels and so many at the highest grade levels, D and F students (those with averages below 1.5) combined into a single category. A distinction was also made between B- students (those with averages from 2.5 through 2.9) and B+ students (those with averages from 3.0 through 3.4). Overall, more than half the students reported B averages, and 40 percent B+. Over a quarter of all students reported A averages (teachers in both schools confirmed this level of performance). C averages were much less common, 17 percent of the total, and students with averages of D or F were rare, accounting for only 4 percent of the total.

For the sake of clarity, we collapsed the measure of reading and writing skills into four categories: "not at all or very little," "a little," "fairly well," and "very well." Thirty-one percent of the students reported that they read and wrote their parental native language (Vietnamese) very well, 29 percent fairly well, 26 percent a little, and 14 percent could not read or write Vietnamese at all. With regard to ethnic identification, more than half the students reported having strong ethnic identification, and only 4 percent of them reported having very weak ethnic identification. In terms of effort, only 5 percent of the students reported that they did not spend time on homework after school, in contrast to over half who reported spending two hours or more on homework. Moreover, more than 40 percent of the students reported that their fathers had less than a high school education. The relatively low level of the fathers' educational attainment implied that the students were mostly from moderate socioeconomic backgrounds.

TABLE 5.5 Percentage Distributions of Variables in the Model of Parental Native Language and School Adaptation

Variable	Percent
Average grades	
A	26.2
B +	39.9
B −	13.2
C	16.7
D and F	4.0
	100.0
Vietnamese literacy	
Reads and writes very well	31.3
Reads and writes fairly well	28.7
Reads and writes a little	25.9
Reads and writes very little or not at all	14.1
	100.0
Self-identification with Vietnamese ethnicity	
0 (Lowest level of ethnic identification)	0.8
1	0.3
2	2.8
3	18.9
4	26.6
5	30.6
6 (Highest level of ethnic identification)	20.0
	100.0
Student effort (time spent on homework after school)	
Does not do homework	5.0
Less than ½ hour	16.7
One-half hour to an hour	24.6
One to two hours	28.0
Over two hours	25.7
	100.0
Father's education	
Less than high school	42.1
High school graduate	39.9
Some college	11.2
College graduate or higher	6.8
	100.0

Source: The Versailles Village Survey of 1994.

Findings from Bivariate Analyses

Table 5.6 shows the relationship between self-reported grades and the ability to read and write Vietnamese. We found a strong relationship between average grades and native language proficiency. Those who could read and write Vietnamese well were much more likely to report receiving A's than those who could not. Among those who could read and write Vietnamese well, 47 percent reported themselves to be A students, and among those who could read and write Vietnamese fairly well, 25 percent reported themselves to be A students. Only 8 percent of the students who could not read and write Vietnamese at all reported A averages.

Among those who could read and write Vietnamese fairly well and among those who could read and write a little, the modal grade was B +. Fifty percent of those who could read and write Vietnamese fairly well had B + averages, while only 39 percent of those who could read or write a little had B + averages. For those who could not read and write their ethnic community's language, C was the average, and this group

TABLE 5.6   Average Self-Reported Grades, by Vietnamese Language Literacy

	Read and Write Not at All or Very Little (%)	Read and Write a Little (%)	Read and Write Fairly Well (%)	Read and Write Very Well (%)	Row Total (N)
F-D	20.4	3.3	1.0	0.0	4.0 (14)
C	30.6	24.4	12.0	8.2	16.7 (58)
B −	12.1	21.1	12.0	8.3	13.2 (46)
B +	28.6	38.9	50.0	36.7	39.9 (139)
A	8.3	12.3	25.0	46.8	26.2 (91)
Column Total (N)	14.1 (49)	25.9 (90)	28.7 (100)	31.3 (109)	100.0 (348)

Source: The Versailles Village Survey of 1994.
Note: Chi square significant at .000 (12 df).

had by far the largest percentage of those making D's and F's. The relationship between grades and literacy in the Vietnamese language appeared significant and linear.

While Table 5.6 offers preliminary evidence on the relationship between present academic achievement of Vietnamese students and literacy in the Vietnamese language, table 5.7 presents evidence for a relationship between attitude toward future education and Vietnamese literacy. Among the respondents to the survey, an overwhelming majority (72 percent) of the students reported that going to college was very important for them. Nearly a fifth (17 percent) said that college attendance was fairly important. Only 5 percent of the total responded that college attendance was not very important, and only 5 percent did not intend to go to college.

Students proficient in Vietnamese were most likely to place a great deal of importance on college attendance; 84 percent responded that a college education was very important to them, as did 80 percent of those who could read and write Vietnamese fairly well. By contrast, 60 percent of those who could read and write Vietnamese a little and only 47 percent of those who could not read and write it at all rated college atten-

TABLE 5.7   Attitude Toward College Attendance, by Vietnamese Language Literacy

	Reading and Writing Skills in Vietnamese				
	Read and Write Not at All or Very Little (%)	Read and Write a Little (%)	Read and Write Fairly Well (%)	Read and Write Very Well (%)	Row Total (N)
Definitely does not want to go to college	18.4	5.6	1.9	3.1	5.3 (20)
Not important	4.1	11.1	4.6	2.2	5.3 (20)
Fairly important	30.6	23.3	13.1	10.5	17.0 (64)
Very important	46.9	60.0	80.4	84.2	72.4 (273)
Column Total (N)	13.0 (49)	23.9 (90)	28.4 (107)	34.7 (131)	100.0 (377)

Source: The Versailles Village Survey of 1994.
Note: Chi square significant at .000 (9 df).

dance as very important. These results suggested a significant and positive effect of ethnic language on orientation toward higher education.

There are two possible explanations for the positive effects of literacy in the parental native language on present academic achievement and future academic aspirations. One may argue that smarter students who are more likely to make good grades and to make college plans are more likely to excel in other areas, such as learning to read and write the language of their ethnic group. In this case, the causal relationship may be spurious. Using "smartness" or "intelligence" as an explanation of accomplishments introduces a variable that is difficult to define and makes an argument that may, to some extent, be tautological. Defining intelligence is largely a matter of *de fructibus cognoscentum*: we say that a student is "intelligent" because that student manifests a certain level of accomplishments in classroom activities or on standardized tests, such as I.Q. tests. The word "intelligence" then is no more an explanation of academic achievement than the word "gravity" is an explanation of why objects attract one another. Still, we cannot completely reject the possibility that there is some ambiguous quality of mind that can be the cause of excellence in disparate fields of endeavor.

Alternatively, one may argue that the process of acquiring parental native language literacy allows children to communicate more effectively with their non-English-speaking parents who stress the value of education and promote habits and attitudes conducive to academic excellence. In this case, the students who can read and write their parental native language may be more receptive to parental guidance and thus more likely to display a positive attitude toward future education. Table 5.8 suggests a more concrete and defensible explanation of the relationship between scholastic accomplishment and parental native language literacy than that of innate intellectual ability: Vietnamese students who read and write Vietnamese well spend more time on homework than those who do not.

The trend shown in this table is clear: The better the students read and write their ethnic language, the more time they spend on homework. Almost 82 percent of those with good ethnic language skills reported spending an hour or more every day on homework. The largest percentage of these students (46 percent) spent over two hours daily on school work out of school. About 20 percent of those who could read and write Vietnamese fairly well said that they put in over two hours a day, compared with only 11 percent of those who could read and write a little. By contrast, those who lacked Vietnamese literacy not only were the most likely not to do homework but were also the least likely to spend more than two hours per day after school on schoolwork. More

TABLE 5.8 Time Spent on Homework, by Vietnamese
Language Literacy

	Reading and Writing Skills in Vietnamese				
	Read and Write Not at All or Very Little (%)	Read and Write a Little (%)	Read and Write Fairly Well (%)	Read and Write Very Well (%)	Row Total (N)
Does not do homework	22.0	6.8	0.9	0.8	5.0 (19)
Less than ½ hour	22.0	28.4	17.6	6.1	16.7 (63)
One-half hour to an hour	26.0	35.2	31.5	11.3	24.6 (93)
One to two hours	20.0	18.2	29.6	36.3	28.0 (106)
Over two hours	10.0	11.4	20.4	45.5	25.7 (97)
Column total (N)	13.2 (50)	23.3 (88)	28.6 (108)	34.9 (132)	100.0 (378)

Source: The Versailles Village Survey of 1994.
Note: Chi square significant at .000 (12 df).

than a fifth (22 percent) of those with no Vietnamese literacy reported that they did not do homework and only 10 percent reported that they spent more two hours on homework daily.

It seems evident that Vietnamese literacy in some way promotes the kind of effort that can lead to academic excellence. It remains to be established what literacy in Vietnamese indicates. In this case, ethnic language literacy may be an intervening variable. The ability to read and write Vietnamese may be a result of socioeconomic background; parents with higher educational achievement, which implies higher occupational attainment in Vietnam, may be more likely to provide their children with opportunities to acquire skills in the parental language as well as more likely to stress education in the host country than are parents from lower socioeconomic backgrounds.

We have seen that the shift toward English and away from Vietnamese is positively related to family socioeconomic background. It is possible, however, that parental-language literacy, as a higher-order language skill, may be an exception to this rule. Perhaps young people whose parents had high levels of educational attainment in their native country are more likely to be encouraged to study the native language. Thus, Vietnamese literacy may be a function of the parent's past, rather than present, socioeconomic status. It could be, then, that family background in the native country accounts for the relationship between skills in the parental language and school performance. We therefore investigated the possibility that the level of Vietnamese literacy of high school students might be a function of the father's education, which in Vietnam is treated as an indicator of family status.

One clear problem with using family educational background as an explanation for the relationship between ethnic language literacy and academic achievement in this group is the uniformly low levels of education of the fathers, as can be seen in table 5.9. Forty-two percent of the students who were able to answer the question about their father's education had fathers with less than a high school education, and 40 percent had fathers who had completed no more than high school. Even when these two categories were compared, the percentage differences between those whose fathers were high school graduates and those whose fathers had not completed high school did not show any pattern of association.

TABLE 5.9   Vietnamese Language Literacy, by Father's Education

	Less Than High School (%)	High School Graduate (%)	Some College (%)	College Graduate or Higher (%)	Row Total (N)
Reading and writing Vietnamese					
Not at all or very little	11.3	16.2	7.5	4.2	12.4 (44)
A little	24.7	22.5	15.0	20.8	22.5 (80)
Fairly well	32.7	25.4	25.0	33.3	28.9 (103)
Very well	31.3	35.9	52.5	41.7	36.2 (129)
Column total	42.1	39.9	11.2	6.8	100.0
(N)	(150)	(142)	(40)	(24)	(356)

Source: The Versailles Village Survey of 1994.
Note: Chi square significant at .271 (9 df).

It does not appear that the ability to read and write the parental language can be considered an indicator of elite family status or that elite family status can be considered an explanation of the association between academic achievement and ethnic language skills. We do not have evidence, then, that these higher order language skills are primarily a function of socioeconomic background, so we can safely dismiss the suspicion that the impact of reading and writing abilities on scholastic achievement may be nothing more than an artifact of past family socio-economic status.

Table 5.10 suggests an alternative explanation of Vietnamese literacy. This table shows the relationship between the abilities in question and a scale of identification with Vietnamese ethnicity. This table presents fairly clear evidence that ethnic language literacy is highly associated with ethnic identification. Sixty percent of the students with the highest degree of ethnic identification could read and write Vietnamese well, compared with 40 percent of those at the next highest level. The four respondents in the two lowest levels of ethnic identification were all unable to read and write Vietnamese. In contrast, only 4 percent of those with the highest degree of ethnic identification could not read or write the ethnic language. The strong association of Vietnamese literacy with a sense of identification with ethnic membership hence indicates that language is an important dimension of ethnicity.

Findings from Multivariate Analyses

The tabulations we have just presented make possible a clear and readily comprehensible portrayal of bivariate relations, but they cannot capture complex interrelations among the variables under study. Therefore, we recast these relations into a multivariate regression model to examine the suggested multivariate relationship between these variables based on our 1993 survey. Grades and college plans are two connected but distinct aspects of academic performance, with grades representing an outcome and attitudes toward college representing future orientation and an influence on outcomes to which both time spent on homework and grades are relevant. Ethnic identity and Vietnamese literacy come logically prior to these three aspects and are therefore treated as exogenous variables.

Figure 5.1 shows that there is a significantly positive relationship between an identification with Vietnamese ethnicity and the ability to read and write Vietnamese. In fact, the relationship is so strong ($r = .437$) that the two should be seen as indicators of a single underlying dimen-

TABLE 5.10 Vietnamese Literacy, by Self-Identification with Vietnamese Ethnicity

Vietnamese Language Literacy	Lowest Degree 0	1	2	3	4	5	Highest Degree 6	Row Total (N)
Reading and writing Vietnamese								
Not at all or very little	100.0	100.0	50.0	20.6	13.5	5.5	4.2	12.5
								(45)
A little	0.0	0.0	30.0	38.2	29.2	17.3	12.5	23.6
								(85)
Fairly well	0.0	0.0	10.0	27.9	27.1	37.2	23.6	28.9
								(104)
Very well	0.0	0.0	10.0	13.3	30.2	40.0	59.7	35.0
								(126)
Column total	0.8	0.3	2.8	18.9	26.7	30.5	20.0	100.0
(N)	(3)	(1)	(10)	(68)	(96)	(110)	(72)	(360)

Source: The Versailles Village Survey of 1994.
Note: Chi square significant at .000 (18 df).

FIGURE 5.1   Causal Relations Between Ethnic Involvement and
School Adaptation

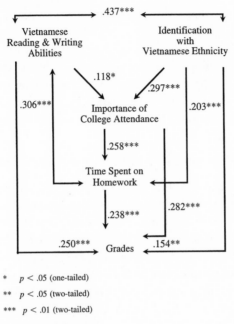

* $p < .05$ (one-tailed)
** $p < .05$ (two-tailed)
*** $p < .01$ (two-tailed)

Source: The Versailles Village Survey of 1994.

sion of ethnicity. It seems difficult, moreover, to establish a causal order
between these two variables. Strong ethnic identification motivates and
improves the learning of an ethnic language, but the process of learning
and the immersion in one's culture afforded by the experience of reading
one's language can also reinforce the sense of group identity. Therefore,
we treat the relationship between identity and language as a correlation
without attempting to establish a causal order between them.

Ethnic identification yields a strong positive influence on orientation
toward future education. Taking ethnic identification into account
weakens the relationship between the importance of college and Vietnamese literacy (significant only at the .05 level, one-tailed test), suggesting that much of the association between ethnic language literacy and
orientation toward education results not from the skills of literacy per se,
but rather from the ethnic membership that is closely tied to those skills.

Both ethnic identification and literacy strongly affect time spent on
homework. Since both measures serve as indicators of involvement in

ethnic membership, it can be inferred that ethnic membership produces positive attitudes toward education at present while promoting constructive behavior that can make both present and future achievement possible. The feeling that college is important also leads students to put more time into their homework. The finding that Vietnamese literacy has the strongest effect on spending time on homework suggests that the contribution of bilingualism to academic performance involves more than cognitive transference, but rather that achieving mastery of higher order skills in the parental native language generates work habits and attitudes that can be transferred to the mainstream school environment.

The Sociological Meaning of Language Use

While there is a definite shift toward English, most Vietnamese children retain the language of their parents. Native language retention may be associated with continual contact with new arrivals, living with household members with limited English, and residence in Vietnamese communities. Most importantly, native language retention is strongly associated with adaptive rather than maladaptive outcomes. This finding falls in line with previous research, which shows that ethnic language abilities contribute to greater overall scholastic achievement (Cummins 1991; Lindholm and Aclan 1991; Willig 1985). Clearly, skills developed in learning to read the parental language may be transferred to other areas of intellectual endeavor, such as history, geography, or mathematics. But ethnic language literacy involves broader effects related to specific social context. As our case study shows, such factors as ethnic identification and ethnic language literacy correlate closely with academic effort and academic achievement and appreciations. These findings tell us that advanced ethnic language skills can connect children to a system of ethnic supports that encourage and direct accomplishments by promoting effort and reinforcing attitudes conducive to learning. In this way, present and future orientations come together; plans for future education and the effort that results from these plans lead to present-day achievements, in the form of higher grades; higher grades then make future education possible; and continued education can later turn upward socioeconomic mobility into a reality.

It is true that parental native language retention does not always yield such positive effects. In our view, the fact that families and the community promote academic achievement is a powerful conditioning influence. But our results do resonate with the broader literature. For example, Nathan Caplan and his associates found that Vietnamese literacy helped families to cope with a variety of problems by strengthening emotional ties between non-English-speaking parents and fully or partially bilingual children, by allowing for shared wisdom in stories read in Vietnamese, and by reinforcing mutual and collective obligations among family members (Caplan, Choy, and Whitmore 1992). Vietnamese children also resemble the Punjabi children in California studied by the anthropologist Margaret A. Gibson (1989), who showed that Punjabi children outperformed American children in school because of the influence of their ethnic culture.

Nevertheless, not all immigrant children benefit from bilingualism. In an earlier study, the sociologist David E. Lopez (1976) found that the use of Spanish depressed occupational attainment indirectly by lowering educational achievement among Chicanos, especially in areas and occupations that allowed few benefits to the knowledge of Spanish. The sociologists Roberto Fernández and Francois Nielsen (1986) also reported that the positive effect of bilingualism tended to diminish with longer duration of U.S. residence and that the frequent use of Spanish was negatively related to academic achievement, after controlling for English and Spanish proficiency. They attributed the contradictory outcomes to a specific handicap associated with Hispanic membership. Thus, parental native language retention may or may not facilitate adaptation; rather specific outcomes vary with the mode of incorporation and the structure of the ethnic community, which in Versailles Village transformed native language retention into an instrument of academic success.

——— Chapter 6 ———

Experiences in Adaptation
to American Schools

Thuy Trang Nguyen, 14, of Harvey, Louisiana, was chosen as the 1995 Middle School Student of the Year in the Jefferson Parish School District. Nguyen had won the school district's Superintendent's Award every year since 1987 and first place in her school's social studies fair and second place in the regional competition. Teachers praised her character as humble but determined. Nguyen herself gave all the credit for her school success to her refugee parents. "I don't ever want to let them down," she wrote in an essay for the Student of the Year competition. "When my parents first immigrated from Vietnam, they spent every waking hour working hard in order to support a family. They have sacrificed for me, and I am willing to do anything for them" (*New Orleans Times-Picayune*, April 20, 1995).

T he preceding chapters have shown that Vietnamese children in the United States suffer from a lack of proficiency in English and from straitened socioeconomic circumstances. For both these reasons, we might expect Vietnamese children to lag behind their American peers in academic achievement. On the contrary, Vietnamese children have adapted surprisingly well to the American educational system in a relatively short period of time. Over the past ten years or so, Vietnamese children have come to excel academically not only by the standards expected of a new refugee group but also by comparison with segments of the established population. They have been particularly successful in science and mathematics, which are weak areas for native-born students, and have started to win top awards at schools across the country (Caplan, Choy, and Whitmore 1991; Rumbaut 1995; Rutledge 1992; Skinner 1984; Spence 1985). They have been doing so well, in fact, that teachers and educational researchers often see them as bringing new life into deteriorating urban public schools, and their parents have been proud to see them attain prestigious occupations as doctors, lawyers, college professors, and engineers.

This chapter examines what determines who will actually achieve academic success. It focuses on the changing social environment of American schools into which Vietnamese children are received and on the various levels of the social structure that most immediately affect these children's experiences in schools.

THE AMERICAN PUBLIC SCHOOL: CHANGES AND CHALLENGES

For the second generation, acquiring skills and credentials is a crucial step in upward mobility in American society. Since immigrant groups arrive in the United States with the hope of moving ahead, education often comes to occupy a central place in their aspirations (Ogbu 1974, 1983, 1989, 1991). The same motivation holds true for refugees, notwithstanding their initially involuntary flight and their lack of preparation for permanent resettlement in a foreign land. In short order, most of them orient themselves toward adaptation to their host country, rather than toward a return to their land of origin. They are therefore likely to establish goals for themselves and for their children in ways similar to those of immigrants.

The availability of education in America and its consequences for mobility in the host society have profoundly reshaped the traditional expectations that Vietnamese refugees brought with them. Vietnamese culture, influenced by Confucianism, traditionally placed a high value on education, but educational opportunities in Vietnam were limited by class and gender; only young men of privileged families were encouraged to obtain an education and were able to do so. In the United States, by contrast, the refugees have found schooling available not only to the privileged classes but also to those from largely uneducated rural backgrounds and to women. Consequently, the traditional Vietnamese view of education as a source of prestige has made parents eager to make use of the American school system. The pattern of response among the Vietnamese cannot be understood, however, without reference to the changes in urban American schools that have come to challenge parents' expectations about educational achievement.

Inequality and Polarization in American Public Schools

In America, public education is open to all, but availability does not guarantee that children of immigrants will succeed in school as well as their parents expect. Children of different racial/ethnic and class backgrounds face profound inequalities in their educational experiences, despite the school desegregation movement in the 1950s and 1960s and numerous federal educational reforms. The influential Coleman Report, released in 1966, reported that most children continued to attend schools segregated by race and class, even after twelve years of reform following the 1954 *Brown* v. *Board of Education* decision by the U.S. Supreme Court outlawing school segregation. The report concluded that social class was the chief determinant of school success, that inequality in educational opportunities had persisted and that schools functioned to reinforce racial disadvantage, at best, and had themselves become sources of inequality, at worst.

The years following the 1970s have seen alarming trends of resegregation of minority and immigrant children in urban schools, rising racial inequality in schooling, and rapid deterioration of school environments in schools that serve poor and minority children. School resegregation is a direct consequence of poverty concentration by the process of "white flight" and economic restructuring (Wilson 1978). The political scientist Jennifer L. Hochschild (1984) found that native minorities and immigrants were disproportionately concentrated in urban schools that were suffering rapid deterioration as members of the middle class continued to abandon the city for the suburbs. She also observed that while racial segregation at the school level might have been reduced, it was reinforced at the classroom level by tracking or ability grouping; the result was greater inequality. At the national level, black and Hispanic students represented 42 percent of the student population in central cities in the early 1970s. This figure increased substantially to 53 percent in the early 1990s (U.S. Department of Education 1994). In large metropolitan centers, the withdrawal of white students has been dramatic. For example, 40 percent of the New York City public school student population were non-Hispanic white in the early 1970s, but by late 1980s, this figure had dropped to less than 20 percent (Reyes 1992). In the mid-1990s, the Los Angeles Unified School District identified 87 percent of the district's students as "minority" and 40 percent as having limited English proficiency (Lopez 1996).

The change in the racial composition of urban public schools has paralleled the concentration of poverty among racial minorities. The 1990 census showed that 46 percent of black children and 39 percent of Hispanic children under the age of 18 lived in families with incomes below the poverty level, compared with 16 percent of white children.

The same census showed that poverty rates for foreign-born children ranged from 21 percent among European whites to 24 percent for non-Hispanic blacks, 27 percent to Asians, and 41 percent for Latinos.

As a result, schools have become "arenas of injustice" that provide unequal opportunities on the basis of class and race (Keniston and the Carnegie Council on Children 1977). While suburban schools are endowed with ample resources, conducive environments, and strong parent-teacher associations (PTA), many urban schools suffer from a wide range of problems; they are underfunded, understaffed, overcrowded, unsafe, and socially isolated, with disproportionate minority-student enrollments. Inner-city schools are even worse; many have become dangerous places where students daily risk being crime victims. A 1992 study by the Carnegie Council on Adolescent Development estimates that about seven million young people, or one in four adolescents, are extremely vulnerable to multiple high-risk behavior and school failure, and another seven million are at moderate risk. Because of segregation by race and social class, minority and immigrant children are overrepresented in this high-risk group.

The deterioration of urban schools has diminished the opportunities of minority children and has sustained the gap in learning environments and educational outcomes between suburban children and central-city children who are members of minority or recent immigrant groups. A 1994 report of the U.S. Department of Education showed that black sophomores were more likely than their white peers to report learning disruptions by other students in school, that they were more likely to have trouble getting along with teachers, that they were twice as likely as whites to feel unsafe at their schools, and that they were more likely both to be threatened with and to be injured by a weapon in school. The same report observed that blacks continued to trail whites in "preschool attendance, grade retention, academic achievement, dropout rates, parental involvement, school climate, course-taking patterns, educational aspirations, labor market outcomes, and adult literacy levels" (p. 9).

Moreover, American public schools exist in a cultural milieu that is not conducive to academic achievement. Many parents, teachers, and policy makers have become concerned about the growth of an adversarial subculture among American youth, even in well-to-do suburban areas. This youth subculture is especially prevalent in urban schools, among those who feel oppressed and excluded from the American mainstream and who are frustrated by the widening gap between cultural values of freedom and materialism and the reality of a bleak economic future. Many of these American children have responded to their social isolation and their constrained opportunities with resentment toward middle-class America, rebellion against all forms of authority, and rejection of the goals of achievement and upward mobility. Because students in schools shape one another's attitudes and expectations, such an oppositional culture negatively affects educational outcomes. School achievement is seen as unlikely to lead to upward mobility, and high achievers are seen as sellouts to oppressive authority. Students who show eagerness to learn, who are making good grades, who are disciplined, or who simply carry books and notebooks around are derogated as "geeks" and "nerds." They are not just uncool or unpopular but frequent targets of ridicule and hate. They are also vulnerable to threats and even to being forced into cheating by doing schoolwork for others and giving out answers during exams.

Of course, much of contemporary American youth culture at all socioeconomic levels tends to be anti-intellectual, but the problem appears to be most serious in classrooms dominated by members of disadvantaged minorities. Several studies of the scholastic performance of minority children have attributed the low level of achievement of these children, at least in part, to the negative views toward learning among their peers (Ornstein and Levine 1989; Reyes and Jackson 1993). One prominent young black attorney recounted how she suffered insults and hatred from her fellow students in her struggle to get the most out of her education (Dickerson 1996). During our own fieldwork in a public school attended by large numbers of Vietnamese, another conscientious young woman, also black, complained, "I try so hard to do my work. But the way all these people act, I just can't. And they laugh at you and make fun of you if you do what you're supposed to."

These trends in American schools pose a challenge to all parents, but the challenge is especially daunting for immigrant parents with limited educational backgrounds, limited English skills, and few resources. For many Vietnamese children, being concentrated in low-income, minority-dominated schools has meant studying in a social environment in which those who attempt to learn are not just discouraged but ostracized.

Schooling in Versailles Village

Predominantly urban and socioeconomically disadvantaged, Vietnamese children are likely to encounter an unfavorable school context like the one just described. The two public high schools serving Versailles Village, Washington High School and Jefferson High School, illustrate the impoverished and disruptive conditions found in many urban public schools.

Washington High is located in Versailles Village (see figure 3.1); all of its students are Versailles residents. At the time of the survey, over half the Vietnamese high school students in the Versailles enclave attended this high school, giving it the largest concentration of Vietnamese high school students of any high school in the city of New Orleans. The school's student population was 20 percent Vietnamese, 77 percent blacks, and 3 percent whites or Hispanics.

Regardless of race or ethnicity, all the students in Washington High came from modest socioeconomic backgrounds. Eighty-three percent of the Vietnamese students and 73 percent of the black students participated in the federal free lunch or reduced-cost lunch programs—a conservative though reliable indicator of the level of poverty in this school. Moreover, over 60 percent of the Vietnamese students and most of the black students lived in government-subsidized private rental housing in the Versailles neighborhood.

Many of the problems of contemporary urban public schools plagued Washington High. A school supervisor whom we interviewed described the school as "having a lot of disciplinary problems"; armed guards patrolled the hall at all times of the school day. The constant turnover in principals, of whom there were three during our study period from 1993 to 1995, reflected a serious problem in discipline and control. One teacher attributed this churning to the search for a leader who could keep order. A Vietnamese social worker from Versailles Village recalled that he was appalled by what he found on his first visit to that school: "It was like a jungle. The students were all walking down the halls, pushing and yelling at each other. There was a guard there, but he didn't say anything to make them behave; he just stood there. I felt sorry for our [Vietnamese] kids that have to go to schools like this."

The other public school, Jefferson High, is located on the fringes of Versailles Village. The school drew about 40 percent of the neighborhood's Vietnamese high school students. Minority youths dominated this school as well; 74 percent of the students were black, 15 percent were Vietnamese, and 11 percent were white. Though located in a middle-class black neighborhood, Jefferson High drew students from some neighboring low-income areas. Socioeconomically, the students at Jefferson were only slightly better off than their counterparts at Washington High; 65 percent of the students participated in the federal free lunch or reduced-cost lunch programs. Among the Vietnamese students, however, 85 percent were in the subsidized lunch programs, an indication of an even higher level of poverty in this population.

Armed guards also patrolled the halls of Jefferson High at all times of the school day. During a semester's employment as a substitute teacher, one of the authors witnessed at least six violent fights, which involved both males and females and had to be stopped by guards and male teachers. None of these fights involved Vietnamese students, among whom fights did occur but with much less frequency and intensity. Active aggression rarely seemed to cross racial or gender boundaries.

The students at both of these schools showed relatively weak scholastic performance. Washington High was a relatively new school, built in the mid-1970s as a junior high school and converted to a senior high in the late 1980s. Possessing an excellent library and a spacious auditorium, it was in good physical condition, showing few signs of the physical deterioration that blight so many urban schools. But these qualities did not suffice to raise the general levels of academic excellence. The students performed very poorly on the California Achievement Test (CAT), a statewide standardized test required of all high school juniors. In 1991, for example, only 16 percent of Washington High's students equaled or exceeded the 50th percentile of those taken the CAT, while 45 percent equaled or fell below the 25th percentile (New Orleans School Board 1993).

Jefferson High compared favorably with Washington High on academic grounds. Jefferson High contained an honors program, referred to as a "magnet component," that enrolled about 10 percent of the student population. To be admitted to the honors program, students were required to have a B or higher average in previous classes or schools and to pass an entry test covering all subjects. Vietnamese students made up about 80 percent of the program's students. In fact, almost 90 percent of the Vietnamese students who attended Jefferson High from the Versailles enclave were enrolled in the honors program, an indication of a conscious mobility strategy among Vietnamese parents, who viewed Jefferson High or other honors programs outside the Versailles enclave as the first step upward for their children.

Despite the magnet component, the overall academic performance of the students at Jefferson High lagged far behind the state average. The results of the CAT given in 1991 showed that only 22 percent of the students in this school equaled or exceeded the 50th percentile of those taking the CAT (6 points over the percentage at Washington High, but still 20 percentage points below that of the state), while 42 percent of them equaled or fell below the 25th percentile (21 percentage points over that of the state) (New Orleans School Board 1993).

Neither Washington High nor Jefferson High is unique. With the exception of a small population with a middle-class background, most Vietnamese children in the United States attend urban public schools, in which most students come from low-income families and are members of racial minority groups. For example, Asians predominated in the two public high schools in Little Saigon, California; most of the Asian students were Vietnamese, with white students making up less than a third of the remaining student population. In San Diego, half the Vietnamese students were enrolled in central-city schools that were predominantly black, Hispanic, or Asian (Rumbaut 1995a).

PATTERNS OF SCHOOL ADAPTATION: ENROLLMENT AND PERFORMANCE

Many adult Vietnamese arrived in the United States with low levels of schooling, mainly because educational opportunities back home were scarce. Overall, adult Vietnamese compared poorly with average Americans in educational attainment. In 1980, 62.2 percent of adult Vietnamese in the United States aged 25 and over had completed high school, and only 12.9 percent had attained four or more years of college, compared with 66.5 percent and 16.2 percent, respectively, of all Americans. In 1990, the percentage of high school graduates among Vietnamese in the United States decreased by a percentage point (to 61.2 percent), but the percentage of Vietnamese with four or more years of college increased significantly to 17.4 percent, compared with 20.3 percent of average Americans.

The decrease in average educational attainment among adult Vietnamese during the 1980s is probably due to the fact that later arrivals were relatively uneducated and unskilled and that those who entered as adults have been unable to make up for their deficient education through formal schooling because of their age. The improvement at the level of college education, however, suggests that those who entered as children or young adults have been able to take advantage of the educational opportunities in the United States to move ahead.

School Enrollment

A look at educational attainment among the young suggests that the Vietnamese embraced education as a means of social mobility for their children. While the average educational level of adult Vietnamese aged 25 years and over remains relatively low, the picture for the younger generation appears more promising. In 1990, for example, 75 percent of Vietnamese young adults aged 18 to 24 were enrolled in school, a rate similar to that found among the Chinese (77 percent), but much higher than that among blacks (43 percent) and among whites (50 percent). Moreover, about 38 percent of the Vietnamese young adults enrolled in school were attending college, on this count outperforming whites (28 percent), and blacks (18 percent) and doing almost as well as the Chinese (43 percent). Overall, 45 percent of Vietnamese in this age cohort reported that they had had at least some college education, compared with 54 percent of Chinese, 30 percent of blacks, and 43 percent of whites. Even after taking family structure and poverty status into consideration, younger-generation Vietnamese from single-parent families and from poor families consistently fared much better in college attendance and educational attainment than their black and white peers. Though still trailing behind the Chinese in this age group, younger-generation Vietnamese appear to follow the Chinese mode of school adaptation rather than that of either native-born American group.

The enrollment pattern for children under 18 years of age resembles that of young adults, as can be seen in table 6.1. In the 1990 census, Vietnamese children under 18 years of age were as likely as their Chinese, other Southeast Asian, black, and white counterparts to attend school. Family structure did not seem to reduce school enrollment for any of the groups, but poverty status slightly affected school enrollment. While public school has been the norm for all American children, Vietnamese, other Southeast Asian, and black children enroll in public schools at somewhat higher levels than Chinese and white children.

Failure to complete high school was much less common among Vietnamese than among native-born Americans; only 7 percent of the Vietnamese aged 16 to 19 years were neither enrolled in high school nor high school graduates, compared with 14 percent of blacks and 10 percent of whites. The pattern was the same for the older cohort; Vietnamese young adults aged 18 to 24 years not only were enrolled in school at a higher rate than their black or white counterparts, as has been discussed, but they also had a much lower dropout rate, as is

TABLE 6.1 School Enrollment of School-Aged Children by Family Structure and Poverty Status, Selected Ethnicities, 1990

	Vietnamese %	Other Southeast Asian %	Chinese %	Black %	White %
Currently enrolled in school					
All children	84.3	80.2	88.7	84.8	84.2
Children from single-parent families	85.6	81.4	90.0	83.8	85.1
Children from families in poverty[a]	84.1	78.2	85.9	81.7	78.9
Attending public school[b]					
All children	91.9	97.2	84.7	93.5	85.6
Children from single-parent families	95.1	97.8	88.1	95.4	90.6
Children from families in poverty[a]	95.6	98.1	94.4	97.8	91.2

Source: U.S. Census of Population and Housing, 1990, 5-percent PUMS.
Note: Sample included children aged 0 to 17 living in family households.
[a] Families living below 1.00 poverty level.
[b] Among those who were currently enrolled in school.

shown in Table 6.2. The dropout rate of Vietnamese young adults (9 percent), though higher than that of Chinese (5 percent), was lower than that of other Southeast Asians, only half that of blacks (19 percent), and similar to that of whites (10 percent). Among single-parent families and families in poverty, the dropout rates of all groups increased substantially, except for other Southeast Asians, but the rates of Asians were still considerably lower than that of either blacks or whites. Although there are differences among Asian American groups in scholastic performance, the relatively high levels of educational achievement among Vietnamese young people appear to be part of the general trend of academic excellence of Asian Americans (Barringer, Gardner, and Levin 1993).

School Performance

Attendance rates hint at the potential for Vietnamese educational success. More important is academic performance. In recent years, the Viet-

TABLE 6.2   High School Dropout Among Persons Aged 18 to 24, by Family Structure and Poverty Status, Selected Ethnicities, 1990

	Vietnamese %	Other Southeast Asian %	Chinese %	Black %	White %
All persons in age group	9.1	15.0	5.4	19.3	10.0
Persons from single-parent families	12.2	14.8	6.8	23.5	14.9
Persons from families in poverty[a]	14.5	15.7	7.7	31.4	26.6

Source: U.S. Census of Population and Housing, 1990, 5-percent PUMS.
Note: Sample included persons aged 18 to 24 and living in family households. Dropouts were defined as those without a high school diploma and not currently enrolled in school.
[a] Families living below 1.00 poverty level.

namese have been succeeding in American schools at a remarkable rate (Rutledge 1992). Though many are still handicapped by their lack of English proficiency, Vietnamese students have averaged scores higher than the national average on standardized achievement tests such as the California Achievement Test, particularly in mathematics and science. Nathan Caplan and his associates at the University of Michigan conducted a study based on a random sample of 536 school-aged children from 200 moderate-to-poor Vietnamese families in five urban areas: Orange County, Seattle, Houston, Chicago, and Boston. They found that one in four of the Vietnamese youngsters had an overall A average, over half had an overall B average, 17 percent had an C average, and only 4 percent had an average below C. In mathematics especially, Vietnamese students seemed to have outstripped other young people; half of them earned A's and another third earned B's. In national standardized tests in mathematics, half the Vietnamese students scored in the top quarter of those taking the tests and 27 percent scored in the top tenth. Even though most were still struggling with English, they ranked close to the national average in language skills (Caplan, Choy, and Whitmore 1992). In his 1992 study of San Diego's immigrant children, Rubén G. Rumbaut (1995a) showed that Vietnamese students had an overall grade point average of 2.87, the highest among second-generation children of all immigrant nationality groups surveyed (the grade point averages for groups under study were 2.74 for Filipinos, 2.73 for Canadians and Europeans, 2.42 for Latino Americans, and 1.94 for Mexicans).

Our Versailles Village study revealed similar results; Vietnamese students made better grades and scored disproportionately higher in standardized tests than their American peers attending the same schools. At Washington High, 52 percent of the majority black student population scored below the state median on the 1990 Louisiana Graduation Exit Examination, and only 18 percent of the black students scored in the highest statewide quartile. Among the Vietnamese, however, despite their language difficulties and their low family incomes, only 33 percent earned scores below the median for all students in Louisiana, and 48 percent earned scores in Louisiana's top quartile (Louisiana Department of Education 1992).

At Jefferson High, where the Vietnamese made up most of the school's honors program, their standardized test scores were even more impressive. Vietnamese students outperformed their black and white peers by significant margins in all major areas; their average scores exceeded their American peers' by at least 17 percentage points in language and arts, 29 percentage points in mathematics, and 16 percentage points in writing and composition (Louisiana Department of Education 1992). In terms of the statewide median, the majority black students did fairly well; 48 percent scored below the state median, 52 percent scored above it, but only 14 percent of the black students scored in the state's top quartile. By contrast, 95 percent of the Vietnamese students scored above the median for all Louisiana students, and 64 percent scored in the top quartile. Despite their disadvantaged socioeconomic backgrounds, Vietnamese students from Versailles Village appear to have been among the best students in the state of Louisiana.

ACADEMIC SUCCESS

The Determinants of Success

What determines who will succeed in school? One widely accepted explanation for academic success emphasizes social class. The socioeconomic backgrounds of families—specifically the father's education, the father's occupation, and family incomes—have been singled out as the most important determinants of scholastic achievement of children (Blau and Duncan 1967). Social class not only has a direct effect but also arguably works indirectly through the formation of a particular kind of social capital. The 1966 Coleman report found that students' achievement was affected least by facilities and curriculum within schools and most by the social environment of schools, in the form of family socio-economic backgrounds of fellow students. The report also indicated that narrowing the gap between black and white schools in resources such as facilities, books, laboratories, experience of teachers, and per-pupil expenditures did not close the black-white gap in academic performance. The report contended that families provided unequal advantages not only through tangible supports, such as income and social positions, but also through intangible supports, such as family stability and expectations for future achievement. These "input factors" (social resources that students bring with them to school) affect performance more powerfully than do "process factors" (the contributions made by school policies, curriculum, methods, and resources) (Coleman et al. 1966).

The economic standing of the family affects school performance contextually; higher-income families can afford desirable neighborhoods that provide access to better schools and a more academically oriented environment. These families also enjoy the resources to provide children with additional support outside school. In contrast, lower-income families are likely to reside in neighborhoods with poor schools, limited resources, and inadequate support facilities.

Family structure is a related and equally important factor that determines children's educational attainment. Previous research has found that dropouts are more likely to come from large families or single-parent households, especially households headed by never-married females (Natriello, Pallas, and McDill 1986; Rumberger 1983; Wagenaar 1987). One of the most common explanations of scholastic performance emphasizes the prevalence of intact and cohesive families that provide constructive value orientations for children. Intact families provide role models, foster belief in the values of education, achievement, and motivation, and make available study aids in the home (Ekstrom et al. 1986). Nathan Caplan and his associates have made some of the most persuasive arguments for this view, seeing the family as the basis of Vietnamese achievement in many areas of life. They even find that family size, a characteristic negatively associated with academic performance in most segments of the American population, promotes a high level of schoolwork among Vietnamese children, since siblings work together in a well-integrated family environment (Caplan, Choy, and Whitmore 1991, 1992; Caplan, Whitmore, and Choy 1989).

An alternative, equally popular explanation of school success highlights cultural influences. This approach derives from research on the educational experience of Asian Americans in general and is based on the assumption that their academic achievement can be attributed to Asian cultural values, beliefs, and practices (Sue and Okasaki 1990). Many Asian Americans, particularly Chinese, Japanese, Koreans, and Vietnamese Americans, come from backgrounds heavily influenced by Confucianism. For these groups, the home culture emphasizes education as a means to mobility. It values consensus, respect, discipline, hard work, the centrality of the family, and social harmony. Advocates of the cultural approach contend that these particular home cultural values have been transplanted to America with few modifications and have been used by Asian American families in socializing the younger generation in accordance with traditional expectations (Ogbu and Matute-Bianchi 1986). Such accounts have dominated attempts to explain the scholastic achievement of the Vietnamese. Caplan and his associates attributed the successful school adaptation of Vietnamese children to the family's respect for education, hard work, and cooperative family patterns, arguing that "cultural values are as important to successful adaptation as gravity is to physics" (Caplan, Choy, and Whitmore 1991, 156). Similarly, the anthropologist Paul J. Rutledge's 1992 study of a Vietnamese community in Oklahoma provided anecdotal evidence for a cultural interpretation of educational success based on strong family values and hard work.

Culture has been a convenient explanation for the clear but unsettling differences in educational achievement and attainment among ethnic and racial groups. The psychologist Laurence Steinberg (1996) has recently revealed the prominent role apparently played by ethnicity in structuring adolescents' lives, both in and outside of school. He found that Asian American students outperformed European American students who in turn outperformed African American and Latino American students by significantly large margins; the ethnic differences remained marked and consistent across nine different high schools under study and after controlling for social class, family structure, and place of birth of parents. He also found that the ethnic effect persisted in important explanatory variables of school success, such as the belief in the payoff of schooling, attributional styles, and peer groups. Steinberg concluded that the ethnic group to which a student belonged was just as important a factor as social class and gender in defining scholastic performance.

An Empirical Test: Explaining High School
Dropout Rates

Among school-aged children aged 16 to 19 in the United States, Vietnamese youths show lower dropout rates than those of the two major native-born racial groups—black and white. As of 1990, only 6.5 percent of Vietnamese youths were identified as high school dropouts, compared with 13.7 percent of non-Hispanic black youths and 9.8 percent of non-Hispanic white youths, a pattern of interracial differences similar to that found in table 6.2 among young adults aged 18 to 24.

Why do Vietnamese children drop out of high school at lower rates than black or white children? We used logistic analyses to examine the effects of social class and home culture, using the 1990 census data.[1] We specifically focused on whether the same situations that made blacks and whites more likely to quit school also made Vietnamese children more likely to quit school. Since, as has been discussed earlier in the chapter, Vietnamese educational accomplishments are often considered in the context of Asian educational accomplishments in general, we also included evidence on why younger-generation Chinese quit school. The Chinese are the largest and most established Asian American group and share with Vietnamese similar home cultural values deriving from Confucianism. If similarities exist between the Chinese and the Vietnamese, we can attribute these similarities in part to the effect of Confucian culture. We would expect to find a different pattern among other Southeast Asians (Cambodians, Laotians, and Hmong), whose home cultures are not so heavily affected by Confucianism.

In our logistic model, we classified all of those who were aged 16 to 19 (that is, within school age and old enough to quit school legally), not currently enrolled in school, and not high school graduates as "dropouts," and all those aged 16 to 19 and currently enrolled in school as "stayers." The dependent variable "dropout" was thus coded 1 for dropouts and 0 for stayers. Following the social class and the cultural approaches, we hypothesized that the probability of dropping out of high school was primarily a function of the student's family socioeconomic backgrounds and his or her ethnicity. Family backgrounds were measured by father's education (coded 1 as completion of high school or more), family structure (coded 1 as living in single-parent family), poverty (coded 1 as living below poverty level). We used ethnic/racial group membership as a proxy for home cultural influence.[2]

Our logistic model also included some of the major individual characteristics that were found to affect dropout rates: age (in years), sex (coded 1 as female), marital status (coded 1 as currently married) (McDill, Natriello, and Pallas 1985). We also introduced three variables measuring exposure to American culture: English fluency (coded 1 as English proficient) and generation status indicated by the 1.5 generation (coded 1) and the second generation (coded 1), with the first generation as the reference category. The exposure variables should enable us to examine how dropout rates are affected by familiarity with American society (Steinberg, Blind, and Chan 1984). Finally, we introduced a Vietnamese residential concentration variable into our model.[3] If social relations among coethnic members influence children's educational attainment, then we should expect living in an area that contains many other Vietnamese to have an impact on dropout rates. Moreover, if Vietnamese have comparatively low dropout rates because of coethnic contacts, then much of the difference between Vietnamese and whites should disappear when we take this residential factor into consideration.

Table 6.3 presents percentage differences among Chinese, Vietnamese, other Southeast Asians, and blacks in the probability of being a high school dropout. Since we were interested in how particular minority group membership raised or lowered the likelihood of being a dropout, we used whites as a reference category. The first step in this analysis showed that the Chinese in this sample were the least likely to be dropouts: being Chinese, rather than being white, lowered the probability of becoming a dropout by 4.8 percent; being Vietnamese lowered the probability of becoming a dropout by 2.5 percent; being Southeast Asian had no significant effect; being black, on the contrary, raised the probability of becoming a dropout by 2.7 percent.[4]

Step 2 controls for the effects of major individual characteristics of young people. Individual characteristics strongly influence dropout rates; nonetheless, race/ethnicity retains its basic effect even after factoring personal characteristics into account. Step 3 controls for the effects of exposure to American society. For the Chinese and Vietnamese, exposure lowers the probability of being a dropout still further, indicating that, were it not for matters such as limited English proficiency or recency of immigration, the Chinese and Vietnamese would stay in school at an even greater rate relative to whites.

Step 4 brings the family background variables into the analysis. Father's education significantly lowers the probability of being a dropout and poverty status significantly increases this probability. Single-parent family structure appears relatively insignificant since poverty status is

TABLE 6.3   Percentage Differences in the Probability of Becoming a High School Dropout

Predictors	Logistic Models				
	Step 1	Step 2	Step 3	Step 4	Step 5
Chinese	−4.8**	−4.8**	−4.7**	−4.9**	−4.9**
Vietnamese	−2.5**	−2.5**	−2.3**	−3.0**	−1.7
Other Southeast Asian	−0.04	−0.1	−0.2	−1.9*	−2.0*
Black	2.7**	2.6**	2.6**	−0.4	−0.4
Age		2.6**	2.5**	2.6**	2.6**
Sex		−1.5**	−1.5**	−1.6**	−1.6**
Marital status		9.2**	9.4**	8.1**	8.3**
English proficiency			−3.5**	−3.3**	−3.3**
1.5 generation			−3.5**	−3.4**	−3.3**
Second generation			−3.6**	−2.8**	−2.8**
Father's education				−3.8**	−3.8**
Poverty				3.7**	3.8**
Single-parent family				−0.2	−0.2
Vietnamese concentration[a]					−2.4*

Source: U.S. Census of Population and Housing, 1990, 5-percent PUMS.
[a] Defined as living in a PUMS Area (PUMA) containing at least one hundred Vietnamese households in the population.
* $p < .05$ ** $p < .01$

also controlled for. When we take these family background characteristics into account, the effects of race/ethnicity change drastically among other Southeast Asians (from insignificant to significant) and blacks (from significant to insignificant), but not so much among the Chinese and Vietnamese, which means that family background variables do not seem to determine dropout rates for the Chinese or Vietnamese as much as they do for other Southeast Asians or blacks.

These results seem to indicate that an inherited Confucian culture keeps Chinese and Vietnamese students in school (the other Southeast Asians come from the non-Confucian cultures of Laos and Cambodia). Finally in Step 5 we controlled for the Vietnamese residential concentration variable, to probe whether something other than the home culture affects educational attainment. As shown in the table, living in an area that contains large numbers of Vietnamese households does significantly lower the probability of being a high school dropout. Moreover, the difference in dropout rates between Vietnamese and whites becomes insignificant. We still, of course, have not accounted for the educational attainment of the Chinese, and it would be interesting to see what would happen if we undertook the substantial labor of computing a Chinese residential concentration; because this book focuses on the Vietnamese, we have not done so. The findings presented so far suggest that young Vietnamese are more likely to finish high school than their other Southeast Asian, white, or black peers; that socioeconomic handicaps do not lower the probability of young Vietnamese staying in school; and that living around other Vietnamese significantly decreases the likelihood of dropping out of high school.

ETHNICITY IN CONTEXT

The evidence from the U.S. census indicates that social class factors alone cannot explain why Vietnamese and Chinese children show higher levels of educational attainment. In fact, the data suggest that if the Vietnamese and Chinese were not laboring under socioeconomic disadvantages, their dropout rates would be lower still, particularly among the Vietnamese. Further, census data suggest that living around coethnics promotes educational attainment among the Vietnamese, a finding that is consistent with cultural explanations; where would it be easier to find Vietnamese culture than in a Vietnamese neighborhood? Census data do not, however, provide any information about the norms and values of ethnic groups. Therefore, it is necessary to look more closely at a specific group of Vietnamese people to explain why ethnic residential concentration appears to be associated with educational attainment.

Is the ethnic or cultural effect a matter of family characteristics or family values? The psychologists P. L. Ritter and S. M. Dornbusch (1989) suggest that "something associated with being Asian is having an impact on school performance independent of the family process variables that may work so well in predicting performance among whites" (p. 70). Certain family characteristics that prevail in Asian families in general and Vietnamese families in particular, such as high levels of parental authoritarianism, low levels of parent-teacher interaction and parental school involvement, and discouragement of independent behavior, usually predict low rather than high academic achievements (Dornbusch et al. 1987). Moreover, families are not the only sources of cultural influence; even in families that may hold high expectations for achievement and stress hard work and discipline, children may still perform poorly in school, especially when they have close ties to youths from disadvantaged native minorities (Portes and Stepick 1993). It seems unlikely, then, that family values alone can account for scholastic excellence.

To address the difficulty of using family as an explanation for Asian school performance, the psychologists Stanley Sue and Sumie Okazaki (1990) have proposed a model of "relative functionalism." According to this model, Asian educational success derives not simply from strong traditional family values or the belief among Asian parents that schooling is the key to success. More important is the parents' own experience or perception of blocked mobility by discriminatory laws and practices in the host society, particularly in areas where education does not have a direct effect, such as leadership, politics, entertainment, and sports. The more the parents experience "blocked mobility," or the more limited the noneducational avenues, the more the parents will focus on their children's education and pressure their children to excel in school as the means to mobility; and consequently, the higher the educational achievements.

While the experience or perception of blocked mobility may influence the life choices of Asian Americans, however, relative functionalism does not seem to account for trends in other racial or ethnic groups, such as African Americans, that also experience blocked mobility. We need, therefore, to take into account the meanings of membership in racial or ethnic groups, meanings that lead to different reactions to similar circumstances. Recently, the psychologist Claude Steele (1995) has enunciated a theory of "stereotype threat." On the basis of his empirical tests, he has found that the stubborn problem of black underachievement has been due mainly to the effect of stereotyping rather than to genetics, social class, family dysfunction, or values. He argues that "the possibility of being judged by a stereotype—or inadvertently fulfilling it—can cause an anxiety so disruptive that it impairs intellectual performance" (quoted in Los Angeles Times, Dec. 11, 1995). He also contends that the victim may consciously reject the stereotype and yet not be able to avoid its effects. Steele's theory points to the detrimental effect of pervasive negative stereotypes of blacks' intellectual inferiority; by implication, positive stereotypes may be beneficial to members of an ethnic minority group. As a new group to American society, the Vietnamese may enjoy a halo effect; that is, generally positive stereotypes of Asian Americans as high achievers may be helping Vietnamese students in their adaptation to school. Thus, ethnicity, or being Vietnamese, may be an important contextual variable that is associated with both the ethnic community and the larger society, not simply with defining behavior within families and among group members.

In our view, racially or ethnically based roles define how individuals behave toward other members of their own group and toward outsiders. A particular pattern of behavior within an ethnic group can be interpreted as an ethnic social structure. Therefore, if we want to understand why ethnicity or race can be associated with a goal such as academic achievement, we must consider the kinds of social relations that exist within an ethnic or racial group and place these ethnic social relations in the context of the surrounding society.

The Theory of Ethnic Social Relations

How may membership in a particular ethnicity, such as being Vietnamese, provide the younger generation with a competitive advantage in school? In addition to looking at how being Vietnamese shapes attitudes—particularly those toward the family—that promote academic achievement, one can look at how ethnic social relations, embedded in ethnic institutions, bind individuals to the group and thereby provide them with support and control by coethnic group members. A theory that attempts to explain why individuals in different racial or ethnic groups adapt to a society in different ways and with different outcomes, therefore, should consider the kinds of social relations that racial or ethnic membership provides and the types of behavior and attitudes produced by those social relations.

If one is interested in explaining upward mobility, one must go further and consider how those types of behavior and attitudes fit the opportunities for mobility that exist in the larger society. When the cultural values of an ethnic minority group lead to behaviors that meet the demands of the mainstream society and are reinforced through a well-integrated ethnic community, these values may become a source of advantage that leads to favorable outcomes of adaptation, even when some of the cultural values, such as parental authoritarianism and collectivism, are in conflict with those of the mainstream culture. The point is that it is not the values per se that cause the favorable outcomes but rather the patterns of social relations among individuals, in which nonconforming is severely condemned, that cause these values to have positive effects on outcomes.

For children who come from modest socioeconomic backgrounds and live in a marginal social environment where the culturally defined goals of their parents' social world are in fierce competition with those of their American peers' social world, the types of social relations engaging these children may be more important in affecting their adaptation to school than individual characteristics or family background factors. Thus, the theory of social relations may best enable us to understand the scholastic performance of Vietnamese children. Our theoretical model emphasizes the effects of various aspects of ethnicity—values, attitudes, and involvement—as indicators of ethnic social relations, controlling for the effects of individual characteristics, family structure, and family socioeconomic characteristics.

We believe that the source of Vietnamese academic achievement lies not primarily in the immediate family, but in the larger ethnic social context that contains the family, most importantly in the Vietnamese community (especially the form in which it has been emerging around the United States for the past two decades). The social ties among members of the community establish the meaning of "authoritarian" behavior on the part of parents and "independent" behavior on the part of children. If Vietnamese children maintain close ties to their ethnic communities through their parents, they are likely to be supported or constrained by the systems of social relations that confer specific meanings on cultural concepts, codes of conduct, and behavioral standards. This is why we expect that the differences between Vietnamese children and their American peers cannot be accounted for by family or individual-level characteristics alone.

Educational attainment in American society is primarily determined by the interaction among group characteristics, the socioeconomic background of the family, and the receiving social environment. If the social environment surrounding immigrant children is rich in resources and if its goals are consistent with those of the immigrant family, then ethnic resources may be relatively less important, but those ethnic resources may still count. For example, many middle-class immigrant parents move into affluent white neighborhoods, send their children to schools mainly attended by white students from similar or more affluent socioeconomic backgrounds, and still insist on enrolling their children in weekend or after-school ethnic schools or involving them in religious or cultural activities. The children then benefit both from privileged socioeconomic contacts with members of the dominant group in mainstream American society and from the group-specific expectations of and opportunities for intellectual development.

An alternative scenario operates where the social environment is not so rich. In this situation, a tightly knit, cooperative ethnic community becomes a crucial source of social capital for its young people. The extent to which young people are integrated into this community also becomes a major determinant of school adaptation, especially when the social environment otherwise places children at risk. The following section examines the empirical findings from our case study in Versailles Village to solve the puzzle of why Vietnamese children succeed, even when they attend poor urban public schools.

The Effects of Ethnic Social Relations

As has been described in detail in chapters 3 and 4, the high level of integration of families into the community stands out as the most conspicuous characteristic of the Vietnamese enclave in Versailles Village. Not only did many of these families know each other before reaching American shores, but once in Versailles Village, they interacted closely on a daily basis when shopping, attending church, and participating in social events. Their overlapping interpersonal connections reinforced the network of relations in the community, which in turn functioned to establish and reinforce community standards. The integration of families was reflected in a high degree of consensus over value and behavior standards (see table 3.2). Vietnamese parents and students whom we interviewed in Versailles Village consistently reported that their families emphasized obedience, industriousness, and helping others but discouraged egoistic values of independent thinking and popularity, which were most commonly associated with contemporary American society. These conservative Vietnamese family values constituted a source of direction, guiding children to adapt to American society the Vietnamese way. Children were constantly reminded of their duty to respect their elders, to take care of younger siblings, to work hard, and to make decisions only with the approval of their parents. Children were also pressured to avoid associating too much with non-Vietnamese children in the neighborhood, not to date non-Vietnamese, and not to become too American.

The results of our 1993 surveys indicate that Vietnamese students not only maintain a high level of consensus on the values held by their families, but also a high level of involvement in their ethnic community. Although value consensus among individuals does not require social control, it becomes a mechanism of control when individuals are deeply involved in a system of social relations. To measure the effects of ethnic involvement, we constructed five indicators reflecting the core aspects of ethnic involvement: language spoken at home, literacy in the parental native language, self-identification, ethnicity of close friends, and the likelihood of endogamy.[5] Vietnamese spoken at home and literacy in the parental native language represent the most intense forms of involvement in an ethnic culture, while identification of oneself as a member of the ethnic group, keeping mostly coethnic friends, and commitment to marrying within the ethnic group all indicate a clear identification with group membership.

As is shown in table 6.4, Vietnamese students in this community displayed high levels of ethnic involvement on all of our indicators. Over 90 percent spoke Vietnamese at home, 55 percent of them reported that they were able to read and write Vietnamese well, over half of them unequivocally identified themselves as Vietnamese rather than Vietnamese American or other, 80 percent reported that their close friends were Vietnamese, and almost 60 percent of them said that it was likely that they would marry someone of Vietnamese origin.

TABLE 6.4   Measures of Ethnic Involvement Among Vietnamese Youths

	Percentage
Language spoken at home	
Vietnamese	91.9
English	8.1
Ability to read and write Vietnamese	
Quite well	54.5
A little	33.3
Not at all	12.2
Self-identification	
Vietnamese	51.0
Vietnamese American	27.3
Other [a]	21.7
Ethnicity of close friends	
Vietnamese	80.3
Other	19.7
Likelihood of endogamy	
Certain	59.0
Uncertain	34.4
Unlikely	6.6

Source: The Versailles Village Survey of 1993 (*N* = 198).
[a] This category includes 15.6 percent who identified themselves as "Asian American" and 6.1 percent who identified themselves as "other." No one identified himself or herself as "American."

If we add family value orientations and work orientations of Vietnamese students in Versailles Village (see tables 3.2 and 3.3), we can see a coherent, complex Vietnamese American culture that includes a range of related orientations and practices among Vietnamese youth, which can be shown in the results of a factor analysis. In table 6.5, all the variables under consideration are clearly loaded on four factors. By creating scales of these four indicators, we can see that while traditional family values, commitment to a work ethic, and ethnic involvement are positively related to one another, they are all negatively related to egoistic value orientations. Therefore, we can interpret the complex of cultural orientations as consisting of a strong adherence to traditional family values, a strong commitment to a work ethic, a high level of ethnic involvement, and a weak adherence to egoistic values.

How does this cultural complex affect the adaptation of Vietnamese

TABLE 6.5   Factor Analysis of Selected Characteristics of Vietnamese Youths

Selected Characteristics	Factor 1	Factor 2	Factor 3	Factor 4
Eigen value	2.409	1.775	1.399	1.134
Factor loadings of selected characteristics				
To obey			.524	
To work hard			.773	
To help others			.718	
To be popular		.785		
To think for oneself		.690		
To help with housework				.731
Time spent on homework daily				.715
Language spoken at home	.741			
Ability to read and write Vietnamese	.559			
Self-identification	.619			
Ethnicity of friends	.639			
Commitment to endogamy	.556			
Correlation matrix				
Factor 1 (ethnic involvement)	1.000			
Factor 2 (egoistic values)	−.002	1.000		
Factor 3 (traditional family values)	.055	.019	1.000	
Factor 4 (commitment to a work ethic)	.125	−.071	.143	1.000

Source: The Versailles Village Survey of 1993 (*N* = 198).

children to American schools? Specifically, how does it affect academic outcomes? Table 6.6 presents a set of bivariate relations between Vietnamese cultural orientations and school adaptation as measured by current academic performance and plans for future education using our 1993 survey. To measure current academic performance, we asked respondents to report grades that they most often received. Possible answers were A or B, C, D, and F. To measure plans for future education, we asked respondents if they planned to attend college. Possible answers were a definite no, uncertain, and a definite yes. As is shown in table 6.6, almost all of the bivariate relationships between traditional family values, commitment to a work ethic, and ethnic involvement with each of the school adaptation measures were significant (one-tailed level).

TABLE 6.6   Self-Reported Grades and College Plans by Selected Ethnic Characteristics of Vietnamese Youths

	A's & B's as the Most Frequently Received Grades %	Plans to Go to College %	N
Traditional family values			
Weak	33.3	50.0	6
Average	69.8	60.5	43
Strong	78.5	78.5	149
p	.080	.051	
Egoistic values			
Weak	76.0	80.0	75
Average	72.7	70.5	88
Strong	80.0	68.6	35
p	.523	.640	
Commitment to a work ethic			
Weak	61.1	63.9	36
Average	76.3	72.2	114
Strong	83.3	89.6	48
p	.100	.053	
Ethnic involvement			
Weak	38.9	50.0	18
Average	75.9	72.2	79
Strong	81.2	79.2	101
p	.006	.054	

Source: The Versailles Village Survey of 1993 ($N = 198$).

Specifically, students having strong traditional family values, commitment to a work ethic, and ethnic involvement tended disproportionately to receive A's and B's and to have definite college plans. Egoistic values had no significant effect on school adaptation.

In order to examine the independent effect of each of the variables and describe the apparent system of causal relations at work, we used a regression model controlling for sex, age upon arrival, number of siblings, living arrangement, work status of parents, and father's education.[6] Table 6.7 shows the means, standard deviations, and standardized multivariate regression coefficients of major variables predicting school adaptation.

When all other effects were taken into account, adherence to traditional family values, commitment to a work ethic, and ethnic involvement all had significant effects on grades and college plans. The largest of all these standardized coefficients was the one representing the effect of ethnic involvement. These results supported the view that the involvement in an ethnic community could lead to desirable school adaptation.

Our controlled variables, which do not show significant influence, imply possible explanations of the behavior and performance of this group of Vietnamese students. It is often suggested that some young people do better than others because they have the support of unbroken—that is, two-parent—families. Similarly, it may be argued that children who have two working parents ("latch-key" children) lack support and direction and therefore are likely to show problems in developing constructive habits and in school performance. Our results support neither of these explanations at the level of the individual family. Neither having two working parents nor living in a two-parent family has a significant effect. Moreover, the father's education has no significant effect on any of the endogenous variables under consideration. This finding is contrary to the general belief that children's school performance may be attributed to the level of the parents' educational attainment, suggesting instead that children's ethnic involvement is more important than the financial and human capital of parents in determining the outcomes of school adaptation for this particular group.

Tangible Supports from the Ethnic Community

Why may the greater degree of ethnic involvement lead to more desirable outcomes? Vietnamese children gain specific benefits from the involvement in their ethnic community. As we have discussed in previous

TABLE 6.7　Means, Standard Deviations, the Range of Values, and Multivariate Regression Coefficients of Major Variables Predicting School Adaptation of Vietnamese Youths

	Mean	Standard Deviation	Minimum	Maximum	Regression Coefficient (S.E.)
Dependent Variable					
School adaptation	4.525	1.191	0	6	—
Predictors					
Traditional family values	10.869	1.268	0	12	.181** (.070)
Egoistic values	3.929	1.559	0	8	−.026 (.056)
Commitment to a work ethic	4.126	1.768	0	7	.111* (.053)
Ethnic involvement	11.303	3.165	0	15	.063* (.028)
Control Variables					
Sex (male)	.500	.501	0	1	−.102 (.173)
Age upon arrival (12 years or older)	.424	.495	0	1	−.255 (.195)
Number of siblings	3.167	2.447	0	12	.001 (.037)
Living with both parents	.747	.436	0	1	−.119 (.209)
Having both parents working	.232	.423	0	1	.005 (.204)
Father's education (high school or more)	.288	.454	0	1	.162 (.186)
Intercept					1.686*
R^2					.129

Source: The Versailles Village Survey of 1993 ($N = 198$).
* $p < = .05$ (two-tailed) ** $p < = .01$ (two-tailed)

chapters, the younger generation in Versailles Village is supported by various ethnic organizations, the most important of which is the Vietnamese Educational Association. This association focuses on promoting academic achievement among young Vietnamese and provides after-school classes and annual awards to young Vietnamese. The leaders of the association are prestigious, influential, and knowledgeable figures in the Vietnamese community. During the time when our study was conducted, the association was led by Brother John Nhon and Mr. Ngoc Thanh Nguyen. Both men were teachers working in the local public school system. Because of their experience with the formal school system, they were able to utilize that system more effectively and established appropriate means of preparing students for school.

Although there is a limit to our ability to measure quantitatively all the ways in which ethnic organizations facilitate school adaptation, we examined two major academically oriented programs—after-school classes and the annual awards ceremony—that are made available by the Vietnamese Educational Association and that affect young people directly. We suggest that participation in these community-based activities is likely to lead to desirable school outcomes. After-school classes are an important ethnic resource in the Versailles enclave. Unlike families in affluent middle-class communities, who can provide children with adequate after-school care and a variety of choices in after-school activities offered by private institutions, such as music, dance, and sports, families in poor communities lack economic resources to provide after-school care and activities. Poor children are more likely than their middle-class counterparts to be either left home alone without supervision or hanging out on problem-prone streets, at risk in either case. One advantage that young Vietnamese in Versailles Village have over their American peers is that they are supported by after-school classes offered by their church and other ethnic organizations, which function to help them with schoolwork on the one hand and to keep them off streets on the other.

The after-school classes include several offerings—Vietnamese, English, and schoolwork tutoring—that draw many Vietnamese students. According to our survey, almost 70 percent of Vietnamese students reported that they participated in these classes regularly; among these participants, over half attended Vietnamese language classes. While Vietnamese is not taught or tested in New Orleans public schools, we find that learning Vietnamese fosters cognitive skills and good study habits that can carry over to the learning of school required subjects as discussed in the previous chapter. English classes are designed to provide students extra help in their language skills with which many Vietnamese students have difficulty. Twenty-seven percent of the students reported that they had attended English language classes. About 30 percent of the students have attended other classes outside the regular school day.

Another program offered by the Vietnamese Education Association is the annual awards ceremony at which high-achieving students are honored. This ceremony is held in June right after the end of the school year and serves as a formal expression of encouragement. Attendance at this ceremony may be seen as ritual participation to show the community's collective commitment to education. For young people, such attendance reinforces their dedication to schoolwork. According to our 1994 survey, 85 percent of the students reported that they attended the ceremony, and 37 percent reported that they attended it twice or more.

The effects of after-school classes and attendance at the awards ceremony are both positively related to academic performance measured by self-reported grades ($r = .343$ and $.208$, respectively). On the basis of our multivariate analysis in table 6.7, we have found that participation in these community-offered activities is highly associated with involvement in the community (measured by the five aspects of ethnicity described earlier in the chapter). These findings suggest that in a socially and economically marginal environment, the ethnic community is crucial in providing help and direction to enable young people combat the disadvantages associated with immigrant status and poverty and counter the negative influence of the adversarial youth subculture that permeates urban public schools. In this sense, ethnicity is reflected in the pattern of ethnic involvement of families and individuals in their community and serves as an important form of social capital in facilitating positive school adaptation.

We recognize that social capital in the family and the ethnic community is what the sociologist M. Patricia Fernández-Kelly (1995) calls "internally heterogeneous." Poor families in low-income neighborhoods may provide support and encouragement to their children. But their attempts to generate social capital are often defeated by their isolation and by the social disorganization that surrounds them. This problem is exacerbated when the formation of constructive social relations among young people is undermined by persistent racism and negative racial stereotypes in the larger society. In contrast, when poor families are connected to one another in the community that actually reinforces the efforts of parents and acts as a bridge to the mainstream society, as in Versailles Village, the children can benefit from these social relations. If the densely knit set of social relations found in a community shapes attitudes and behaviors in ways that are conducive to upward mobility, these social relations can produce cultural values that fit the opportunities for mobility afforded by the larger society.

This examination of how an ethnic community can promote academic achievement provides an explanation of why Vietnamese children seem to be excelling in American schools and why this phenomenon appears to be related to living among coethnics. It also offers a concrete example of a concept that has become popular in the social sciences, the concept of social capital. As previous chapters have shown, many of the newly arrived Vietnamese settled in ethnic communities built from reformulated extended family ties. These communities have promoted productive behavior in the schools and may therefore be seen as sources of social capital, or social relations that result in desirable outcomes. Community organizations such as the Vietnamese Educational Association provide educational resources such as after-school classes. Beyond these specific benefits, however, the densely interknit social ties of the Vietnamese community control the behavior of young people through continual vigilance, maintain a high level of consensus on values, and reinforce parents' goals of upward mobility for their children.

—— Chapter 7 ——

Straddling the Gap:
Bicultural Conflicts and
Gender Role Changes

As a boy in Vietnam, Xuan Tran was accustomed to his father's beatings. He did not question this punishment, which often was carried out with a wire or cord and left welts on his skin. He shared the belief held by others in his village that the whippings and canings were his father's right as a parent, and Tran's role was to be submissive. Years later, when he became a parent himself, he continued to believe in a father's right to whip his child. So, enraged at what he felt was his 16-year-old daughter's misconduct last fall, the father of four grabbed an electrical cord and beat her about the arms, legs and buttocks. But Tran was no longer in Vietnam. He was living in America . . . and conduct that once was sanctioned had become a crime (*Cleveland Plain Dealer*, May 29, 1994).

Tran's use of corporal punishment on his child exemplifies the clash of two cultures in Vietnamese families as well as in other immigrant families. Like other immigrant children, Vietnamese children confront cultural differences in their families that often put them at odds with their parents and widen the generation gap. This chapter first looks at the bicultural conflicts that Vietnamese children encounter on an everyday basis and explores some of the main sources of these conflicts. It then considers the changes and complications in gender roles that have occurred as Vietnamese families have modified their original cultural patterns to fit into American society. The focus is on how ethnic social control creates difficulties and paradoxical consequences for intergenerational relations.

CONTRADICTIONS IN TWO SOCIAL WORLDS

The chapters thus far have told a story of successful adaptation to school and, through school, to American society. Success comes at a price, however. For many Vietnamese children, even the best-adjusted, the pressures of immigrant adaptation, on the one hand, and of American adolescence, on the other, feel like two opposing forces. Vietnamese youth find themselves straddling two different social worlds; the one from which they or their parents came and the one in which they are maturing. Often they feel the urge to rebel against their parents in order to fit into their adolescent world as "Americans," but they also experience a strong tug pulling them back to their own families and to their culture of origin. Like other immigrant children, Vietnamese refugee children struggle to find answers to a set of difficult questions: Why do my parents object to my acting like other American kids? What's wrong with it? How can I fit in with my friends without offending my family? Can I ever grow up as an American in a Vietnamese family? These questions reflect considerable confusion over the nature of being American and over the meaning of Americanization.

"American" Versus "Un-American"

At times, Vietnamese children fight with their parents over parental demands that the children consider "un-American," but often the children do so without knowing exactly what is "American." As part of growing up, the young people whom we studied struggled both to learn American ways and to decide what American meant to them. When asked what was considered American, a Vietnamese high school senior scratched his head a little and replied, "I don't know exactly. I guess whatever is cool." When asked to define what was considered "cool," he said,

You look *cool* when you are free to do anything a white boy would be able to do, or when you are able to go do things on your own rather than on your parents' instructions like most Vietnamese do.

His peers from the same high school added:

Well, there are a lot of things that can be considered cool—say, wearing nice clothes, like Calvin Klein . . . and that sort, driving a car to school, going out on dates or parties, hanging out with friends, getting drunk occasionally, and having your own apartment so that you don't have to put up with all your kin, and doing exciting things.

To me, being American is doing things like other American people do—say, going to the ball games, baseball and football, eating hamburgers and French fries, taking family vacations, and having fun.

I feel that being an American involves having American cultural ways such as celebrating Christmas, Thanksgiving, Easter, July 4th, and things like that.

Not all the Vietnamese students agreed. Some offered alternative views of what it meant to be American:

Being an American doesn't simply mean that you can have many dreams about living luxurious lifestyles you see on TV or movies and that you can even own some of those nice things. For me, it has to do with the freedom to choose whatever is best for you, the ability to make your own decisions and to be yourself, and the courage to challenge authorities.

An American is not Bill Clinton or Bill Gates or Shaquille O'Neal. Being an American is being ambitious, competitive, and hardworking. You can never become an American if you just lay back and wait for things to be handed over to you. You have to aggressively pursue what you want.

Being American can take on many different faces. One thing that really sets an American apart from a Vietnamese is the idea of independence. In America, you don't have to do what your parents tell you to.

These quotes illustrate a distinct pattern of response. Vietnamese youth pinpoint precisely those practices, beliefs, and objects of consumption that are typically absent from their own families but are central in today's American youth culture. Their notion of being American tends to mix materialism and idealism. For them, becoming American means adopting visible expressions of youth culture; it combines display (wearing fashionable hair styles and name-brand clothing) and behavior (going on dates, to parties, and on vacations, or making one's own decisions about whom to befriend, what to do, and where to go), both of which make one look "cool." The youth also embrace the core American values of individualism, freedom, and independence.

But these adolescents know that America is full of contradictions. Enthusiastic about American ways, they are ambivalent about their own relationship to things American. A Vietnamese high school girl remarked in a cynical tone, "Looking cool doesn't make you an American. A typical American is blonde, blue-eyed, white, and beautiful. I can never be an American." Her boyfriend echoed, "She's right. An American is white. You often hear people say, 'Hey, so-and-so is dating an American.' You know she's dating a white boy. If he were a black, then people would say 'He's black' rather than 'American.' You see what I mean?" Another young person said, "Being an American can be a little bit of everything, like the stuff in a salad bowl. For me? I guess to be an American is to be oneself—me or you."

Still others pointed to a dilemma, as one said,

> Of course I want to look cool and don't want to be somebody's laughing stock. But being an American is not your choice. Even if you speak English without an accent, people may not think of you as American. To tell you the truth, I don't even like the apple pie. I am Vietnamese in my blood and my gut, that's something I cannot choose. But sadly, I am not fond of being Vietnamese, either.

In these remarks we see considerable ambivalence and confusion that betray young people's unending effort to straddle the gap between Vietnam and America and to make sense of the contradiction between the goals and expectations of their families and those embraced by the new culture in which they are growing up.

In the struggle to find a place of their own, Vietnamese youth often come up against the views of their parents, for whom "American" is defined in rather different terms. Being cool bears little relationship to their parents' perspective on what it means to be American. For the parents, being American has to do with getting ahead in society, which translates into hard work and school success. One parent told us when asked what "American" meant:

> I say, education. You can't become an American if you drop out of high school and get stuck in here [Versailles Village]. To be an American is not just to wear baggy pants or Nikes, but something more important. It's not like in Vietnam. Back in Vietnam, you didn't have much opportunity for a good education, and you were fine without finishing high school. But in America, if you don't finish high school and go on to college, you can't get a good job. If you don't have a good job, you can't raise a family. How can you be an American if you can't support yourself and your family?

Another parent voiced similar sentiments:

> A true American is not someone who is uneducated and poor like me. Some of these kids just don't get it. All these things that they are going for would not make them Americans if they don't pay attention to school.

The parents also differ from the children in their judgment of American ways. What youth regard as cool parents consider superficial, unimportant, or even harmful. A Vietnamese parent told us:

American ways are two-sided. We want our kids to adopt the good ways and avoid the bad ways so that they can become good Americans. These kids are too ready to get Americanized on their own terms. They are too young to distinguish what is good and what is bad and they don't know what it takes to become a real American. To me, real Americans are those who are hardworking, polite, willing to sacrifice, and doing well in school, but not those who are lazy, disrespectful, irresponsible, or self-centered, like those you often see on TV.

In the words of yet another parent:

I don't have any problem with democracy, independence, and freedom and all that my children often complain about lacking in the family. These kids think they have many choices in America—land of the free, right? You think my children have that many choices in America? No, not now. If they don't do well in school, they are finished. Once they get through college, then they may have many more choices and then they may be able to do whatever they want. But now I have to make sure they bring home decent grades. The point is that if I don't emphasize obedience, don't give them strict instructions, they will easily get lost or get stuck here.

These stories sound familiar; they might just as easily have been told by the middle-class or working-class parents of any American child. Of course, the generation gap is nothing new but in Vietnamese refugee families it looms larger and takes a different form. The children of Vietnamese refugees are immediately plunged into American life, placed in the American educational system as soon as they arrive. They learn English and other American ways quickly through interacting with American peers in school and watching TV at home. The pressure to fit in is overwhelming, even among first-generation immigrant youth.

By contrast, the parents are in, but not of, America. Work and the need to reestablish a stable family come first, and that effort is a constant struggle, requiring long hours of toil with little time for learning English or socializing with other Americans. Parents are rarely able to provide the resources required for American lifestyles, they have two priorities:

putting food on the table and making sure that children do well in school. These contrasts in their experiences lead Vietnamese parents and children to divergent assessments of the value and meaning of American ways.

Where Do the Two Cultures Clash?

Tension between the individualism of American society and the collectivism of Vietnamese culture lies at the heart of the conflicts between Vietnamese refugee parents and their children. With its emphasis on competitiveness and creativity, American individualism is bound up with a particular form of social organization characterized by the nuclear family, loose kinship ties, and fluid and relatively weak traditions. The care and nurturing of children is the primary focus of American family life. Parent-child obligations flow in one direction; parents are obliged to raise children to be caring parents, productive workers, and good citizens; but the obligations children owe parents are few and ill-defined. Taught to be independent, competitive, and self-supporting, American children are encouraged to leave home and to be on their own as they grow into adulthood.

Vietnamese culture orients parents and children in very different ways. In Vietnam, the extended family, tightly knit kinship networks, and deeply rooted traditions prevail, leaving little room for individualism. The individual is considered part of the extended family, and the individual self is treated as a part of the family rather than as the self's own. The culture dictates that parent-child obligations should be mutual and lifelong. Not only do parents raise children to be productive grownups, they expect their children to be their lifetime "social security"—to provide emotional and financial support in old age. In this sense, it is in the parents' interest to raise children who will live up to parental expectations.

Vietnamese children often cite this family-centered culture to distinguish between what is Vietnamese and what is American. A six-foot-tall Vietnamese of the 1.5 generation, who was the only Asian player in the women's volleyball team at a university in Louisiana, told us:

Everybody says I am very Americanized: tall, athletic, and playing college volleyball. Most of my friends are Americans indeed. But I sometimes don't consider so. I would consider anything that is not tightly related to family American. You know, the family is so central and so important in the lives of the Vietnamese people.

She went on to tell us the following story about her cousin, who grew up in the same household but was "becoming so Americanized":

She acts so independent, and she puts so much emphasis on the self— "me" instead of "us." Not that this is wrong. Independence is greatly admired in Vietnamese culture because it shows maturity and growth, but she is so "free" and never seems to care about her own parents [who were still in Vietnam] and her family.

Another Vietnamese young woman, also a college student, said:

This may sound very silly, but a youngster who is becoming too American is the one who is having too much fun, too much fun in doing nontypical Vietnamese things such as enjoying yourself, unwilling to do hard work, and not obligating yourself to your family's best interests. To be an American, you may be able to do whatever you want. But to be a Vietnamese, you must think of your family first.

The Vietnamese high school students whom we interviewed agreed that attitudes toward the family distinguished "Vietnamese" from "Americanized Vietnamese." Striving to become American, many young Vietnamese men and women have, ironically, found themselves growing up Vietnamese in America. Some are torn between the individualism of growing up American and the community or parental demands to fulfill family obligations; others manage to balance the two, as suggested by the story of Dr. Ninh, the brother of one of our interviewees. The eldest of five children, Ninh arrived in New Orleans with his parents and his younger siblings at age 18. Like many other Vietnamese teenagers, he was older than his classmates, beginning American public school in the tenth grade. He lacked English language proficiency, but not literacy; he quickly caught up with others in his school, graduated from high school with honors, and went on to college. From there, Ninh continued on to medical school. Again, he did well in medical school and moved on to Atlanta, Georgia, to do his internship. Everyone in the community was proud of him, but they thought that he would leave home for good. Ninh's sister recalled:

In the last year of his internship, my brother got married in Georgia. The bride was his high school sweetheart—a Vietnamese girl from New Orleans. He didn't allow the family on either side to hold a big traditional Vietnamese wedding in New Orleans; instead, he had a small American wedding at a Catholic church in Georgia attended by close families and a few American friends. There were actually more Americans than Vietnamese at the wedding. People in our neighborhood all knew about his success but thought that he was too Americanized to return home. A few years later, he joined a family practice in Macon, Georgia, and he and his wife moved there and bought a big home. Guess what? He moved the whole family to Georgia—my parents, my youngest brother and sister who were still in school. My older sister and I stayed here for college. We may all end up moving to Macon. My big brother always feels he should support his family and keep everybody together under the same roof.

Whether Dr. Ninh's story is atypical remains to be seen, but this example suggests that individualism and family obligations may not always be incompatible and that becoming a mainstream American may not necessarily require abandoning the culture of origin; family obligations may sometimes spur individuals on to success. But if the pressure to oblige the family is too great, it may become oppressive. For some young Vietnamese, individualism may mean the ability to do whatever they want, in which case the resentment of parental pressure builds up, gradually alienating children from their families. And even accepting familial or community expectations and finding ways of living up to these expectations within an American context can place burdens on individuals that would be seen as onerous in the American value system.

Authority and control provide a second area for parent-child conflict. Deeply influenced by Confucianism, Vietnamese culture places a high value on parental authority and respect for parents and elders that presupposes mutual obligations and lifelong interdependence. Vietnamese children are expected to submit to the discipline of elders in the belief that the older people are wise and experienced and possess a superior understanding of right and wrong. Even when they have grown to adulthood and become parents themselves, offspring remain children in the eyes of their parents. Grown sons and daughters are expected to submit to the authority of elderly, frail, sometimes even dying parents.

American culture also values parental authority, but in a circumscribed and instrumental way. While parents exert control over their minor children, they encourage independence from an early age. A former Vietnamese teacher explained the difference between the two cultures:

> It is not that American parents don't exercise authority and control over children; they do. But their authority is built on the fact that their children are on their "payroll." Once children grow up, they are on their own; they are not children any more. In the Vietnamese family, parental authority is not simply based on custodianship but also on lifetime moral obligations. We have a saying that "one is always a child in the eyes of the parent." Your father could slap you, if he thought you did something wrong, even when you were forty years old. Plus, you have to take care of parents when they get old. You simply cannot just leave home and be on your own.

While many Vietnamese parents in the United States find it hard to discard traditional ways, children experience difficulty accepting traditional discipline from their parents. As in the case of Tran cited in the beginning of the chapter, corporal punishment, common in Vietnam, continues to be practiced by Vietnamese parents. In the eyes of the original culture, children need stern guidance from their parents; they are too young to be on their own and cannot yet tell right from wrong. Parents take the credit when a child behaves and makes progress, but parents also take the blame when a child does wrong. Stern discipline is thus a socially accepted instrument for ensuring that children bring only honor to the family, and not shame.

In the United States, children expect to be treated as individuals, who are owed respect and who have some measure of control over themselves. They are protected by law from forms of punishment that Americans generally interpret as physical or psychological abuse. As the judge who heard Tran's case remarked, "Corporal punishment is not illegal, but what you get it done with may be. He [Tran] hit her with an electrical cord" (*Cleveland Plain Dealer*, May 29, 1994). Apparently, the cultural clash involves different assumptions about the individual rights of children and divergent interpretations of physical harm. While Vietnamese families in the United States still accept the idea of corporal punishment, the use of it is much less frequent than in the old country, because parents have increasingly become aware that American ways are not their own, that their children are Americans, and that they cannot cane or beat these American children. But the gradual easing of corporal punishment does not mean that the generation gap is disappearing. Open challenges to parental authority makes parents feel estranged from their children. One parent lamented: "In Vietnam, you are not supposed to look at parents in the eye and talk back. Here, when children disagree with us, they open their eyes wide and shout back, sometime even in front of other people. When they do that, I see a little monster in their eyes."

This parent was also disheartened by what he perceived as a lack of respect for teachers in American or Americanized children. He said, "The students do whatever they want to do, because [they have] too much freedom. They don't care about the teachers. In my country, the teacher is the second parent. Anything the teacher says, they listen." Another parent made an equally explicit connection between the authority of the parent and the authority of the teacher when he said, "I do not see how American teachers can keep good order without a stick. The father must use his stick at home. The teacher must use his stick at school."

Just as Vietnamese concepts of family obligations can actually promote upward mobility in America for individuals who manage to balance two sets of values, Vietnamese ideas about parental authority can sometimes be useful in American life. One Vietnamese college student explained: "I feel like I have to do whatever my teacher says. The teacher is like my father or mother, they know what's best for me to do. I see a lot of my American classmates, they don't do what the teacher tells them, and I think that's why a lot of them don't do too well in school. They don't know how to listen."

Conflicts over parental authority often flare up over issues of dating and curfews. Dating in high school is an important part of American youth culture. Vietnamese high school students are no different from their American peers in this respect; they generally socialize within their own ethnic circles, but they adopt the dating patterns of American youths, to the chagrin of their parents. A 19-year-old college student recalled:

> When I was in high school, my parents did not allow me to go out on dates because they were afraid that I might get hooked up with bad guys, that I might be taken advantage of, and that I might get distracted from my study. They worked all the time and never seemed to know that there was such a thing as popularity. When they finally agreed that I could go out, they set a time when I should be home. If I was a little late, they would get really upset. They always told me that they worried, and that I was a girl, and that girls shouldn't be out late. I had always hoped that my

parents would someday open up just a little to realize that we are living in America and not in Vietnam.

The weakening of parental authority bemoaned by Vietnamese parents does not simply result from Americanization alone but also from the change of parent-child roles. The language barrier cuts many parents off from the larger society, leaving them socially isolated. Many non-English-speaking parents have to rely on their children to guide them into American society, in effect becoming the children of their children. These parents have to depend on their children to answer phones, shop, deal with household bills, contact people outside the home, and even read and sign notes and report cards sent home from school. One young man expressed the alienation from his parents and family produced by this parental dependency: "I don't see why I should listen to her (his mother). Like, she needs me a lot more than I need her. She can't even talk to anybody that calls on the phone. So I just do what I like. Who's gonna tell me I can't?"

Even parents and children who do not undergo such extreme role reversals may find that poor communication makes for troubled relationships. Long work hours leave parents with little time for their children; in the evenings, the parents either are too exhausted to talk to their children or sometimes even come home too late to see any children awake. A 22-year-old college senior described her relations with her parents:

> In a way, I guess my mom and dad are foreigners to me in addition to being foreigners to America. I am Vietnamese, but I'm also American, and sometimes I just don't understand what my parents want from me. Maybe if we could talk more . . . But my dad especially, he works so hard all the time that we never have time to talk. And my mom works too. Maybe when I get older we'll know each other better.

These family tensions often have undesirable outcomes, but the act of balancing between Vietnamese and American values can actually be productive. The pressure of family obligations can push young people forward in American society. Respect for authority, transferred to the classroom, can be an educational advantage. We are not, of course, making a case for the virtues of authoritarian families; the intent in this section has been to describe the difficulties often inherent in Vietnamese family relations, even when these relations may lead to achievement in school and in later life. The following section looks more deeply at a particular aspect of Vietnamese family relations—gender roles—in order to see how traditional Vietnamese culture patterns, modified by the American setting, can be a source of tension and stress for young people and at the same time lead to upward mobility through the educational system.

CHANGES IN GENDER ROLES

One might be tempted to interpret our account as a story of conflict between parents' unchanging traditionalism and their children's attempts to abandon those traditions. The reality is a good deal more complex, however, for both parents and children are struggling to adjust to the demands of their new environment. Those struggles yield patterns of adaptation that combine the old and the new and that are sources of tension. A clear illustration of these new developments can be seen in gender roles.

Studies of the Vietnamese have shown that gender roles among Vietnamese refugees in the United States differ markedly from those in Vietnam, which are characterized by the subordination of women (Freeman 1989; Kibria 1993; Muzny 1989; Nash 1992; Rutledge 1992). The anthropologist Gerard C. Hickey's classic ethnographic study of Vietnamese village life in the late 1950s testified to the second-class status of women in Vietnam (1964). Hickey observed that rural Vietnamese women were expected to marry early, bear children, and serve their husbands. Except for a few Catholics, families widely accepted polygamy. Most of the villagers were poorly educated; but women were four times as likely as men to be illiterate, since in the past only men received a formal education, while women were taught household arts. Although significant improvements in educational facilities have been made in contemporary Vietnam and more villagers agree that women deserve a basic formal education, educational opportunities for women have remained strictly limited.

With migration to the United States, gender roles have changed in significant ways. We can trace these changes to two sources: necessity and opportunity. The economic situation of Vietnamese families no longer permits men to function as sole providers. At the same time, Vietnamese women encounter many more opportunities for education and employment outside the home, establishing an identity that includes greater independence from their husbands than they had in Vietnam. Vietnamese women's work outside the home has also greatly narrowed the male-female power gap within the home (Kibria 1993). Despite these changes, researchers generally agree that traditional ideas about family and gender have not been completely abandoned by the Vietnamese. The anthropologist James M. Freeman's collection of short autobiographies of the Vietnamese show a people profoundly attached to their family traditions and troubled by challenges to them (1989). And Jesse W. Nash's participant observation in a Vietnamese community portrays the idealization of women as a core value of the community (1992).

The Changing Educational Achievements of Women

Virtually all the researchers who have studied the issue of gender relations among the Vietnamese in America have interpreted the increasing entry of Vietnamese women into the nondomestic spheres of employment and education as a straightforward matter of conflict between traditional Vietnamese cultural attitudes, which promote male dominance, and contemporary American attitudes and economic structures, which create pressures for gender equality (Kibria 1993; Muzny 1989; Rutledge 1992). Our observations in the Versailles Village, however, provide a different, more nuanced perspective, with a look at changing but conflicted views of the education of young Vietnamese women.

Do traditional Vietnamese social relations advance or inhibit the education of women? To the extent that tradition promotes academic achievement among both men and women by providing encouragement and discipline, the answer is yes (Caplan, Whitmore, and Choy 1989; Caplan, Choy, and Whitmore, 1991, 1992). Table 7.1 provides data from the 1990 census on educational attainment among adult Vietnamese by date of arrival. Among the most recent arrivals, both women and men had extremely low levels of educational attainment, and the gender gap was substantial; these findings reflect both the lack of education and the gender bias in education. Among those who had been in the United States for five years or longer, however, both men and women showed noticeably higher levels of educational attainment, despite a persistent gender gap. The selective immigration among the earliest arrivals, mentioned in earlier chapters, accounts for part of the difference, but another important part results from the educational opportunities that younger refugees found upon arrival in America.

Gender differences in high school dropout rates and current college attendance rates among young people aged 16 to 24 look radically dif-

TABLE 7.1   The Gender Gap in Educational Attainment Among
Adult Vietnamese (Aged 25 or Over) by Date of
Arrival, 1990

	Female	Male
Arrived in 1985 or later		
Less than high school (%)	60.2	43.2
High school graduate (%)	18.4	18.4
Some college (%)	15.7	27.0
College graduate (%)	5.7	11.4
N	2,397	2,451
Arrived before 1985		
Less than high school (%)	40.4	25.8
High school graduate (%)	19.6	15.7
Some college (%)	25.3	31.7
College graduate (%)	14.7	26.8
N	4,480	4,816

Source: U.S. Census of Population and Housing, 1990, 5-percent PUMS.

ferent, as can be seen in table 7.2. Because marital status is often negatively associated with educational attainment, especially for women, and
because Vietnamese women tend to marry younger than men do, this
factor is controlled for. Indeed, those who are married tend to show
higher high school dropout rates and lower college attendance rates than
those who are single, regardless of gender in this age group, and Vietnamese women are four times as likely as Vietnamese men to be married.

Controlling for marital status yields a sharply diminished gender gap.
Among those who are married, women's dropout rate is almost identical
to men's. Among those who are unmarried, women drop out at a rate
lower than men. Gender differences in current college attendance are even
more marked, again showing higher levels of educational attainment
among young Vietnamese women than among men; while married
women are as likely as married men to be currently enrolled in college,
unmarried women are significantly *more* likely than their male peers to be
enrolled in college. These census data indicate a convergence of educational attainment among younger-generation Vietnamese women and
men.

Results from the Versailles Village study provide corroborating evidence. Table 7.3 shows two measures of school adaptation: average
grades and attitudes toward college attendance. Overall, female students
earned significantly higher grades than did their male peers; only 9 per-

TABLE 7.2   The Gender Gap in High School Dropout Rate and
Current College Attendance Among Young
Vietnamese by Marital Status, 1990

	Married		Unmarried	
	Female	Male	Female	Male
High school dropout (aged 16 to 24) (%)	29.6	28.6	8.4	10.4
N	334	105	2,212	3,038
Currently enrolled in college (aged 18 to 24) (%)	19.4	18.6	42.3	36.7
N	330	102	1,556	2,278

Source: U.S. Census of Population and Housing, 1990, 5-percent PUMS.

cent of the girls reported receiving grades averaging C or lower, half the
proportion of their male peers; by contrast, 28 percent reported receiving A averages, substantially more than their male peers. Similarly,
young Vietnamese women placed as much importance on college attendance as did young Vietnamese men. Interestingly, among those who
said that they definitely would not go to college or that college was not
important, there was a slightly higher percentage of girls than of boys,
perhaps as a result of the younger ages at which young women marry, as
seen in the census. Nevertheless, women's attitudes toward future education are generally quite similar to men's.

In contrast to adult Vietnamese women, handicapped by the educational disadvantages they brought with them from Vietnam, younger-
generation Vietnamese women in the United States no longer trail their
male peers in schooling. Why is it that these young Vietnamese women
seem to have attained levels of education that are at least equal, and
possibly superior, to the levels attained by men? Our fieldwork in Versailles Village pinpoints the factors behind this reversal. Since gender
roles are fundamentally matters of interpretation of the kinds of behavior considered appropriate to men and women, we focused on how fathers, mothers, young men, and young women themselves have perceived the importance of women's education and how perceptions of
women's education may be related to broader views about changes in
gender roles. In addressing the broader views about gender roles, we pay
special attention to whether the refuge in the United States has brought
about a break from the traditional Vietnamese ways of thinking about
men and women or whether these ways of thinking have somehow been
adjusted to new circumstances.

TABLE 7.3 The Gender Gap in Levels of Adaptation to School Among Vietnamese Youths

Measures of Adaptation	Female	Male
Average Grades		
A (%)	28.1	21.4
B to B+ (%)	57.9	52.9
C+ to B− (%)	4.7	8.6
C or lower (%)	9.3	17.1
Attitude toward college attendance		
Definitely do not want to go to college (%)	4.9	5.2
Not important (%)	7.1	4.3
Important (%)	88.0	90.5
N	215	187

Source: The Versailles Village Survey of 1994.

The Father's View

Most of the Vietnamese fathers interviewed considered obedience as the most desired quality and achievement as the second most desired quality to be expected from or desired in their daughters. But the fathers did not view obedience and achievement as mutually inconsistent. From the father's perspective, obedience produced achievement. One father told us:

It is important that all children obey their parents. But it is more important for daughters to obey. The daughters will be mothers one day and they must be good mothers. So, they must obey their parents today.

Obedience from all children, both sons and daughters, is generally expected in Vietnamese families. In Vietnam, fathers might have expected obedience throughout life, but in the United States, they hoped that it would last until marriage. Fathers worried that the greater level of personal freedom in American life might undermine obedience among daughters and sons, but they overwhelmingly agreed that the perceived need to protect the sexual purity of daughters made the obedience of daughters even more important than that of sons. A father remarked:

Of course a boy can get away with more than a girl. A boy can do more before he gets a bad name. A boy can get a bad name and still become good later. But if a girl gets a bad name, I don't know what she can do to get over [it].

The fathers whom we interviewed not only tolerated the idea that their daughters would be educated but encouraged it. They pointed out that women had always participated in the household economy in Vietnam, but mostly in agriculture, a pursuit that required little formal education. But farming was not part of the Vietnamese experience in the United States, as one father explained:

> In Vietnam, the girls helped with the rice, sure, but here nobody's a farmer. You got to have a job to get money. A good wife needs to help her husband. She got to have a job to help and she got to go to school to get a job.

Having experienced so much hardship in the United States, fathers knew the importance of a two-income family. Most of the fathers whom we interviewed worked as fishermen or in low-skilled manufacturing; their wives either did not work outside the home or were employed at relatively low-income part-time jobs. As low-wage workers, the fathers realized that their wives' lack of job skills made it all that much harder to get ahead. They had also learned that living well in America required a relatively high income, a goal that only families with multiple earners could hope to attain. For these reasons, fathers had come to see education as a way that would allow their daughters to contribute to family well-being, as expected by the traditional Vietnamese family, but in a manner suitable to American needs and wants. A father said:

> It is very hard for me being the only one in the family who works. I am a fisherman. I make enough money for us to live, but I worry all the time. My wife, her English is not good, and she cannot work. So, I want my daughter to go to school so that she and her future family will not have these problems. My daughter is good, so she will do what I say and her life will be better than ours.

Fathers struck a clear note when discussing their desire for their daughters to do well in school—namely, the expectation that education would make a young woman an appropriate match for a relatively high-status husband. Several fathers outlined the following contrasting scenarios. In Vietnam, an uneducated woman had no other options but marriage into a working-class or peasant family; in the United States, an uneducated woman would face a similar option, and she would have a hard time finding a husband with good prospect of doing well. In the minds of most fathers, pushing daughters toward academic achievement did not subvert traditional gender roles, but rather affirmed those roles under changed circumstances. As one father explained:

> I want my son-in-law to be a doctor or an engineer. A doctor or an engineer does not want a wife whom he has to be ashamed of. Say, nursing would be a decent job for my daughter; and she would work with doctors. If she found a husband who's a doctor, she would help him in his job. I always tell my daughter to study hard so that she will be someone who can be part of a good family.

Furthermore, Vietnamese fathers expected personal and familial rewards to accrue from their daughters' success in school. How daughters did made little difference as long as education was largely limited to men, as in Vietnam. But the very availability of education to women in the United States made daughters' education a matter of status competition for the fathers. The educational accomplishments of sons and daughters reflected on the fathers themselves. With daughters there was actually a keener edge; expecting higher levels of obedience from girls, the fathers were more likely to take personal responsibility for their daughters' success or failure in school. With sons, in contrast, fathers generally took a more laissez-faire approach, treating their sons as individual actors rather than as dependents. A father said:

> The daughter of my neighbor finished college last year. I would feel ashamed before him if my daughter had not also finished college. If my daughter does less than the daughter of my neighbor, that means I am a less good father than my neighbor.

On the issue of relative control over sons and daughters, another father explained:

> Of course I want both my son and my daughter to do well in school. But my son, he is a man, and if he do not do what I want him to do, others will understand. But my daughter, she must do what I tell her to do, and how can I explain if she does not do good?

Overall, the Vietnamese fathers whom we interviewed voiced support for their daughters' educational pursuits for three important reasons: (1) educated daughters have high earnings potential and can thus contribute to the incomes of their future families; (2) educated daughters can make suitable wives to relatively high-status husbands and ensure quality child-rearing; and (3) educated daughters can be status symbols for their birth families.

The Mother's View

Gaining access to mothers was more difficult, since fathers were generally presented as the spokesmen of the Vietnamese families. But the mothers opened up when their husbands were not present, and they told us a similar, though distinctive, story. Like the fathers, the mothers whom we interviewed saw their daughters' education and eventual employment as an affirmation, not a rejection, of traditional Vietnamese gender roles. Whereas fathers stressed educational achievement as an outcome of the obedience they required from the daughters, however, mothers usually perceived education as a means of enhancing opportunities and thereby improving their daughters' bargaining position within traditional gender roles. The mothers stressed the importance of academic achievement as did the fathers, but they went even further, linking women's education to a version of the Vietnamese image of feminine virtue as modified by the encounter with American culture.

The mothers whom we interviewed desired independence for their daughters, understanding that dependence on men was not good for their daughters growing up in America. They generally held the idea that men should hold more power in the family than women, but they felt that women should get more involved in family decision making than they did in Vietnam. These mothers reasoned that education would increase their daughters' earnings potential and thereby improve their status within the family, while remaining within "traditional" gender roles. One mother remarked:

> If my daughter no have good job and she marry, the husband can go off with other woman and do what he like. Maybe he good, OK, but if my daughter go school, get good job, make money, then she no have to put up with anything husband do, and he have to be good.

Other mothers whom we interviewed commonly echoed this view. They did not seem to seek complete independence for their daughters, nor did they hope that their daughters would abandon a Vietnamese identity. They universally expected that their daughters would marry and would maintain what was seen as Vietnamese culture through their roles as mothers.

The mothers also shared fathers' views that daughters required greater control than sons. They accepted the sexual double standard and the part that this double standard played in determining the marriageability of young women. One mother reflected a view similar to that of the father cited earlier:

> My daughter must be a good girl. That means she must do good in school and she must not go out alone at night with boys. Sometimes my son is bad, but not very bad. He can always do better. But if a girl is bad, people will always see her as bad, so it is very important to be careful with daughters.

The mothers seemed to not only accept but even to expect a certain amount of acting up from their sons. A mother told us that if a boy was "too good," never rowdy or disorderly, she would worry that his excessively unproblematic behavior might suggest a lack of spirit. Parents indulged unruly sons, even at a very early age. As we observed, mothers allowed little boys to play and run around public places, at church functions, or in shops, only admonishing them when their play became excessively energetic. By contrast, little girls and young women often showed a quiet self-discipline, inculcated by parental control. Such parental control may stem from fathers, who are seen as the chief authority figures in these Vietnamese households, but it is exercised primarily by mothers, who have the immediate responsibility for raising children.

Housework illuminated the mothers' divergent expectations of daughters and sons. In the older generation, women were almost exclusively responsible for housework. When wives worked outside the home, their paid work was usually simply added onto their household responsibilities; and these dual responsibilities were carried over to the younger generation, since mothers looked to their daughters for help with the housework. In Versailles Village, as in other Vietnamese communities, when girls came home from school, they were expected first to help with the housework and care of younger siblings and then do their studying (see Muzny 1989). Unlike boys, who were allowed to participate in relatively uncontrolled activities outside the home, girls often had to stay home doing household chores. Thus, mothers' expectations kept girls more tightly bound to their mothers and to the domestic sphere, ensuring that young women spent a greater amount of time under the control of the family.

Views of Young Men

Vietnamese adolescent men in Versailles Village generally agreed with the idea of a strict gender separation and accepted the gender double standard that expects young women to be morally superior. Our field observations of young men and young women in the schools and in the community indicated a strong tendency toward gender-segregated friendship groups. One young man expressed a common attitude:

> Yeah, sure, girls are more good than boys. Everybody knows that. Not too many girls smoke or drink. So sure they act better in school and get better grades. It's different [for boys and for girls].

Though often preferring traditional ways, these young men whom we interviewed seemed more flexible in their ideas about gender roles than were the older men. They were acutely aware of the tensions between the Vietnamese ideals presented to them by their elders and the American ideals they adopted from the popular media and from exposure to their non-Vietnamese peers. The young men also frequently expressed allegiance to both sets of ideals. They wanted girlfriends who would dress fashionably and who would be "fun," not stodgy. But as wives, they would desire sexually inexperienced women who would put a priority on motherhood. One young man put it this way:

> I guess I want a girlfriend who is very American but a wife who is very Vietnamese. I think girls can be both of these things, though. They can wear okay clothes and listen to okay music and still be Vietnamese inside.

Young men also explicitly associated the "Vietnameseness" of young women with better school performance. They generally agreed that a "good girl" should do well in school; they also thought doing well in school was more important for girls than for boys, reasoning that girls could not afford to have a "bad name." Thus, the women's identity as

Vietnamese has a unique twist. Unlike their mothers and grandmothers in Vietnam, the young women were encouraged to acquire an education, and this encouragement was reinforced by strong family control and pressures from the surrounding community, including those from their male peers.

Views of Young Women

Not surprisingly, Vietnamese young women themselves showed the greatest awareness of the contradictions, complications, and frustrations inherent in the changing meaning of appropriate gender roles. Like their mothers, many young women voiced a general acceptance of traditional gender roles but felt that role expectations were perplexing and frustrating matters complicated by the pressures to conform. Some young women sought to rebel but found it very difficult to do so, given the authoritarianism of many families and the nature of tightly knit communities.

Almost all the young women with whom we spoke told us that parents enforced discipline more strongly among girls than among boys, even in the use of corporal punishment, the form of parental discipline permitted and commonly practiced in Vietnam. While corporal punishment was considered appropriate for all children, almost all the young people we interviewed who said that they had been spanked or beaten at home were young women. By contrast, the only young man who said that his father had tried to use corporal punishment also reported that he had actively resisted his father's attempt at force.

One young woman, aged 16, whom we spoke with in school and later interviewed in greater depth by telephone, explained that her father allowed her to speak with the interviewer on the telephone because he knew that the interviewer was a non-Vietnamese researcher (also a substitute teacher in the girl's school at the time) who was attempting to learn about Vietnamese people. Cooperating with an outside researcher was seen as working with someone who represented authority and school. Had the interviewer been a young Vietnamese man calling on her socially, she would not have been allowed to speak with him. This girl made it clear that her social life was highly controlled at home. She was permitted to visit with female friends in their homes but was not allowed to "hang out" in local restaurants or other public places. When she disobeyed her father or did anything that did not meet with her father's approval, she said, corporal punishment would follow. If she had

had a non-Vietnamese neighbor to whom she could complain about her father's beating, or if she had called 911, her father might have been jailed for child abuse, as was Tran in the case cited in the beginning of the chapter. But unlike Tran's daughter, who lived in a mixed neighborhood and had many non-Vietnamese neighbors, this Versailles Village girl did not consider corporal punishment as abuse and was therefore not likely to report it as such. When asked how she felt about corporal punishment, she said that she did not like it but that she understood that there were many dangers facing Vietnamese girls in America and that her father used it for her own good. While it is difficult to gauge just how common the use of corporal punishment on girls may be in Vietnamese communities in the United States, the fact that girls are subjected to it more often than boys is an indication of the stricter social controls imposed on young women. These social controls exist because of the importance of the Vietnamese ideal of "the virtuous woman," which calls not only for passive obedience but also for living up to higher behavioral standards than are expected of men.

But these higher behavioral standards have generated greater pressures for academic achievement. One high school teacher, an American Vietnam War veteran who had close ties to the Vietnamese community, candidly discussed the grades of his students with us in an interview. He commented on one particular young Vietnamese woman who almost never made grades below an A. "She has to," he explained. "If she brings home a B, her father beats her."

Young women were often frustrated by the stricter parental control to which they were subject and the higher moral standards expected of them. A common complaint was that parents were "old-fashioned" or "too Vietnamese." One girl complained to the interviewer:

It's just not fair. My brother can stay out all night with his friends and they [the parents] don't say anything about it. But for me, I have to tell them where I am and what I'm doing all the time, and they get real mad at me if I don't.

Another girl added:

They don't understand about life here. They want us to do everything they way they did things when they were in Vietnam. And it isn't the same.

Though uncomfortable with their parents' cultural expectations, our young female interviewees were not prepared for an open confrontation with parental authority. But they were ready for—and indeed often embarked on—challenges of an indirect sort. For example, most of the young women whom we interviewed reported that their parents disapproved of the American custom of dating. Many said that rather than rebel openly against their parents, they would leave the house with a group of female friends and then later go off alone with a young man.

Parents, of course, are not the only source of social control, and they are not the sole object of this frustration. If neighbors and other social contacts do not back up parental authority, young people will be more likely to rebel. But adolescents generally go along with their parents' expectations when the surrounding community echoes these expectations. Many young women spoke about the effect of public opinion in their tightly knit little community. A young woman said:

> It's so easy for girls to get a bad reputation here. You really have to watch everything you do. There's gossip all over the place. All my neighbors know everything. They even know some things that never happened.

This observation can help us understand why it is that young Vietnamese women accept gender role expectations that they themselves see as unfair and also why young Vietnamese in general often conform to the expectations of their elders rather than to the expectations of their American peers. As has been discussed in previous chapters, young Vietnamese do not live in isolated families, nor are they surrounded by an alien culture. Instead, they are embedded in a complex system of Vietnamese social relations that reinforces and also enforces parental expectations.

With this description of the current situation of Vietnamese women, we do not mean to justify gender inequality, nor to defend patriarchy. We find the subjection of women undesirable. But intrinsically undesirable situations may have desirable consequences, consequences that in the end subvert those situations. If social control plays an important part in bringing about a certain pattern of behavior, such as academic achievement, then those who are subject to greater levels of social control may exhibit this pattern of behavior to a greater extent. Clearly, the social controls imposed on young Vietnamese women do not make their lives more pleasant; the young women whom we interviewed agreed, for the most part, with the ethical evaluations that many Americans would make regarding their treatment: it is unjust and unfair. Whatever case can be made for densely interknit systems of ethnic social relations, these ethnic systems also create numerous problems and sources of stresses for those who live with them.

On the other hand, orientation toward upward mobility of the Vietnamese means that social control no longer prevents women from acquiring schooling; instead, it pushes them toward educational excellence. Paradoxically, it is women—the young people most controlled by traditional Vietnamese expectations—who do better in school. Thus their situation, though inherently undesirable, yields a desirable outcome—academic excellence—that in the long run is likely to subvert traditional Vietnamese patterns of gender roles.

——— Chapter 8 ———

Delinquency: Insiders and Outsiders

Tinh Ngo was only 11 when he was put on a refugee boat by his parents who hoped that he could find a decent life outside wartorn Vietnam. He spent twenty-two months in a camp in Thailand before resettling in America. In the United States, he was placed in three difficult foster homes. Feeling lonely and longing to be "somebody," he found Born to Kill, a notorious Vietnamese youth gang based in New York's Chinatown, and adopted it as his family. His troubled life then turned violent; he was involved in terrorism, beatings, and murders. Later, he assisted a government task force to destroy the gang. Now, under the witness protection program, the former gang member has disappeared (English 1994).

Stories such as Tinh's appear regularly in the American press. One day we read about Vietnamese youths who consistently make good grades, win academic prizes, and gain entrance into the nation's elite colleges; the next day, there are stories of ruthless youth gangs committing the worst sorts of crimes. These real-life stories reflect two contradictory images of Vietnamese young people: valedictorians and delinquents (Kibria 1993). How have these antithetical images come about? Previous chapters have discussed the factors that promote behavior and accomplishments likely to lead to upward mobility among Vietnamese adolescents, focusing on school adaptation. School, however, is only part of adolescent life. Not all Vietnamese youths are well adjusted to school. Some do poorly in the academic area but manage to adjust quite well in other areas of American life, while others are maladjusted both in and outside of school. This chapter examines the factors that are related to delinquency—that is, maladaptation in and outside of school.

VIETNAMESE DELINQUENCY AS AN EMERGING SOCIAL PROBLEM

Substantial anecdotal evidence points to delinquency as an issue of growing significance among younger-generation Vietnamese. While Vietnamese youths have made remarkable academic achievements, they have also showed relatively high rates of juvenile delinquency and youth gang involvement. The following startling incidents suggest the depth of the problem:

- Little Saigon is prey to teenage Vietnamese gangs like the Santa Ana Boys and Cheap Boys, or the Wally Girls and Pomona Girls, their female counterparts. Armed with knives, pistols, and even semi-automatic weapons, they steal cars, rob stores, and extort from merchants. They specialize in "home invasions," breaking into the homes of affluent Vietnamese and forcing them to hand over their concealed valuables by torturing children, raping women in front of husbands, or killing a family member. Some graduate into nationwide Asian crime syndicates engaged in big-time rackets like prostitution, illegal gambling, check scams, and narcotics (Gropp 1992).

- On an evening in 1986, members of the Pomona Boys, a Vietnamese youth gang based in Southern California, opened fire on Vietnamese diners at the My Nguyen Restaurant in Garden Grove, striking six patrons and killing two of them. The reason given was that a patron had flirted with one gang member's date (*Los Angeles Times,* October 21, 1990).

- On the afternoon of April 4, 1991, four Vietnamese youths (three brothers and a best friend) armed with semiautomatic pistols stormed into a Good Guys electronic store in Sacramento and held forty-one people hostage. Speaking heavily accented and broken English, they issued a series of "bizarre" demands. They wanted a helicopter to fly to Thailand so that they could fight the Viet Cong, and they also demanded four million dollars, four bulletproof vests, and forty pieces of thousand-year-old ginseng roots. The eight-and-a-half-hour stand-off ended in tragedy: three hostages were killed and eight wounded by a gunman, and three gunmen were killed and one seriously wounded by the SWAT team (*Sacramento Bee,* March 27, 1994).

- In early 1992, young Vietnamese and ethnic Chinese from Vietnam, armed with automatic weapons and machetes, invaded the homes of Asian businessmen in the Boston area, beating, stabbing, and robbing the businessmen and their families. Nguyen Toan Phuo, 17 years old, was arrested after he and two other youths broke into the home of a Chinatown restaurant owner, knocked his wife to the floor, punched and kicked him, and stabbed the couple's 13-year-old child, in an effort to learn where he kept his money (*New York Times,* February 7, 1992).

- In the early 1990s, Vietnamese gangs and grudges have left a river of blood from Houston's "Little Saigon" to Port Arthur's Ninth Avenue. Retribution killings have brought an old-world style of justice and honor to the refugee-dominated cafes and pool halls where unemployed Vietnamese pass the hours (*Houston Chronicle,* September 18, 1992).

In truth, the process of adaptation to the United States yields delinquency and youth gangs as one of its by-products. According to anthropologists James Diego Vigil and Steve C. Yun (1990), Vietnamese youth gang activities generally involve grand theft automobile, home robberies (mostly of affluent Vietnamese), and extortions of local ethnic businesses. "These Vietnamese youths bought new clothes and cars and spent much of their social and recreational time at traditional coffee shops and pool rooms. Following a rational plan of securing money, they created fluid and mobile gangs, often traveling throughout the region or in nearby states to conduct their crimes. As wayward street children with hardly any semblance of family influence or control from authorities, they often teamed up with a group, including females, went on a rampage of crime, with a motel room as their headquarters" (Vigil 1993, 101–102).

The youth gang and crime problems have naturally become the number one concern in Vietnamese communities across the nation, and that concern has increased over time. In the first of two polls conducted by the Immigration and Refugee Planning Center in Orange County, California, in 1981, about 45 percent of the respondents reported that crime was a major concern; in the second survey, that number had risen to 64 percent. By 1989, a *Los Angeles Times* poll found 87 percent of the Vietnamese polled in Orange County considered crime a serious problem, and 41 percent of the Vietnamese (compared to 10 percent of those polled from the general population countywide) ranked gangs the worst problem (*Los Angeles Times,* October 21, 1990).

In the *Los Angeles Times* survey of 1994, by far the greatest number of respondents named crime, street violence, and gangs as their chief community problems. Among parents with children under 18, gangs were identified as the most important problem, second to school, facing their children. Given fourteen possible problems, over a quarter (27 percent) of the parents identified achieving academic excellence as the most important problem for their children, and one-fifth identified staying away from gangs as the second most important problem; none of the other twelve possible problems came close to these two in the minds of Vietnamese parents. Among those parents who named more than one problem (30 percent of the total), the greatest number (33 percent) named staying away from gangs as the most important problem facing children, while 19 percent named studying and doing well in school as the second most important problem facing children. Again, no other potential problem came close to the avoidance of delinquency and academic achievement in the eyes of parents.

Information from the U.S. census on persons living in institutional settings suggests that Vietnamese parents are worried for good reason. Although in absolute numbers relatively few Vietnamese adolescents were confined to correctional institutions of various sorts, they were nonetheless a larger presence than their other Asian counterparts, constituting a quarter of all Asian institutionalized adolescents.[1] In terms of rates of institutionalization, the Vietnamese situation looked grimmer still. As can be seen in table 8.1, Vietnamese adolescents ranked second among ethnic groups, after blacks, and higher than all other Asian groups.

Comparison with adults shows that this phenomenon is a problem of youths; as of 1990, Vietnamese adults had low rates of institutionalization. This contrast takes on additional meaning if we remember that Vietnamese adults are almost all foreign-born or -raised, whereas the youths are, at least in part, products of the U.S. experience. Thus, although the pressures of growing up in American put many Vietnamese on the road to success, they lead others to go astray, for reasons to be explored in greater detail in the sections that follow.

DELINQUENCY IN VERSAILLES VILLAGE

The Vietnamese of Versailles Village have little trouble identifying delinquents. According to our informants, the "problem" children, or the "bad kids," are those who lack respect for parents and elders. Typically they come from a single group—those who were born in the United States or arrived here before age 13. These youths can usually be found idling in the medians on Dwyer Boulevard and Alcee Fortier or in local restaurants or coffee shops. As Lieutenant Jack Willoughby (1993), in an internal training document about Vietnamese gangs used by the New Orleans Police Department, notes, "Being a gang member involves a lot of 'hanging out.' Gang bangers hang out in pool halls, coffee shops,

TABLE 8.1 Institutionalization by Selected Ethnicities, 1990

	Vietnamese	Other Southeast Asian	Chinese	All Asian	Black	White
All minors under 18	209,257	192,235	386,290	1,951,392	8,364,035	32,728,160
All minors under 18 in correctional institutions	439	149	177	1,821	58,160	32,422
Per 100,000 all minors	210	78	46	93	695	99
All persons	614,547	386,507	1,645,472	6,934,689	26,153,444	143,807,279
All persons in correctional institutions	860	154	895	5,960	508,084	506,131
Per 100,000 all persons	140	40	54	86	1,943	352

Source: U.S. Census of Population and Housing, 1990: General Population Characteristics, tables 35, 45, 48.

game rooms, and on the street." A middle-aged Vietnamese man in the neighborhood, remarked, "The bad ones are the ones that hang out on Alcee Fortier [one of the main streets in the neighborhood, see figure 3.1]. Even though they're in public, you can see them just sitting down on the sidewalk, drinking and smoking cigarettes."

It is difficult to determine the extent of formal gang activity in New Orleans. Most Vietnamese residents of Versailles Village either deny that there are formal youth gangs or insist that the serious gang activity involves outsiders coming through the community on special occasions, such as Tet, the Vietnamese New Year. But gangs do exist, although they are generally not well organized, and many are ephemeral (Gropp 1992). The most common activities of Vietnamese delinquents in New Orleans, aside from "hanging out," are petty theft and robbery, although more violent criminal activities, including murder, are not unknown. Neither local police nor community members willing to discuss the subject are able to say with certainty which young people belong to gangs and which ones simply follow behind—"hangers-on" or "wannabes."

Both serious gang members and casual followers affect a certain presentation of self; many wear extremely baggy shorts, oversized T-shirts or sweatshirts, baseball caps, and sandals or sneakers, and some wear earrings and jewelry in their noses or on other parts of the face. Gang members and those who want to look tough also have professionally or semi-professionally drawn tattoos on different parts of their bodies, with dragons and tigers among the most common symbols. They also wear three-dot or five-dot tattoos on their hands or lower arms, the three-dot symbol usually stands for "My Crazy Life," "I Don't Care," or "I'll Take Any Dare," and the five-dot symbol has the meaning of "A Group of Good Friends." The dots may also be burned into the hand or arm with a cigarette, rather than tattooed. One of the gangs that was identified to us was known as *Thanh Sang*, which was believed to have connections with Vietnamese criminal organizations in Biloxi, Mississippi. The close ties among the Vietnamese communities scattered around the country provided a natural network for the delinquents in these communities (see Fox Butterfield's report "Gangs Terrorize Asians in Boston," *New York Times*, February 7, 1992). In Little Saigon, California, community service officers with the Garden Grove police department usually identified those youngsters in punk haircuts and expensive tennis shoes in cafes and pool halls as gang members (also see Willoughby 1993).

Gang members and followers usually skip school; they spend their days in the swampy forests of the Bayou Sauvage Wildlife Refuge that surround the Vietnamese neighborhood, smoking marijuana and cigarettes and hiding out from the police and from parents looking for truants. Within the neighborhood, they hang out in places with no family or adult supervision, including one reputed "crash pad"—a nondescript brick house in the middle of the neighborhood that is occupied by a revolving group of male teenagers. This house is believed to be the center of local gang activities. The police have made several raids on it, arresting occupants for possession and sale of marijuana and cocaine.

In a sense, the term "bad kids" is a misnomer, since most of the youths falling into this category are male. A social worker from Associated Catholic Charities who worked with teenage girls in the area told us that there were groups of girls who skipped school together and sometimes associated with delinquent young men but that, for the most part, falling behind in school and eventually dropping out were the most serious offenses of the girls, who liked to say, "At least we're not as bad as the boys." While young women are less frequently engaged in deviant behavior, they also have much further to fall once they become known as "bad." Prostitution is a fairly common recourse among young women who have established an irreparably bad reputation. These young women usually work in massage parlors.

Our Versailles Survey of 1994 did not include questions about arrests or other standard indicators of delinquency, but it did ask about alcohol use, illicit drug use, and confrontations with legal authorities, which are consistently identified by both adults and young people in this community as characteristics of the "bad kids." Taken in isolation, any one of these three items would provide little evidence of delinquency. But if all three are highly correlated with each other, that is, if the same individual reports frequently using alcohol to the point of drunkenness, engaging in frequent use of illicit drugs, and having been stopped by the police numerous times, then these three items can logically be taken as indicators of some underlying commonality and thus as tentative indicators of delinquency. In our survey, the correlation between self-reported drug use and alcohol use is .676; the correlation between drug use and being stopped by the police is .587; and the correlation between alcohol use and being stopped by the police is .641.

Table 8.2 shows that Vietnamese youths are indeed visibly present at the high end of each of the three indicators of delinquent behavior. Responses to the first two items tend to be bimodal, with concentrations at the low and high ends, indicating that the students tend not to have used drugs or alcohol at all, or that they tend to be heavy users. The

192   Growing Up American

responses to the third indicator about having been stopped by the police show somewhat more variation in the middle ranges. But this item too shows a U shape, with the greatest numbers at the low and high ends. It is possible that Vietnamese youths in the poor neighborhoods may be more likely to be stopped by the police than other American youths in the suburbs because of the stereotypical images of Asian gangs and the poor. The point here, though, is that some young Vietnamese may be more likely than others to have experiences with the police, and those who report having been stopped by the police may also be more likely to report having used drugs and alcohol. The high degree of correlation, together with the fact the Vietnamese themselves identify these as characteristics of delinquents, should make these items reasonably reliable indicators.

Cluster analysis shows that not only are some young Vietnamese

TABLE 8.2 Frequency of Drug Use, Alcohol Use, and Confrontations with the Police Among Vietnamese Youths

	Percentage	N
Drug use		
Never	89.3	359
Once	.5	2
Two to 3 times	1.0	4
Four to 5 times	.5	2
Five times or more	8.7	35
Alcohol use to the point of drunkenness		
Never	77.4	311
Once	4.2	17
Two to 3 times	3.0	12
Four to 5 times	.7	3
Five times or more	14.7	59
Number of times stopped by police		
Never	77.9	313
Once	6.5	26
Two to 3 times	2.7	11
Four to 5 times	5.7	23
Five times or more	7.2	29

Source: The Versailles Village Survey of 1994.

more likely than others to score high on each of these items but also that responses to these three items divide our respondents rather neatly into two separate groups. In table 8.3, the two clusters are crosstabulated with their three component elements. Cluster 1, which we call the "delinquents," consists of young Vietnamese with extensive experience with drugs, alcohol, and being stopped by the police. In contrast, Cluster 2, which we call the "nondelinquents," consists of youths with virtually no experience with drugs or alcohol and few experiences of police confrontation.

The technique of cluster analysis divides respondents into categories on the basis of their responses to several survey items. This procedure allows us to move beyond considering drug use, alcohol use, and experi-

TABLE 8.3 Drug Use, Alcohol Use, and Confrontations with the Police, by Delinquency Clusters Among Vietnamese Youths

	Cluster 1 "Delinquents" (%)	Cluster 2 "Nondelinquents" (%)	χ^2
Drug use			390.085**
Never	0	98.1	
Once	0	.5	
Two to 3 times	0	1.4	
Four to 5 times	5.6	0	
Five times or more	94.4	0	
Alcohol use to the point of drunkenness			192.67**
Never	0	85.0	
Once	2.7	4.4	
Two to 3 times	2.8	3.0	
Four to 5 times	2.8	.5	
Five times or more	91.7	7.1	
Number of times stopped by police			161.40**
Never	19.4	83.6	
Once	0	7.1	
Two to 3 times	0	3.0	
Four to 5 times	33.3	3.0	
Five times or more	47.3	3.3	
N	36	366	

Source: The Versailles Village Survey of 1994.
** $p < .01$

ences with the police as isolated variables. We are not looking at whether or not an adolescent has ever experienced substance abuse or has ever been confronted by the police but at whether or not this adolescent is a member of the category characterized by *frequent* drug and alcohol use and *numerous* confrontations with the police. The fact that cluster analysis divides young people into two clear categories on the basis of their responses to these highly correlated items gives us confidence in using these indicators for the purpose of classification. Further, our interviewees have identified these same indicators as distinguishing the "bad kids" from the other young people in the community. The two clusters, then, should be seen by any unbiased investigator as adequate reflections of "delinquent" and "nondelinquent" groups among Vietnamese adolescents in Versailles Village.

As has been discussed earlier in the chapter, many Vietnamese whom we have interviewed consistently identify what they call the "bad kids" as "over-Americanized kids." We therefore considered the generation effect, which would reflect the level of exposure to American society. As can be seen in table 8.4, while those characterized as delinquents by high levels of alcohol and drug use and frequent confrontations with the police made up less than 10 percent of the group, over 12 percent of those who are U.S.-born or who have lived in the United State since infancy fall into this problematic category, which is more than twice the percentages of first- or 1.5-generation adolescents. The generation effect indicates that, while the majority of Vietnamese youths are adjusted well, an unignorable number of them are not as well-adjusted, and the ill-adjusted ones are, ironically, overrepresented in the second generation.

Table 8.4 also reveals the effect of family socioeconomic backgrounds. As has already been pointed out, socioeconomic situation is fairly uniform in this community, so our survey already has something of a built-in control on social class in our survey. Still, some families do come from somewhat more privileged backgrounds in Vietnam. In the table, parental education is used as a proxy for social class. Overall, there is a weak, though statistically significant, relationship between father's education and classification by clusters. The association of mother's education is statistically insignificant, but this finding appears to be a result of the fact that so few mothers (5 percent) had educational credentials beyond high school. Indeed, only 17.4 percent of the fathers had any educational experience beyond high school. It should be noted, however, that those youths classified in the delinquent cluster were more likely to have fathers or mothers without a high school education. Family structure

TABLE 8.4   Generation, Parental Education, and Family
Structure, by Delinquency Clusters Among
Vietnamese Youths

	Cluster 1 "Delinquents" (%)	Cluster 2 "Nondelinquents" (%)	Row Total (N)
Generation			$\chi^2 = 11.05^{**}$
First	2.8	24.0	89
1.5	5.5	10.9	42
Second	91.7	65.1	271
Father's education			$\chi^2 = 8.36^*$
Less than high school	47.2	37.2	153
High school graduate	52.8	43.7	179
At least some college	0	19.1	70
Mother's education			$\chi^2 = 3.32$
Less than high school	69.4	56.8	233
High school graduate	30.6	37.7	149
At least some college	0	5.5	20
Family structure			$\chi^2 = 4.68$
Single-parent or parent- absent family	30.8	17.9	77
Two-parent family	61.5	66.4	265
Two-parent with grand- parent	7.7	15.7	60
N	36	366	402

Source: The Versailles Village Survey of 1994.
** $p < .05$
** $p < .01$

does not have a significant association with delinquency clustering, but
it is in the expected direction; those in the delinquent cluster are more
likely to come from single-parent or parent-absent families.

So far, our data show a strong significant effect of generation, but a
lack of significant effects of parental education and family structure, on
how well Vietnamese young people adapt to American society. While the
socioeconomic limitations of families may put children at risk, these
limitations would seem inadequate to explain the central issue of why
problematic behavior seems to be most common among those born or
reared in the United States. To answer that question, it is necessary to
look at the issue of acculturation.

ACCULTURATION AND MALADAPTATION

Exposure to American Youth Subcultures

In Versailles Village, both adults and young people have specific stereo-typed ideas about what they regard as "bad kids," and they usually give concrete descriptions of the behavior of these bad kids: spending too much of their time "hanging out" in public places, rather than staying at home; while at home, not getting along or cooperating with parents or other family members, much less contributing to household chores; dressing and acting like other American youths attending the same school and acquiring the tastes and interests of other American youths, such as carrying around portable radios or tape players and playing loud American-style music; and showing little interest in Vietnamese culture and Vietnamese ways of doing things. In matters of dress and musical taste, for example, Vietnamese and black youths often appear nearly identical. Since these are fashions favored by teenagers not just within the black community neighboring Versailles Village but throughout the United States, their adoption by the Vietnamese can be interpreted as indicating that Vietnamese youths have been culturally assimilated into the American youth culture.

Our interviewees, including young people themselves, repeatedly identified those who fit the above descriptions as delinquents, and they also consistently regarded these delinquents as becoming too "Ameri-canized." It should be noted that exposure to American culture in Ver-sailles Village was limited to a very underprivileged neighborhood and that the Vietnamese generally considered such exposure undesirable for their children. The descriptions of problem youths given by Vietnamese people prompted us to include in our survey a number of items regard-ing tastes and preferences. We asked respondents how much they liked listening to traditional Vietnamese music, helping around the house, reading, participating in school clubs, watching television, wearing gold necklaces, having their noses pierced, and listening to rap music. These items are reported in table 8.5 in a three-point scale, ranging from "dis-like very much" to "like very much."[2] These items were chosen only because both our interviewees' descriptions and our own observations suggested that they might be associated with delinquency; we did not particularly approve or disapprove of any of these preferences and did not attempt to make value judgments.

Table 8.5 shows a clear split between the delinquents and nondelin-

TABLE 8.5 Tastes or Interests by Delinquency Clusters Among Vietnamese Youths

	Cluster 1 Delinquents (%)	Cluster 2 Nondelinquents (%)	χ^2
Traditional Vietnamese music			103.59**
Dislikes or dislikes very much	61.9	8.5	
Indifferent	28.6	23.8	
Likes or likes very much	9.5	67.7	
Helping around house			81.87**
Dislikes or dislikes very much	54.7	9.1	
Indifferent	26.2	32.1	
Likes or likes very much	19.1	58.8	
Reading			71.47**
Dislikes or dislikes very much	64.3	16.1	
Indifferent	28.6	34.1	
Likes or likes very much	7.1	49.8	
Participating in school clubs			28.30**
Dislikes or dislikes very much	33.3	11.5	
Indifferent	52.5	35.6	
Likes or likes very much	14.2	52.9	
Watching television			13.91**
Dislikes or dislikes very much	2.4	2.4	
Indifferent	2.4	15.3	
Likes or likes very much	95.2	82.3	
Hanging out			33.56**
Dislikes or dislikes very much	0	4.8	
Indifferent	4.8	12.4	
Likes or likes very much	95.2	82.8	
Gold necklaces			15.66**
Dislikes or dislikes very much	14.2	33.2	
Indifferent	40.5	40.9	
Likes or likes very much	45.3	25.9	
Pierced noses			57.84**
Dislikes or dislikes very much	33.3	79.1	
Indifferent	45.2	18.2	
Likes or likes very much	21.5	2.7	

(Table continues on p. 198.)

TABLE 8.5   (*Continued*)

	Cluster 1 "Delinquents" (%)	Cluster 2 "Nondelinquents" (%)	χ^2
Rap music			81.95**
Dislikes or dislikes very much	9.5	34.7	
Indifferent	7.1	31.8	
Likes or likes very much	83.4	33.5	
N	36	366	402

Source: The Versailles Village Survey of 1994.
** $p < .01$

quents in their tastes and interests. The delinquents tend to dislike listening to traditional Vietnamese music, helping around the house, reading, and participating in school clubs, while the nondelinquents tend to favor these things. The delinquents are also more likely than the nondelinquents to favor gold necklaces, hanging out, jewelry in pierced noses, and rap music. It is notable that the interest most strongly associated with the delinquents is a liking for rap music, a unique form of musical expression that has emerged from American youth subcultures; over 80 percent of the delinquents said that they liked rap or liked it very much. In contrast, the interest most strongly associated with the nondelinquents is a liking for traditional Vietnamese music; almost 70 percent of the nondelinquents said that they liked this type of music or liked it very much.

This look at the tastes and interests of Vietnamese adolescents provides some insight into what the Vietnamese in Versailles Village mean when they describe their problematic young people as being too "Americanized." The two sets of interests fairly neatly distinguish young people who are highly acculturated into the local youth subculture from those who remained strongly attached to the Vietnamese community. Certainly rap is more closely associated with contemporary American youth subcultures than is traditional Vietnamese music. The emerging portrait of Vietnamese youths, then, does strongly suggest that the problem youths are more acculturated than the nondelinquents; in this case, they are more acculturated into the subculture of their American peers.

Peer-Group Association

Acculturation is a matter of social contact, or peer group association, as well as a matter of cultural expression. Table 8.6 provides information on the social contacts that characterize Vietnamese adolescents in each of the two clusters. As has been seen in earlier chapters, there are relatively few whites in this neighborhood. It is entirely understandable that in neither cluster did the Vietnamese adolescents report having many white friends and that the association between having white friends and delinquency clusters is not significant. It is also notable that the few respondents who reported that at least half of their friends belonged to the socioeconomically privileged white racial group, were all nondelinquents. In response to the question about black friends, neither category reported having many black friends, but the delinquent adolescents were significantly more likely than their nondelinquent peers to report that at least half of their friends were blacks. At the same time, the delinquent adolescents were significantly less likely to have exclusively coethnic friendship than their nondelinquent peers. This finding is consistent with our field observation that the problem kids tend to hang out with other coethnics but maintain extensive social contacts with the non-Vietnamese young people in the neighborhood and in the school.

The results reported in table 8.6 are admittedly a rather rough measure of social ties to local non-Vietnamese youths. Given their consistency with the qualitative observations, however, they do support the popular view of the Vietnamese in Versailles Village that the delinquents in this community are too Americanized in part because of their association with a particular segment of American society, the native minority youths in an underprivileged neighborhood. Nevertheless, the adolescents in both clusters reported that most of their friends were coethnic. Were the Vietnamese friends of the delinquents more Americanized than those of the nondelinquents? To explore this possibility, we looked at the language use among coethnic friends. As can be seen in table 8.7, the delinquents are more than three times as likely as the nondelinquents to report infrequent usage ("never" or "seldom") of Vietnamese with their friends. If we take language use as an indicator of acculturation, then, it appears that the problem adolescents not only have more social contacts with non-Vietnamese but are also more likely to associate with other Americanized Vietnamese.

The pattern of peer-group association and the acculturation process among Vietnamese adolescents of Versailles Village is quite unusual; the Vietnamese adolescents, who lean toward the tastes and interests of American peers and display forms of behavior similar to those of non-Vietnamese peers, also tend to retain separate ethnic identities and to

TABLE 8.6 Distribution of Vietnamese, Black, and White Friends, by Delinquency Clusters Among Vietnamese Youths

	Cluster 1 "Delinquents" (%)	Cluster 2 "Nondelinquents" (%)	χ^2
White friends			2.84
None	36.1	32.0	
Some	63.9	63.4	
About half	0	2.5	
Most	0	.8	
Almost all	0	1.3	
Black friends			27.06**
None	2.8	20.2	
Some	63.9	70.2	
About half	19.4	6.1	
Most	2.8	1.9	
Almost all	11.1	1.6	
Vietnamese friends			21.53**
None	8.3	.5	
Some	8.4	8.8	
About half	16.7	9.3	
Most	30.6	23.5	
Almost all	36.0	57.9	
N	36	366	402

Source: The Versailles Village Survey of 1994.
** $p < .01$

TABLE 8.7 Reported Frequency of Speaking Vietnamese with Friends, by Delinquency Clusters Among Vietnamese Youths

	Cluster 1 "Delinquents" (%)	Cluster 2 "Nondelinquents" (%)	Row Total (N)
Never	16.7	2.5	15
Seldom	22.2	9.0	41
Sometimes	27.8	31.7	126
Usually	30.6	39.9	157
Always	2.7	16.9	63
N	36	366	402

Source: The Versailles Village Survey of 1994.
$\chi^2 = 28.42$; $p < .01$

associate more with coethnics than with non-Vietnamese. In our field observations, we frequently noted that the Vietnamese adolescents who dressed almost the same as black adolescents in the neighborhood rarely interacted with their black peers on an individual basis but rather on a group basis. Our interviewees reported that fights between young Vietnamese and blacks were fairly common, though we did not observe any while gathering data for this study. We often saw members of the two racial groups standing or sitting together, sharing cigarettes or beer. They obviously all knew each other by name and had frequent social contacts with each other. But they also obviously remained separate cliques, and their individual dealings were predicated on their separate clique memberships.

The young Vietnamese, who have acquired American language, dress, and tastes that differ from traditional Vietnamese culture, may be characterized as "culturally assimilated but not structurally assimilated" into the native youth society of their local social environment. Such a generalization, however, may be misleading. A more accurate way of understanding the process of Americanization is to take into account the race-based clique memberships in which the social structures of the age-segregated youth culture of both racial groups are rooted. If a young Vietnamese man reports that he has many black friends, he may not necessarily mean that he has become a part of any local black peer group. More often, he will consider himself a member of a Vietnamese peer group that engages in frequent social interactions with members of black peer groups.

The Vietnamese adults have different opinions about these patterns of peer-group associations than the youths. They singled out only the ones who showed no interest in their own ethnic culture and who did not participate in the ethnic community as "bad kids," and, ironically, the separate ethnic identity these "bad kids" had developed was also rejected as being too Americanized. The social worker whom we quoted earlier in the chapter expressed this view. He perceived the young Vietnamese with whom he worked in the Vietnamese community as a group who "want to be American." He remarked, "But what they know about America is usually the worst part of it. They listen to rap songs about shooting policemen and watch movies with everybody killing each other. A lot of the American kids they know are kids who skip school, or quit school, and get in trouble a lot. So I think the problem is that they're becoming part of the wrong part of America." In our view, the so-called "bad kids" have not just failed to find a place in the ethnic community; they also have their own social networks, their own systems of support and constraint, and their own accepted attitudes. In other words, their experiences take place largely within a socioeconomically marginal local environment, in which a youth culture is a prominent aspect. Vietnamese youths in this situation are members of an American minority group at the fringes of American society, rather than members of an immigrant group seeking upward mobility in American society. Their identities are shaped by their participation in the disadvantaged minority fringe, rather than by participation in an immigrant community or in the larger society.

Finally, we looked at how the adolescents of different delinquency clusters fared in their adaptation to school. As can be seen in table 8.8, we found a strong correlation between academic performance, as measured by self-reported average grades, and delinquency clusters. Not surprisingly, the delinquents were low achievers; over a third reported grades averaging C or lower. In contrast, only a few of the nondelinquents reported C averages or lower, whereas about 85 percent had B averages or higher. These findings indicate a strong relationship between delinquency and maladaptation.

REASONS FOR DELINQUENCY: THE MULTIPLE CONTEXTS OF ALIENATION AND INTEGRATION

The data on rates of institutionalization presented earlier in this chapter suggest a generational gap among the Vietnamese in the United States; whereas the general Vietnamese population has comparatively low rates of institutionalization, its younger cohort shows higher rates than those of most other ethnic groups. Moreover, the case study reported in the last section indicated that the Vietnamese adolescent cohort tends to bifurcate into delinquent and nondelinquent clusters and that bifurcation is associated with acculturation. The Vietnamese in Versailles Village often describe their problem children as too "Americanized," and our field observations and survey data indeed show that the problematic behavior seems to be more common among those who have spent all or almost all their lives in the United States and have become highly acculturated. How can one account for the peculiar phenomenon that acculturation produces consequences contradictory to what is generally expected? We suggest an approach that takes into account the effects of alienation or integration at four contextual levels: the family, the ethnic community, the local environment, and the larger society.

Alienation from the family is perhaps one of the chief sources of

TABLE 8.8   Average Grades Received in School, by
Delinquency Clusters Among Vietnamese Youths

Average Grade	Cluster 1 "Delinquent" (%)	Cluster 2 "Nondelinquent" (%)	Row Total (%)
A	3.9	27.9	24.9
B	35.3	58.7	55.7
C+ to B−	23.5	4.0	6.5
C or below	37.3	9.4	12.9
Column Total (%)	12.7	87.3	100.0
N	36	366	402

Source: The Versailles Village Survey of 1994.
$\chi^2 = 67.681; p < .000$

delinquency. Maintaining smooth relations between parents and children is always difficult for families with adolescents, but it is especially so for immigrant or refugee families, in which children frequently face conflicting sets of expectations from their parents and from the members of the larger society with whom the children are in most immediate contact. Communication between non-English-speaking parents and almost exclusively English-speaking schools poses a further problem, undermining the ability of parents to keep abreast of their children's school progress and maintain control over their attendance and behavior at school. In Versailles Village, we have observed certain family features that render some children more prone than others to problems in relating to their parents. In order to understand how patterns of parent-child relations have varied effects on children, it is helpful to conceive of the family as a subsystem contained in larger social systems, namely the ethnic community, the local social system, and the larger society. Ideally, these interdependent systems involve ongoing processes in which each system promotes adaptation to a larger environment (Bronfenbrenner 1979). Interactions between individuals and their families enable family members to function in a community setting, and interactions among families and other primary social units in that setting mediate the individual's adaptation into the larger social system.

Figure 8.1 displays an ideal case of multilevel integration. The oval represents the individual, who overlaps all of the systems, participating in his or her own family, the ethnic social system, the local social environment, and the larger society. Ideally, the family lies at the very center of the systems in which the individual participates, and each larger circle

FIGURE 8.1   Multilevel Social Integration, an Ideal Case

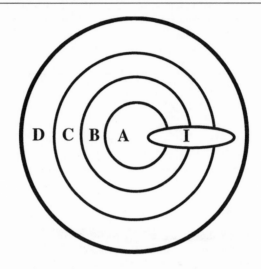

I. individual
A. family
B. ethnic community
C. local social environment
D. larger society

symmetrically contains the smaller subsystems. As is shown in figure 8.1, the family (A) is well integrated into the ethnic community (B), the ethnic community is well integrated into the local social environment (C), and the local social environment is well integrated into the larger society (D), given that the goals and means of achieving these goals prescribed by the larger society are accepted by each of the lower-level subsystems. But reality usually departs from this ideal situation. In the worst case scenario, an individual is insufficiently integrated into the family, the family is insufficiently integrated into the ethnic social system, the ethnic social system is insufficiently integrated into the local social environment, and the local social environment is insufficiently integrated into the larger society.

The immigrant experience often lies somewhere between the ideal and the worst cases. Earlier in the century, Italian Americans were characterized by integration of the individual into the family and the family into the ethnic community, which largely coincided with the local social environment. While the peasant familial system of the Italian Americans bound adolescents to the community, it also distanced them from the mainstream American society and its goals, thus jeopardizing academic

FIGURE 8.2   Multilevel Social Integration, in the Marginal Local
Social Environment

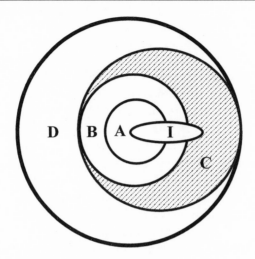

I. individual
A. family
B. ethnic community
C. local social environment
D. larger society

success among the second generation (Child 1943; Covello 1972; Perlmann 1988). Like the Italians, the Vietnamese of Versailles Village display a high level of individual integration into the family, and familial
integration into the ethnic community. But this particular ethnic community resides in a local social environment that is marginal to (or at
odds with) the larger society—a common situation confronting other
contemporary immigrant children—as illustrated in figure 8.2. Under
these conditions, successful integration will depend on the fit between
the familial and ethnic social systems on the one hand and the goals and
means prescribed by the larger society on the other. Unlike the Italians,
the familial and ethnic social systems of the Vietnamese of Versailles
Villages often provide that consistency. Therefore, integration into these
ethnic systems can help young people bypass the marginal local social
environment and prepare them for successful integration into the mainstream American society.

From this perspective, delinquency among Vietnamese youths of Versailles Village occurs when integration problems occur in the lower-level
structural contexts. Where an individual is poorly integrated into the

family, or the family is poorly integrated into the ethnic community, conflict with and rejection of the larger host society is likely to be the result. Our fieldwork illustrates how these patterns emerge.

THE FAMILY CONTEXT

Problems in family relations that may lead to delinquent, or deviant, behavior on the part of Vietnamese children can be categorized into three groups with reference to the systemic level at which integration has failed. In the first category, the "absent or partially absent family system," the family relations that make possible adaptation to larger systems are not present. In the second category, the "community-marginal family system," individual families are distant or alienated from the ethnic community, so that family-community linkages are inadequate to provide constraints and supports to the family. In the third category, the "society-marginal family system," individual families are oriented more toward the homeland than toward integration, so that the linkage between the family and the larger society is inadequate.

The Absent or Partially Absent Family System:
The Cases of Hanh and Ngoc

Hanh was 17 years old when we interviewed him. He was jobless, out of school, no longer living with his family, and spending most of his time on the street. Hanh was born in a coastal fishing village in Vietnam; his father, a South Vietnamese soldier, was killed in the war. Hanh lived with his mother, several younger siblings, and his maternal grandparents until the age of 10. Not yet an adolescent, he left the village one night with two adult uncles in a fishing boat, leaving his mother and siblings behind in Vietnam.

At sea, Hanh and his uncles were met by a commercial ship, which took them to a refugee camp in Hong Kong. After several months in the refugee camp, Hanh was sponsored by another uncle, already in the United States, and was resettled in the United States with his uncle's family. Hanh reported that he found classes difficult and often skipped school, so that he was falling further and further behind in his studies. Although his uncle, with whom he still lived, provided him with housing and food, his adult relatives took little interest in his progress in school.

Hanh spent most of his time with a group of young men who were also truants from school. He did not admit to any criminal activities, but he and his friends were suspected of engaging in acts of petty theft. Adults in the community who knew Hanh and his friends clearly identified them as "bad kids." We had seen Hanh and his group of friends smoking marijuana openly on the street. In speaking of his friends, Hanh said, "These dudes are my real family. They look out for me and I look out for them. If anybody messes with me, they gonna jump in, and if anybody messes with them, I gonna jump in too."

Like Hanh, Ngoc, 16, spent much of his time hanging out on the street. At the age of 3, he left Vietnam by plane with his father and an older brother under the Orderly Departure Program. Ngoc's mother was left behind in Vietnam for unknown reasons. After being initially resettled in Wisconsin, Ngoc's family moved to New Orleans because of family connections.

A fisherman in the Gulf of Mexico, Ngoc's father spoke little English and was rarely at home. He had very little to do with the other Vietnamese people in the community. When asked about his father, Ngoc responded, "Well, I see him sometimes when he's in. We get along okay, I guess. But, you know, we don't really talk to each other that much."

Though still enrolled in high school as a sophomore when we talked with him, Ngoc was frequently absent and seemed to show little interest in school. Much of his time was spent on the streets or in the dense swampy woods surrounding the Vietnamese neighborhood. Like Hanh, Ngoc saw his group of friends as a substitute family. Although his close friends were all Vietnamese, Ngoc reported that he and his pals knew all of the non-Vietnamese kids in the neighborhood. They had few ties to the adults in the ethnic community. In Ngoc's words, "I don't have that much to say to the old people around here. Their heads are all back in Vietnam, and I'm here. So we just don't have that much to say to each other."

The situation in which Hanh and Ngoc and some of their friends find themselves is typically an absent or partially absent family system surrounded by a marginal local social environment. Without a family system adequate to center them in their own community, young people in this situation tend to be alienated from their own community and to drift in the surrounding local social environment. Therefore, they are more likely to be influenced by the local social environment—the one that is marginal to the mainstream society in this case—than by their own ethnic community, as illustrated in figure 8.3.

FIGURE 8.3   Multilevel Social Integration, the Absent or Partial
Family System in the Marginal Local Social
Environment

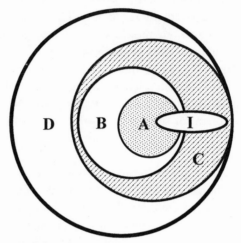

I. individual
A. family
B. ethnic community
C. local social environment
D. larger society

The Community-Marginal Family System:
The Case of Man

Man, born in the United States, was a 16-year-old high school sophomore. Soft-spoken and with a gentle manner, he was always eager to
talk, volunteering his home telephone number so that we could talk
with him outside of school. For these reasons, we found it difficult to
believe that Man was seen as a delinquent and a troublemaker in school,
but his teachers assured us that this was indeed the case. Later on, during our fieldwork in Man's school, Man was expelled from school for
allegedly slashing a teacher's tires. He was readmitted but then expelled
again for bringing a knife to school.

Man lived with his mother and father on the fringes of the Versailles
enclave. His father was employed in a technical profession and earned a
good salary but maintained few ties to the Vietnamese community. Man
reported that his father almost always spoke English to him, although
his mother and father spoke Vietnamese with one another.

Adults in the community who knew the family described it as a family with many problems. The father was said to have a girlfriend, with whom he spent much of his time. One teacher who knew Man's family reported that Man seemed to feel a great deal of resentment toward his father. Man indeed confirmed the teacher's view when we interviewed him, saying, "Sometimes I think I don't really like my dad that much. He's always trying to push me and tell me what do, and I don't see why I ought to do what he says. He ought to run his life and let me run mine. He says I owe him respect and I don't see it that way." Man also told us that he had no sense of himself as being Vietnamese, "I've never been to Vietnam and I don't think I want to go. They wouldn't have the TV programs that I like there, and life there is probably pretty boring. I'm American."

Despite this disavowal of his Vietnamese identity, Man's own group of friends were all Vietnamese. He denied that he and his friends constituted a gang and claimed that they had no name for themselves (one knowledgeable teacher warned that we should be skeptical of these claims). Nevertheless, Man admitted that fighting was one of the activities for which he and his friends were known. For the most part, he said, they fought with young Vietnamese from West Bank, a smaller Vietnamese community on the other side of New Orleans: "They're afraid of us 'cause they know we're bad. We can beat them any time, any place. We have to fight them so they respect us and respect our territory. We don't want them to come over here. We don't go over there alone either, but if it's a group of us, no problem, because we know we can take them on."

While Hanh and Ngoc looked to their peers as a substitute family because of an absence of family relations, Man apparently was drawn to his peers because of weak relations within his family. It is notable that Man's family was essentially a family of outsiders, standing alone. While his father had a good job and therefore a source of economic capital, he seemed to be alienated from his coethnics and therefore lacked "social capital." Man, alienated from his own family and from the adult Vietnamese community, adapted to the host society through a delinquent peer group. Vietnamese adolescents like Man who find themselves in a community-marginal family system are inevitably affected more by the marginal local social environment than by their own community, precisely because their families are alienated from the ethnic community, as illustrated by figure 8.4.

FIGURE 8.4   Multilevel Social Integration, the Community-
Marginal Family System in the Marginal Local
Social Environment

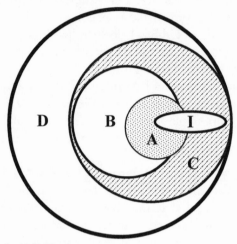

I. individual
A. family
B. ethnic community
C. local social environment
D. larger society

The Society-Marginal Family System:
The Cases of Thanh and Dai

Thanh was a 15-year-old freshman in high school who had arrived in
the United States as an infant, the youngest in a family of six children,
with no memory of Vietnam. Thanh's mother was almost fifty years old
and her father about sixty; neither parent spoke any English.

When we met her, Thanh was having trouble keeping up in school,
primarily because she skipped school frequently. She would dress for
school in the morning, but instead of going there, she would meet a group
of girlfriends to eat and chat at a restaurant or take the bus to a shopping
mall. Thanh's parents were unaware of the extent of Thanh's truancy,
because they spoke little English and could not establish effective contact
with school authorities. Thanh expressed exasperation with her parents,
"They're just kinda out of it. They don't know anything about life in this
country and they're always talking about what it was like back in Vietnam.
What has Vietnam got to do with me? Sometimes I don't even get what it
is they're talking about." An experienced social worker who had worked

with problem teenage girls in the neighborhood told us that young people in Thanh's situation eventually dropped out of school, because they fell so far behind that they could not catch up and got frustrated and quit.

Dai was a 14-year-old high school freshman whose parents had arrived from Vietnam a year before his birth. His father spoke some English but worked at two different jobs and was rarely home. His mother had not learned to speak English and Dai had to act as her interpreter on the rare occasions when she found it necessary to speak with non-Vietnamese people.

Dai also had problems with school. He not only missed school frequently, but often slept in class when he did attend, because he often stayed out all night with his friends. When asked how his mother felt about his ways, he shrugged, "What does she have to say about it?" He said, "She doesn't take care of me, I take care of her. I don't have to make explanations to her or anybody."

When an ethnic community is oriented toward integration into the larger society but is located in a marginal local environment, such as a disadvantaged neighborhood, the community system must help its young members bypass the marginal local social environment and facilitate their integration into the larger society. For example, an ethnic community may provide its young members with special programs and motivation that encourage upward mobility in the larger society. Young people in society-marginal families, however, tend to receive little control from their parents, because of the cultural distance of parents from both the local and larger social environments in which adolescents operate. The lack of parental control and support weakens the family's ability to help their children overcome the disadvantages associated with the marginal local social system and gain social acceptance in the larger society. This situation is shown in figure 8.5.

On the basis of our fieldwork in the Versailles enclave, we have suggested a model for understanding why two extreme tendencies—delinquents and valedictorians—have developed among Vietnamese youths and why the youths tend to adapt to American society in one or the other of these two contradictory ways. Since Vietnamese communities are so often located in economically disadvantaged and socially marginal neighborhoods, the ethnic social structures such as the family and the ethnic networks of social relations must act as alternatives to the underprivileged local environments in order to promote desirable forms of adaptation to the larger society. Whether adolescents make use of these alternatives or become part of the youth culture of the marginal local social environment depends largely on how their families connect them to the ethnic community and to varied levels of the surrounding society.

FIGURE 8.5   Multilevel Social Integration, the Society-Marginal
Family System in the Marginal Local Social
Environment

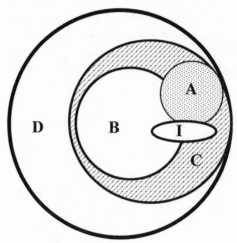

I. individual
A. family
B. ethnic community
C. local social environment
D. larger society

THE ETHNIC COMMUNITY CONTEXT

The above description of Vietnamese problem youths implies an interesting twist on the sociologist Robert E. Park's theory of "the marginal
man" (1928). These young people appear to be "marginal," but marginal with regard to their own ethnic group rather than, as in Park's view,
marginal to the larger society as a result of being caught between the
ethnic group and the larger society.

In Versailles Village, these problem youths are labeled as "bad kids"
and clearly distinguished by the community as "outsiders." This interpretation found support in interviews with Vietnamese community
leaders. Monsignor Dominic Luong, pastor of the Vietnamese Catholic
church in New Orleans, had observed that the youths who spent their
time idling on street corners or using drugs were those who were alienated from the society of their adult coethnics. Dr. Joseph Vuong, a Vietnamese counselor at a New Orleans junior high school, referred to the
youth on the margins of the Vietnamese community as "overadapted" to
American society. "They have become Americans in their own eyes, but

they do not have the advantages of white Americans. So, they lose the direction that their Vietnamese culture can give them. Since they do not know where they are going, they just drift."

The alienation of Vietnamese youths from adult members of their own ethnic group may be seen from two perspectives: youth alienation and community rejection. Having grown up in America, younger-generation Vietnamese may see their foreign-born elders as alien to their own lives, in which they are pushed to stress relationships with their own peers. Like the young people described by the anthropologist Elijah Anderson in his ethnographic study of the youth culture in Chicago (1990), these youths lead age-segregated lives. In the case of troubled Vietnamese youth, however, cultural distance from their elders intensifies solidarity with peers. One young man explained, "I ain't gonna go against my partners. If the old people don't like something we do, that's their problem. I don't care what they think. I care what the kids I hang out with think."

Although these troubled youths were extremely secretive and disliked naming or discussing gangs, we learned that some of them organized themselves into formal gangs; others rebelled against the behavioral standards prescribed by the larger society and reinforced by the ethnic community in less organized ways. Such youth alienation, however, suggests that the young people are not simply rejecting conformity to the expectations of the adult community in favor of completely anarchic orgies of individualistic antisocial behavior but that they are replacing the adult society with a society of peers by distinguishing themselves with their baggy-panted uniforms and close-cropped hair.

The community's response to its deviant youths mirrors the alienation of the young from the adult Vietnamese community. The tradition-minded Vietnamese elders often label those steeped in a "foreign" American youth culture as outsiders and reject them. A Vietnamese social worker whom we interviewed bemoaned the fact that once young people were labeled as "bad kids," they became outsiders to the community, not just because the young people themselves had trouble fitting in but because the community itself no longer accepted them. He explained to us the difficulties he had in getting adult Vietnamese to support a youth program that he had designed. "I had real trouble in getting the adults here to support my project," he said. "Once they identify a young person as a problem, they don't want to have anything to do with them, they want to just forget about them. They don't want to let them [the problem adolescents] take part in the life of the community."

Moreover, members of the Vietnamese community in Versailles Village tend to maintain sharp boundaries of ethnicity; they dichotomize their young people into "good kids" and "bad kids," seeing the former as having Vietnamese forms of deportment and the latter as having local American forms of deportment. "Most of the kids here are good, respectful," remarked one middle-aged man. "But some of them are just not Vietnamese at all." A young man who described the "bad kids" as Americanized, explained that Americanized to him meant rude and disrespectful. "It's in the way that they act," he said. "They're loud when they talk to their friends and act in ways that look rude." Many adults feared that Americanization would undermine the ethnic identity of their youths. In their words, "Our Vietnamese culture is of steel, but yours [American culture] is acid that dissolves the steel" (*New York Times*, March 15, 1992).

Consequently, these youths are increasingly pushed into the company of rebellious peers, where they develop a strong sense of attachment to youths who are also rejected by their adult society as outsiders. The exclusion of these young Vietnamese from systems of social relations in the ethnic community is the flip side of the closely knit social ties that we have described as characteristic of Vietnamese communities in the United States. A high level of integration also means sharp distinctions between insiders and outsiders and a readiness to reject outsiders. Therefore, the situation of younger-generation Vietnamese who have been rejected by their own communities should be understood within the framework of interpretation that has been used throughout this book. The Vietnamese have, for the most part, few measurable resources to invest in their children, as reflected by their low levels of educational attainment. They have generally settled in low-income neighborhoods where incentives and opportunities for advancement are extremely limited. Their children establish social contacts either with other Vietnamese or with native-born Americans, mostly racial or ethnic minorities, in their neighborhoods, and they tend to adopt attitudes, interests, and behaviors similar to those of other American young people with whom they have immediate contact. Their social ties are still with other Vietnamese, but these ties tend to be with other Vietnamese who have also grown up in the United States. In a tightly knit ethnic community, problem youths are shut out of ethnic institutions and networks of social relations and often meet rejection and active discouragement instead. The same ethnic social relations that push and encourage "good kids" (the conformists or nondelinquents) to achieve in American society also label and reject "bad kids" (the rebels or delinquents).

The evidence on delinquency, fragmentary as it is, can shed some light on why youthful delinquency may be high in the very same immigrant group that also shows high levels of academic achievement. It can also, we believe, serve as a caution against romanticizing or idealizing Vietnamese culture or Vietnamese communities and as a caution against an uncritical characterization of Vietnamese in the United States as a "model minority." Our research has led us to conclude that the supports and constraints provided by Vietnamese communities help to promote scholastic excellence among economically disadvantaged Vietnamese youth living in economically disadvantaged communities but that the same tightly knit social networks that encourage achievement among some also exclude others and leave them adrift. Achievement and delinquency, we believe, do not depend on whether young people retain a "good" Vietnamese identity or assimilate into a "bad" Americanized identity. Instead, the social adaptation of the second generation depends not only on the segment of American society into which young people may assimilate but also on how other ethnic group members respond to this segment of American society.

Overall, our approach to explaining the sources of delinquency is exploratory and requires more fine-tuned research; its merit lies in the emphasis on multiple contextual factors in conceptualizing how immigrant or refugee families and ethnic communities lead individuals into delinquent groups or high-achieving groups. While we draw on the idea of social support and control to form the basis of this conceptualization, we also stress that when families and communities are not able to provide adequate social support or control to steer adolescents away from the youth culture that surrounds them, the adolescents tend to identify with the youth culture and learn distinctive patterns of behavior from it. Whether or not this identification and these behavioral patterns lead to desirable outcomes depends on the segment of the American society that receives the immigrant children. Living in poor neighborhoods puts children at higher risk of exposure to adversarial subcultures that marginalized native-born youths have developed to cope with their own difficult situation (Portes and Zhou 1994). Meanwhile, their immediate ethnic social system can also place children in danger. As adults in the ethnic community see young people displaying traits that are associated with underprivileged American youths, these young people are labeled as "non-Vietnamese" or "bad kids" and are excluded as outsiders. Exclusion, in turn, reinforces delinquent identities among problem youths and produces maladaptive outcomes. In sum, the process of adaptation is not a smooth one, and it is one that often involves burdens, conflicts, and contradictions.

——Chapter 9——

Conclusion: Contexts of Reception, Selective Americanization, and the Implications for the New Second Generation

Mom had never seen a turkey in Vietnam, much less ever cooked one. Just this past Thanksgiving, after we have been here for twenty years, she decided to give it a try. We all came home and gathered just like other American families around the table, having our first traditional American dinner with turkey, mashed potatoes, and salad. Mom made the turkey with Vietnamese seasonings and fish sauce and she made seaweed Jell-O for dessert instead of pumpkin pie. . . . For my mom, I guess for us children too, Thanksgiving has changed in meaning. Americans sit down around the dinner table and thank God for their blessings. We sit down to thank the Americans for ours.

The bitter experiences since the fall of Saigon and memories of war and exile have become a matter of the past. For American-born or American-reared children of Vietnamese refugees, Vietnam is far away. These children may understand their parental native language, remember a few ancient proverbs, and eat Vietnamese foods, but they may not fully appreciate these Vietnamese ways or consciously practice them, much less pass them on to their own children. They have been on their way to becoming American; many have moved up in status, but some have been trapped at the bottom of the society and may never be able to find a legitimate upward path.

Our study has focused on the adaptation experiences and outcomes of the children of Vietnamese refugees. Because of the recency of immigration, Vietnamese children are playing an important role in the transformation of their group from refugees to American ethnics. Throughout the book, we have examined several key aspects of the process of growing up American by assembling and analyzing a great deal of information on Vietnamese young people around the country as well as within a specific ethnic community. We have considered how social and eco-

216

nomic structures in the mainstream society as well as in the ethnic community interact with ethnicity and the culture of origin to determine how young Vietnamese strive to become American. Our results, we believe, can provide insight into the subtleties and complexity of contemporary processes of immigrant adaptation.

THE CONTEXTS OF RECEPTION:
NEIGHBORHOODS AND SCHOOLS

Vietnamese America has come about only since the mid-1970s. The U.S. government and its contracted nongovernmental volunteer organizations have resettled thousands of Vietnamese refugees in almost every state in the hope of accelerating their pace of assimilation. Whether the native population responds to the newcomers with sympathy or with hostility and whether public opinion is positive or negative, however, the Vietnamese have encountered a paradoxical host society and have almost always been seen as exotic foreigners.

The Neighborhood Context

Vietnamese refugees risked their lives to flee their homeland in the hope of finding a better place for their families. When they resettled in the United States, they envisioned for themselves and for their children a land of opportunities and a bright future. This has always been the vision of immigrants, but the America that has greeted refugees in recent years has created both opportunities and barriers for newcomers. While many of the Vietnamese refugees have embraced the opportunities, few anticipated the initial hardships in resettlement, and still fewer visualized what has actually awaited them: a reality described by Douglas S. Massey (1996) as "an age of extremes."

The gap between rich and poor, which progressively narrowed for most of the twentieth century, has been widening in recent years. The part of the American work force referred to as "knowledge workers" or "symbolic analysts" has seen its economic advantages steadily increase as information technology and management become more critical to the economy (Drucker 1993; Reich 1992), but at the same time the situation of most other American workers has worsened. Between 1979 and 1989, the average income among the top 5 percent of American wage earners increased from $120,253 to $148,438, while the average income among the bottom 20 percent decreased from $9,990 to $9,431 (U.S.

Bureau of the Census 1984, 1994). Over the course of the 1980s, 80 percent of American workers saw their real hourly wages go down by an average of about 5 percent (Mishel and Bernstein 1992). Blue-collar jobs, the kinds of jobs generally available to newly arrived immigrants, not only pay less than they used to but are harder to find as jobs in manufacturing and in unskilled labor have disappeared at a rapid rate (Mishel and Bernstein 1992). Although the distribution of wealth has not yet taken on the shape of an hourglass, the trend is toward expanding classes of poor and rich and a shrinking middle class. In such an economic structure, even U.S.-born Americans find their chances for economic mobility lessening. The situation for many immigrants is bleaker, except for the unusually fortunate, the highly educated, and the highly skilled (Waldinger 1996).

Contemporary economic hardships in the United States are different from those of the Great Depression and the current hardships in many Third World countries. Although there is a growing class of poor Americans, there are relatively few deaths from starvation in the United States. Until the early 1990s, the welfare state had made access to public assistance relatively easy (Rumbaut 1994b; Tienda and Liang 1994). While opportunities for stable jobs with good incomes were rare for low-income individuals, food stamps and Aid to Families with Dependent Children were readily available. Public assistance did not provide a comfortable way of life, for welfare payments averaged less than half the amount defined as poverty level income (Sancton 1992: 45), but it did provide a means of existence for the chronically poor, the unemployed, or the underemployed. Yet members of this expanding class of poor were not being offered chances for socioeconomic improvement; they were, for the most part, being fed and housed and maintained in their social and economic limbo.

These unfortunate circumstances were exacerbated just prior to the 1996 presidential election when President Bill Clinton signed a Republican welfare reform bill limiting public assistance to two continuous years and mandating a five-year lifetime maximum, with neither public jobs nor child care to help recipients enter the work force, and nothing for their children. The bill also excludes legal immigrants from access to many basic forms of assistance, forcing poor immigrant families to sink or swim. Long-term effects of the welfare bill remain to be seen, but it appears that thousands of children will be thrown into poverty, and chances for the truly disadvantaged to get out of poverty will be even more limited.

The poor are not, of course, evenly distributed across the American landscape. Even before new information technologies and the globalization of production began shrinking the American working class, the automobile industry promoted the exodus of the middle class from the cities. With the contraction of American manufacturing and the suburbanization first of the middle-class population and later of middle-class jobs, poverty has become concentrated in urban areas (Herbers 1986; Muller 1981). These changes have adversely affected not only individual minority members, but also minority communities. In inner cities, the African Americans, Mexican Americans, Puerto Rican Americans, and members of other immigrant minority groups who predominate in entire neighborhoods represent the poorest of their respective groups, left behind when their more affluent coethnics move to suburbia. Institutional discrimination and segregation have exacerbated the social and economic processes of minority concentration in low-income communities (Massey and Denton 1993; Moore and Vigil 1993; Wilson 1987).

The creation of concentrated low-income communities has had social consequences for the people who live in these communities, particularly for the young people, who form their expectations from the world they see around them. William J. Wilson (1978, 1987) has found that increasing joblessness has resulted in a decrease in the number of marriageable men in such communities and a corresponding increase in single-female-headed households. Without middle-class models, without roles in economic production, and without roles in families, young men in low-income communities tend to become marginalized and alienated. Social isolation and deprivation have given rise to an oppositional culture among young people who feel outside the mainstream of American society and oppressed by it (Darity and Myers 1995; Testa and Krogh 1995; Wilson 1987).

This is the neighborhood context, or what we call the local social environment, that has greeted the Vietnamese. With limited economic means, new arrivals from Vietnam have been resettled in America's low-income neighborhoods. Versailles Village, for example, was established in a place that offered cheap housing and was in the process of transition from a working-class, racially mixed neighborhood to a low-income minority neighborhood. Other Vietnamese communities elsewhere have also found themselves putting down roots in socioeconomically marginalized American neighborhoods.

The School Context

The economic and social forces that affect the neighborhoods are also felt in neighborhood schools, where students shape one another's attitudes and expectations. In a disruptive urban environment, caught between rising hopes and shrinking opportunities, younger members of native-born minorities have become increasing skeptical about school achievement as a viable path to upward mobility. While there is a strong anti-intellectual streak in American youth culture at all socioeconomic levels, the rejection of academic pursuits is especially widespread in minority schools, where many students tend to identify teachers and school administrators with oppressive authority. They see little hope of entry into the middle class and rebel against learning. Living in underprivileged neighborhoods, then, means going to underprivileged schools. Young Vietnamese tend to go to schools located in low-income neighborhoods and dominated by other minority students. These schools provide poor learning environments, and they often are even dangerous places. In the schools where we did our fieldwork, fights were frequent, and drugs were commonplace; the halls were patrolled at all times by armed guards. Students displayed scant respect for teachers, and teachers at times even feared for their safety.

It would be wise, we think, to avoid passing judgment on the children in these schools or blaming them for their response to the world around them. The sociologist Robert K. Merton (1938) long ago described rebellion as a response to a gap between socially approved goals and available means of achieving those goals. Limited prospects for mobility create frustration and pessimism for all young people in America, but these emotions are most strongly felt by those at the bottom. When those at the bottom are also members of historically oppressed minority groups, the frustration is compounded by the need to maintain self-esteem, so that rejection of middle-class mores and opposition to authority become important strategies for psychological survival (Fordham 1996).

Vietnamese children are pushed toward educational success by their parents but at the same time are pulled by the oppositional youth culture that surrounds them. The confrontation with poor neighborhoods and disruptive public schools places young Vietnamese in a forced-choice dilemma. If they strive to meet their parents' expectations for academic achievement, they are likely to be ostracized as "uncool," "nerdy," or "acting white" by their American schoolmates, mostly members of racial minorities. If they submit to peer pressure and attempts to become "American," on the other hand, they are likely to adopt the cultural ways, including the language and behavior, of the underclass. This type of assimilation can cause them to be stigmatized and condemned by their own community as well as by the larger society and destroy their parents' hopes for them.

THE WAY OUT: ETHNIC NETWORKS OF SOCIAL RELATIONS

The future seems bleak for those trapped on the bottom rung of society in the age of extremes. Is there a way out? Can parental hopes be realized in the second generation? The adaptation experiences of Vietnamese children seem to indicate a positive answer. Consistent with previous research, our study has found that Vietnamese children have displayed remarkable academic achievement, despite low socioeconomic status, low-income neighborhoods, and poor schools. Their school performance, as measured both by grades and by standardized test scores, is above the averages for both black students and white students, and their rates of college attendance are higher than those of either blacks or whites. Moreover, they are frequently reared by parents who have only limited English proficiency, and some have parents who speak no English at all. The parents' lack of language acculturation makes the children's academic accomplishments all the more surprising.

The apparent success of Vietnamese young people is a puzzle composed of many pieces. While previous research has focused on one piece or another, our study is a first attempt to assemble the main pieces so that we can see the whole picture more clearly. As has been documented throughout the book, successful adaptation of Vietnamese in poor urban neighborhoods has been determined, to a large extent, by distinctive patterns of ethnic social relationships. What follows are several conclusions that have important implications for children of immigrants growing up in post-modern America.

The Ethnic Community as a Locus of Support and Control

The ethnic community is an essential piece of the puzzle. Unlike other recent immigrants whose initial settlement is generally assisted by preexisting family networks and ethnic communities, the Vietnamese who arrived in the United States had no such coethnic assistance. Within a short span of time, however, they have managed to mobilize ethnic networks to build communities that are not simply Vietnamese transplants on American soil but new social structures shaped by the need to use ethnicity as a basis of cooperation for survival in a strange and difficult environment. Yet life in ethnic communities is more than a matter of reliance on coethnic support for survival; as the case of Versailles Village indicates, the dense, multiplex social system of family or kinship ties, religious ties, organizational ties, and work ties weaves its members into a fabric of both supports and controls that is in many ways conducive to successful adaptation to American society.

Community-based institutions provide a prime example. Vietnamese communities contain various ethnic institutions that help adult immigrants get settled and eventually become citizens and help the younger generation adapt to the American educational system and become the type of American expected by the community and by mainstream American society. These institutions are formal expressions of underlying networks of ethnic social relations, which for adult members function to create opportunities missing in the larger society and for younger members offer direction and encouragement in school adaptation.

Systems of ethnic social relations exercise social control over their members, reinforcing both traditional values brought from Vietnam and aspirations to upward mobility. These networks connect families and link parents to like-minded friends and neighbors, lending legitimacy to parental expectations as well as providing a microcosm within which parental values and wishes are not alien or outlandish. An ethnic community can provide children with the image of people like themselves and help them to see their own customs and traditions as worthwhile. As a buffer between the individual family and the larger society, the community can also assist parents in moderating their ways enough to meet host country requirements while retaining something of their own heritage. Thus, being enmeshed in these dense, overlapping networks of social relations based on shared ethnicity creates a high degree of consensus over community-prescribed values and norms and an effective mechanism of social control, which can serve as a special form of social capital. When individuals and families are integrated into the ethnic community, they can be encouraged to adopt positive American ways and can at the same time be effectively shielded from negative American influences. In Versailles Village, Vietnamese children cannot get away with much because neighbors are always around watching them and reinforcing the teachings of their parents.

Of course, adult members of the ethnic community are not the only people with whom Vietnamese young people have contact, nor is the ethnic group the only influence on their attitudes and behavior. Therefore, if systems of social relations in Vietnamese communities promote academic excellence, the young people of a given community who are involved in these systems will have an advantage over those who are not so involved. Once the young people are tied into these networks of relations, their good behavior and achievements receive public recognition and praise, in which their families share. Similarly, their unacceptable behavior or their school failure is met with gossip and reproach on all sides, bringing shame not only on themselves but on their families. These types of supports and constraints can effectively reinforce consistent standards and guide (or push) young people away from the oppositional culture and toward the fulfillment of parental aspirations.

The Role of the Family

The family is another large piece in the puzzle of immigrant adaptation. Social relations in Vietnamese families derive from traditions carried from Vietnam, from the experience of exile and resettlement, and from the pressures of life in America. The flight from Vietnam and resettlement in a strange new country has altered the Vietnamese family in a number of ways, but ties within families remain strong, and Vietnamese Americans continue to cultivate close family relations.

Initially, Vietnamese refugee families were scattered as isolated families in many parts of the country, but they soon formed distinctive Vietnamese neighborhoods, through secondary migration and subsequent family immigration. Strong ties within Vietnamese families serve to ease resettlement hardships and to reinforce parental aspirations and expectations for children. Findings from our study, which are consistent with prior research on the Vietnamese refugees, indicate a positive relationship between the acceptance of traditional family values and school performance. Vietnamese students who have strong orientations to family values tend to spend more time on their schoolwork and to receive better academic grades than their counterparts with weak family-value orientations. While cultural values make a difference in school performance, however, these values are not just mental heirlooms passed down from parents to children. In our view, values and attitudes are shaped by present-day social relations. If we are to understand the impressive accomplishments of Vietnamese young people, we must take into account not just the values and norms their parents have brought from the homeland but also the ways in which these traditional values and norms are moderated and re-created every day by people living together, continually reshaping one another's lives in a new environment.

A "deficient" family, to use James S. Coleman's (1990a) term, can lower the chance for success in school in the second generation, but a "functional" family may not guarantee that parental values and expectations are met. Young people are also influenced by peers, by neighbors, and by the media. A single, isolated family, therefore, exercises a relatively weak hold over its children. If individual families functioned in isolation, the traditional values of obedience, hard work, discipline, and scholastic achievement would have been abandoned by the younger generation as "old fashioned" or "unAmerican." Immigrant parents would have been powerless to protect their children from the negative influences of the popular American youth culture in the larger society and from the oppositional subculture in their immediate local social environment. Their children would have readily adopted alternative values learned from television or from their peers in school, both of which are prime influences on contemporary young Americans.

Our finding—one that we believe makes a significant contribution to the understanding of Vietnamese families—is that these families do not and cannot maintain and pass on cultural values in isolation. Rather, they exist and function in wider webs of social relations in the community. Since the Vietnamese have formed distinctive communities as a way of living in a strange new environment, it is important to see how the pressures of resettlement brought Vietnamese people together into ethnic communities in the United States and how these communities have consequently supported and controlled their members. It is also important to see how these communities have fit into the American society that surrounds them, challenges them, and changes them.

Selective Americanization

A third conclusion concerns the selectivity of Americanization. An ethnic system of social relations is expressed most clearly and meaningfully in the institutions of the ethnic community and the family. But what is it that makes community-prescribed directions and expectations desirable for adaptation? Or to put it another way, are there any alternatives available to Vietnamese young people? To ask this question is to attempt to put another large piece into the puzzle.

Generally, both Vietnamese families and the ethnic community expect the younger generation to assimilate into the mainstream American culture and to take full part in American society as citizens. At the same time, they often use the term "Americanization" in a negative sense. The young people described as "over-Americanized" have been referred to as "overadjusted" kids, which implies that they have adjusted to the local American youth culture so well that they no longer fit into the Vietnamese community. These "over-Americanized" young people are, at best, the ones who fail to show proper respect for their parents and elders; at worst, they are delinquents.

As has been noted earlier, there are different segments of American society into which new immigrants may be assimilated. In other words, they may be Americanized in different ways, depending on the specific context they enter. Since the large majority of the Vietnamese live in low-income neighborhoods where minority members predominate and where oppositional subcultures prevail, their position in the American social structure dictates that there are basically two routes open to the younger generation. One route is to cleave to the communities created by their parents as a response to sudden resettlement in an alien land and to adhere closely to the values and aspirations of these communities, which promote successful adaptation and actively encourage generally accepted mobility goals. The other route, by contrast, is to assimilate into the immediate local social environment, which is often in the alienated segments of American society. Taking the first route, a fairly difficult one, means that young Vietnamese will be both supported and controlled by parents, neighbors, and other coethnic members. They will be obliged to show respect for elders, teachers, and other authority figures and to do well in school. Following the second route, a relatively easy one, means that they will become marginal to their own ethnic community because in abandoning their Vietnamese identity they are likely to violate ethnic codes and show disrespect to their elders. They will also be marginal to the larger American society because in their adopted American identity they are likely to resemble those who are trapped in inner cities and have the least opportunity for upward mobility.

These two routes are reflected in the two widely held stereotypes of Vietnamese young people: "valedictorians" and "delinquents." We suggest that these two stereotypes arise from the two groups in which adult Vietnamese and Vietnamese youths themselves tend to divide their young people: "good kids" and "bad kids." Our survey data clearly indicate that these young people actually do tend to fall into two categories, those who report very little or no alcohol and drug abuse and few or no confrontations with the police, and those who report substantial substance abuse and a number of experiences with the police. Those in the first category tend to do quite well in school, and those in the second category tend to fare poorly.

While selective Americanization can lead to desirable outcomes, bicultural conflict can also yield fruits. In the process of Americanization, many young Vietnamese confront a gap between their own desires and expectations and those of their parents. They need guidance from their families at the same time that they are trying to break away from their families. Moreover, the standard generation gap is compounded by cultural distance between themselves and their elders. The Vietnamese insistence on obedience and lifelong filial obligation is inconsistent with common American ideas of self-fulfillment and self-satisfaction. Despite these intergenerational, bicultural tensions, however, Vietnamese young people tend to adhere to the adapted, rather than the transplanted, versions of Vietnamese ways, and they seem to understand that these Vietnamese ways are actually helpful in their efforts to move upward in American society. The bicultural conflicts are sources of psychological discomfort, but being held back from immediate assimilation into American society and subjected to controls derived from Vietnamese traditions do seem to bring about desirable outcomes.

Another interesting case in point is the educational attainment of Vietnamese women. While older Vietnamese women in the United States tend to have low levels of educational attainment, younger women tend to attain educational levels even higher than those of their male coethnics. This finding has led us to believe that young Vietnamese women are achieving success not because they are becoming Americanized and breaking away from the gender roles of their elders, but rather because the control imposed by traditional gender roles, to some extent, is pushing them to achieve, despite the pain and psychological discomfort of the constraints to which these young women are subject. This is not to say that the Vietnamese have imported male-female relations unchanged from Vietnam. In Vietnam, male-female relationships impede the advancement of women. In America, however, the social controls placed on women are linked to the immigrant goal of upward mobility within densely connected social networks.

In sum, Vietnamese families promote adaptation to American society, but only selectively. They provide young people with the basic tools to get by or to flourish. Families, however, exist in communities, and communities also promote adaptation. We have seen that the Vietnamese formed their communities as a means of helping one another meet the demands of American society, and these ethnic social networks and organizations are helping young people adapt.

American society is complex, composed of a variety of groups, social classes, and influences. Becoming American, then, can have both desirable and undesirable aspects. The social controls provided by families within ethnic communities can steer young people toward the desirable aspects of Americanization and away from the undesirable aspects. To say this is not to idealize Vietnamese cultural traditions or to claim that social control is in all circumstances a good thing. The point is rather that it is the tensions between Vietnamese traditionalism and the quest for social mobility and the tension between community controls and individual opportunities that produce selective Americanization. Without the structure provided by adult coethnic guidance, Vietnamese young people would be conforming completely to the ways of their non-Vietnamese peers. Without the educational opportunities offered by the U.S. public school system, they would simply be maintaining the age-old customs of their elders.

The Theory of Ethnic Social Relations

In an effort to put together the pieces of the puzzle, we have developed a theory of ethnic social relations to explain why some Vietnamese young people become underachievers, or even gang members, while others succeed beyond all expectations. This theory involves the relationships of these young people to their families, their ethnic community, the local social environment, and the larger American society. The varied adaptational outcomes of Vietnamese youths in the extremes of "valedictorians" and "delinquents" are, we argue, based on how they fit into their own families, how their families fit into the ethnic community, how the ethnic community fits into the local social environment, and how their own community and the local social environment fit into the larger American society.

We have tested this ethnic social relations theory by using data from our Versailles Village study. We have found that the Vietnamese young people in Versailles Village tend to show high levels of community involvement and that the more involved they are in their community, the more they adhere to traditional family values and the more committed they are to a work ethic. Community involvement, traditional family values, and a work ethic are all positively related to school performance, but the influence of community involvement appears to be the greatest.

We have also found that the development of advanced Vietnamese language skills, notably literacy, is associated with high levels of academic achievement, the amount of effort spent on schoolwork, and aspirations for future education. This finding, we acknowledge, may in part be due to cognitive development; learning to read and write any language can hone intellectual habits and skills. We have also found, however, that Vietnamese literacy is highly correlated with identification with Vietnamese ethnicity. This finding supports a sociological explanation of the connection between minority language skills and school performance, in contrast to the individual-level, psychological cognitive development explanation. Language joins people and binds them together in groups. Students with advanced Vietnamese language skills are more tightly bound to the social network of the ethnic community than students without such skills.

Our ethnic social relations theory of scholastic achievement has a seemingly paradoxical implication: adolescents adapt to American society to the extent that they are not assimilated into it. To understand why this is the case, it is necessary to reflect that American society is complex and frequently contradictory and that one may be American in many different ways. The reason why the Vietnamese use the term "Americanized" in a pejorative sense is that the Vietnamese young people who become like other American young people become like those around them; they are therefore assimilating into the oppositional culture of low-income, disaffected American youth. If cultivating ties with fellow Vietnamese is an advantage, it is an advantage within a specific setting in American society. Being part of a Vietnamese network offers a better route to upward mobility than the type of Americanization available to most Vietnamese American young people who live in poor neighborhoods.

Thus the main elements of Vietnamese success in the United States can be seen to be a traditional value orientation of dedication to the expectations of others brought from the home country, parental aspirations for upward mobility, and an ethnic system of social relations to enforce the expectations and aspirations. What about those who have failed? Our theory of ethnic social relations has offered a description of the connection between ethnic social structures and contemporary American social structures to examine why some Vietnamese fail to adapt to American society in a constructive fashion.

Ideally, families integrate their members into the surrounding environment and the surrounding environment integrates them into the larger society. Contemporary American society, however, contains marginalized segments. Becoming integrated into a low-income, disadvantaged neighborhood means becoming part of a social group that is alienated from middle-class America and that integration offers few opportunities for becoming part of the American mainstream. In this situation, the ethnic community acts as an alternative to the marginalized segment of the society. Through their families, young people become part of the ethnic community, and the ethnic community enables them to bypass the troubled, marginalized neighborhood that surrounds them and to concentrate on the chief opportunity offered them, public schooling.

Neither families nor communities are successful in every instance, however. In some situations illustrated by cases presented earlier in the book, the Vietnamese family and the Vietnamese community have failed to promote upward mobility for some of their children, especially those who came to the United States as unaccompanied minors or with families disrupted by the flight from Vietnam. Lacking the direction of the family and being rejected by the ethnic community, these young people may become part of the marginalized segment of American society that surrounds them. Some adolescents may grow up in families that have failed to adjust sufficiently to American ways to be able to provide children with sufficient guidance. Others may grow up in families that do not maintain close relations with coethnics, and these young people may also become integrated into the local oppositional youth culture rather than into the ethnic community.

Having failed to be integrated into the ethnic community, the alternative is to be assimilated into the disadvantaged youth culture, where adolescents learn the behavior and attitudes of their marginalized peers and they become "part of the wrong part of America." As we have seen, the "Americanized" adolescents share the tastes associated with American youth culture. Once young people are culturally assimilated into the native youth society, they are recognized as "bad kids." The ethnic community frequently responds by labeling them and locking them into their status as delinquents. This is the other side of the densely knit network of social relationships that we have argued are characteristic of Vietnamese communities. While these relationships can provide means of upward mobility to those who meet with approval, they can also serve to exclude some young people as outsiders. An ethnic identity serves as a basis of solidarity in Vietnamese communities. Young people who act in ways that are seen as "non-Vietnamese" threaten this solidarity and the collective project of adaptation to American society.

We have concluded that the story of how Vietnamese children are becoming American is one of concentric levels of social integration. The young members of this group have generally been successful because, in the process of exile and resettlement, their elders have formed close, mutually dependent social networks that offer control and support. Cultural values brought from Vietnam have aided in the formation of these networks, and cultural values have helped ethnic networks to bind young people closer to their families and to their ethnic communities. Vietnamese culture, however, has been modified by the pressures of American life, and Vietnamese culture alone cannot account for the achievements of Vietnamese young people. Integration through families into Vietnamese communities provides an alternative to assimilation into the most disadvantaged segments of American society. Therefore, Vietnamese ethnicity can be seen as means of bypassing the barriers of contemporary American class structure.

We stress that ethnicity is not simply an ascribed category; it is an identity rooted in distinctive patterns of social relationships. Since ethnic communities consist of individuals and their families cooperating with one another to achieve goals, we consider ethnicity as a form of social capital. Even for middle-class immigrants, ethnicity may provide some competitive advantage. Children of immigrant professionals, for example, may benefit from the attitudes toward education conveyed by their parents and from participating in institutions and programs, such as Korean churches or Chinese or Japanese weekend language classes, created by social relations among coethnics. For Indochinese children, however, ethnicity is not simply a source of advantage; it provides an alternative to ghettoization. To understand how ethnicity produces an outcome for members of a group, therefore, it is necessary to look at what kinds of social relations exist within the group and to consider how family structures and the social structures that surround families guide individuals toward outcomes. It is also necessary to understand how family and community structures fit into neighborhoods and into American society in general and how families and communities change in response to environmental pressures. If, as we maintain, networks of ties among coethnics constitute a major influence on the behavior and attitudes of the younger generation, then ignoring the role of ethnic social relations is a serious oversight.

ANOTHER "MODEL MINORITY"?

Much of the story told here has been one of success. It has not de-bunked the popular myth of Vietnamese children as overachievers but instead has also shown that this myth has some basis in fact. Whereas sociologists generally like to explain why popular wisdom is all illusion, we have concentrated on investigating the truth behind the popular wis-dom. Two objections might be raised to our doing so. First, why write a book that simply confirms what everyone knows? Second, doesn't the book present an overly favorable picture of contemporary Vietnamese Americans, holding them up as a model minority for emulation by other minorities in the United States?

Regarding the first point, we think that it is useful to provide empiri-cal support for, as well as against, common sense perceptions. Our cen-tral theme is not, however, that Vietnamese children have advanced to the heads of their classes. Instead, we have been concerned with how this advancement has come about. Our explanation, we believe, brings out a frequently overlooked dimension in the process of Vietnamese adapta-tion to American society and immigrant adaptation in general. We have discussed the ethnic group as a true social group, a source of identity and a distinctive pattern of social relationships. An individual's destiny cannot be determined merely by individual traits and aspirations; it does not depend completely on either the beliefs and habits held by the indi-vidual and the ethnic groups or the structure of socioeconomic oppor-tunities imposed from the outside. Individuals participate in immediate social structures that influence their beliefs and habits and facilitate or frustrate their making use of the opportunities offered them. We have identified the Vietnamese ethnic community as a critical social structure in explaining the adaptation of young people from Vietnam. This em-phasis on the networks of ethnic social relations rooted in the commu-nity supplies a large piece too often missing from pictures of Vietnamese life in America. It helps to provide a coherent theoretical explanation of the events and processes that have produced the Vietnamese overachiever of popular wisdom.

Regarding the second point, we have not argued that there is any-thing inherently superior about Vietnamese culture, nor have we main-tained that other youths could emulate the industriousness of Viet-namese youths, if only they had the self-discipline and the high moral standards to do so. In fact, we deplore the fact that the model minority argument is often used as a justification for the inequalities in American society. If the Vietnamese can advance themselves by hard work and dedication, the argument goes, why can't Mexican Americans, or Puerto Rican Americans, or African Americans? We have pointed out in some detail that there are Vietnamese children who fail to make it in American society. The same inequalities that frustrate the aspirations of native minority youth frequently trap Vietnamese youth at the bottom of our society. More importantly, though, we have described how the Vietnamese are able to make use of the limited opportunities that are offered them because of the way their social relations with one another has been shaped by historical events. We have further stressed that the explanation for how Vietnamese young people are adapting to American society lies in how ethnic group characteristics and current American social structure fit together. We have not attempted to evaluate the relative moral quality of Vietnamese ways but simply investigated how a people—Vietnamese Americans—have taken on a distinctive social structure and how this social structure affects their destiny in their new homeland.

THEORETICAL AND PRACTICAL IMPLICATIONS OF THE STUDY

Educating Immigrant Children

We believe that our findings in this book have implications for the study of the sociology of education, immigrant adaptation, and ethnic stratification. James S. Coleman (1990a) once observed that families and public schools are, to some extent, institutions with mutually contradictory functions. Families attempt to maximize the life-chances of their own offspring in a competitive world, perpetuating educational inequality. Families are endowed not only with varying material assets relevant to this endeavor but with varying social assets, such as family stability, time for parental involvement, and parental intellectual habits. Public schools, Coleman pointed out, are in theory egalitarian and redistributive in character. Supported by taxes on individuals, they seek to confer equality of opportunity on all citizens.

The egalitarian goals of public education may, however, be frustrated by inequalities outside the school. These inequalities are social as well as economic. A child with a stable family structure and with attentive parents may receive more encouragement to succeed than children without these forms of social capital receive. We have extended Coleman's argument beyond individual families. We maintain that communities can influence school performance by providing social capital. Just as family structure can be connected to the achievement of students, community structure can also be connected to that achievement. Young people who live in communities with explicit educational goals enter the educational arena with advantages.

The implications for the study of immigrant adaptation and ethnic stratification are related to the idea that communities play a major role in education. One way of measuring the adaptation of immigrant children to American society is by looking at how well those children appear to be adapting to the American school system, which has been designed to promote assimilation as well as equality of opportunity. American schools continue to act a bit like giant sponges, absorbing and acculturating children by means of formal education. Doing well in school, and achieving a high level of educational attainment can still be an important way of getting ahead, of assimilating structurally. Our study, however, indicates that in many cases cultural assimilation is inconsistent with structural assimilation into school or into other American institutions.

American public schools offer education to students from a variety of environments. School culture is not simply imposed on these students from above, by teachers and administrators. Students create their own patterns of behavior and their own prevailing attitudes from their experiences in families and neighborhoods. School environments, therefore, are unequal and often segmented by social class and ethnicity or race. Our study has suggested that when immigrant children enter the bottom of a stratified social structure, the forces of assimilation may come directly from the underprivileged segments of this structure and that assimilation then tends to result in distinct disadvantages. In this case, the maintenance of ethnic ties and integration into the ethnic community may enable immigrant children to break the cycle of disadvantage and lead them up the social ladder.

Growing up American

The study of immigrant adaptation to the United States, then, is the study of the different ways in which immigrants can become American. This is not just an abstract, theoretical issue; it is an issue close to the heart of the second-generation quest for identity. "What is an American?" "How am I part of American society?" "Can I ever be accepted as an unhyphenated American?" These are crucial questions of identity for immigrants and for their native born children. Theorists of the assimilationist tradition may tell these young people that they become American—and prosper—to the extent that they distance themselves from their immigrant origins and become indistinguishable from the native-born population. Multicultural theorists may remind them that the native-born population itself is a puzzle of many pieces, that the image of the American as a white English-speaking member of the middle class is largely an illusion, and that people from various parts of the world can retain or rely on their ethnicities while building America and becoming American. Structural theorists may direct their attention to the fact that America is composed of various races and ethnicities but that benefits and opportunities are distributed unequally among these racial and ethnic minorities. They may also remind these young people that there is a rather loosely defined racial and ethnic majority in the United States and that there are distinctive minorities. To be a member of a minority within the ethnic hierarchy is, in general, to occupy a disadvantaged position in this hierarchy.

There are no simple answers to second-generation questions about identity. Identity is a rather slippery matter that depends on how individuals feel about their own groups and other groups in a society. Our research suggests, however, that members of the second generation may identify strongly with immigrant minorities without feeling alienated from the larger American society. If identifying with an ethnic minority community—such as Versailles Village—can help members of the second generation succeed in American institutions—such as the school—then the two parts of an American ethnic identity can come to seem complementary rather than contradictory.

Immigrant adaptation, we suggest, is the study of how the various identities within a country fit together, as well as the study of how the country imposes new identities. Since the United States is, as the history texts constantly remind us, a nation of immigrants, the question of how one people is forged from many is a critical one for this country. The classical answer to this question is the melting pot. New arrivals may set foot on these shores with varied languages, traditions, and ways of interacting with others, but they become American by discarding their exotic habits in favor of the cultural patterns of the native-born. From this perspective, to the extent that they remain distinctive, members of immigrant groups can never really fit in. This is why controversial critics of U.S. immigration policy generally favor a moratorium on immigration;

the country needs time, they say, to assimilate the great numbers of new ?arrivals who are only gradually becoming American (see Brimelow 1995).

As assimilation theorists have long recognized, taking on the culture of a new country and being accepted into the society of the country's majority are often two quite different matters. Some native-born minority groups, such as African Americans and Mexican Americans, have been in North America longer than most European ethnic groups. These native minorities have helped to create American culture, but they have yet to achieve full acceptance in American society. Readily identifiable racial and ethnic groups continue to face barriers to structural assimilation. Accordingly, there is a connection between ethnicity and socioeconomic differentiation. Integration into American society may be more a matter of skin color or eye shape than of time passed since the arrival of ancestors. While the United States does not have a formal caste system, the heavy representation of ethnic and racial minorities among the chronically poor is a situation that should provoke extreme discomfort among those who believe in social mobility on the basis of individual achievement.

For Vietnamese children, however, ethnicity is not necessarily a barrier to becoming American; rather, it is a means of becoming American. An ethnic identity based on social relations with other Vietnamese serves as a springboard for upward mobility by means of education. In contrast to traditional assimilationist theory, structural assimilation to a host country is occurring before cultural assimilation. Indeed, to some extent it appears that young Vietnamese are achieving structural assimilation in America precisely because they have not been fully acculturated.

Multicultural theorists, recognizing the diverse character of North American society, both in the past and at present, have emphasized the fact that the national *unum* has been and continues to be constructed *e pluribus*. While developing a unified sense of national identity, many Americans have kept other identities. Distinctive cultures and religions have provided psychological benefits to a variety of groups, and they have served as bases for cooperation. In many cases, members of ethnic groups have achieved upward mobility because they have cultivated their ethnic identities, and not because they have divested themselves of these identities.

In our view, however, the celebration of diversity must be qualified. Varied ethnic identities may fit together, but they fit together in an unequal fashion. For this reason, we believe that our findings carry serious implications for the study of ethnic stratification. The historical exploitation of ethnic minorities and the restructuring of the American economy have handicapped many minority-group members, and these structural forces have continued to trap some groups to the bottom strata of the society while preserving the privileges of those on the top. Thus, ethnic or racial distinctiveness can be an asset; yet, the fruits of ethnicity differ from one group to another. We argue that a segmented assimilation perspective can enable us to put together a theory of why a particular group becomes Americanized in a particular manner. In this perspective, immigrants find themselves in different segments of American society, and their adaptation depends on what characteristics they bring with them into their new homeland, on what opportunities and restrictions they find in their immediate environment once they arrive, and on how their own characteristics interact with the social structures of the host country.

Race and class, we point out, are closely related to one another and to opportunities for social mobility in the contemporary United States. Minority groups are concentrated in low-income areas, and as a result minority group members, especially young people, develop social relations and attitudes that are geared toward coping psychologically with being the least privileged in their own country. The public schools located in these low-income neighborhoods also become concentrations of disadvantage and resentment. Young African Americans or Latino Americans who excel in school may find themselves reviled by their classmates for "acting white." In this situation, ethnicity can be a relative advantage for Vietnamese and other young people when the ethnic group provides an alternative to the oppositional culture of low-income neighborhoods. Immigrant ethnicity, in other words, can provide an alternative to assimilating into disadvantaged segments of modern society.

Our findings on this new immigrant group suggest that neither politically liberal views nor politically conservative views offer adequate explanations of the socioeconomic inequality among ethnic groups. Liberal theories of inequality tend to ascribe inequality to opportunities offered or denied by the social and economic structure of a society. If members of one group show high levels of achievement, it is because they have enjoyed privileges denied to others; if members of another group experience chronic problems of poverty and low educational attainment, it is because they have suffered systematic discrimination. Conservative theories tend to maintain that individuals in different groups hold different values. If members of one group take a more desirable place in American society than others, it is because the members of that group hold the right set of values and work ethic. If members of another group do not do well, it is because they are lazy or give up too soon.

In our study of Vietnamese youth in America, we have seen that the adaptation of Vietnamese young people is neither completely imposed from the outside nor solely determined by the quality of Vietnamese culture. The process of resettlement has shaped a Vietnamese American ethnicity that is not simply a category of national origin, nor a collection of traditions, nor yet a label that outsiders respond to favorably or unfavorably. It is a system of social relations that has consequences for those who participate in it. In describing this system of social relations, we have made use of both the old Durkheimian idea of social integration and Coleman's concept of social capital. We have indicated that social capital exists in a set of social relations, such as is found in the Vietnamese community, in which participants are tightly integrated into a group with definite shared goals. For the Vietnamese, the tight integration has resulted from the interdependence brought about by the experience of flight followed by sudden resettlement in a new land where ties to coethnics have offered the most readily available resource for survival. The shared goals have been produced by the linking of traditional Vietnamese cultural values to the immigrant goal of upward mobility. The study of immigrant adaptation, or ethnic stratification, then, requires close attention to the social system immediately surrounding individuals, the social system of the ethnic group. The level of social integration and the nature of shared goals within this social system strongly influence how members respond to whatever opportunities they can find in the larger society.

Policy Implications

Drawing policy implications is, perhaps, more dangerous than constructing a theory, since someone may actually put one's suggestions into practice. Nevertheless, we would like to mention a few modest policy-related implications. Although large-scale Southeast Asian refugee migration to the United States appears to have ended, there are still numerous governmental and nongovernmental agencies concerned with Southeast Asians in America. Our findings imply that these agencies would do well to concentrate on helping these new American residents and citizens to develop their own community organizations and on working through these community organizations. Schools with large numbers of Vietnamese among their students can help these young people by offering elective Vietnamese language classes and by supporting clubs and activities based on ethnic identity. These schools should also attempt to secure Vietnamese counselors who can act as bridges between families in ethnic communities and schools.

Social service organizations would do well to recognize the nature of the bicultural conflict confronting young Vietnamese and other young immigrants or members of today's second generation. Like their European predecessors, today's young immigrants are eager to fit in and to become American. The immediate social environment that surrounds most contemporary immigrant children is likely to be the poor neighborhood with its alienated, discouraged residents. Acculturation into this underprivileged segment of the host society may be harmful to immigrant children and their families. Social workers and others who work with troubled second-generation youths, among the Vietnamese or among other immigrant groups, may do well to concentrate on building bridges between the young people and their ethnic communities. Whenever possible, it would probably be best if those who work with these youths could themselves be members of the same community.

It is difficult to say what practical implications we can draw for members of other immigrant minorities or for members of native minorities. Each group is responding to a different set of experiences and pressures. One of the reasons the model minority concept is so unfair is that it compares groups of peoples with entirely dissimilar backgrounds. Nevertheless, we think our identification of the community as a key to individual adaptation to a larger society may offer some generalizable suggestions. Programs to help members of minority groups, whether immigrant or native minorities, often concentrate efforts on individuals. Public assistance benefits and educational programs such as Head Start are directed toward individuals and individual families. Our research may indicate that projects aimed at building interdependent communities may better meet the needs of America's disadvantaged minorities. This is speculation, but it is consistent with our findings on the Vietnamese.

THE FUTURE OF VIETNAMESE AMERICANS

What will the future look like for second-generation Vietnamese? Futurology is a notoriously risky endeavor, but current trends do provide some indications, however unreliable, of things to come. Since we are dealing in this book with young people, with lives that are largely yet to come, it may be worthwhile to think about some of these current trends and plunge into speculation.

The massive twenty-year transfer of population from Southeast Asia to North America is over. With the end of the Cold War, normalization of relations with Vietnam, and growing American discomfort with large-scale immigration, it is unlikely that another influx of refugees will pour into the United States from Vietnam. Given its relative youth and high fertility of the Vietnamese-American population, as well as family-sponsored immigration, however, this population will continue, in the foreseeable future, to grow at a rapid rate. This growth will yield a sizable native-born component. If current trends continue, Vietnamese Americans will in the long run probably resemble other Asian Americans and the general American population.

The predicted cutoff of the refugee inflow from Vietnam will change the process of resettlement for these immigrants. The already well-established communities will offer a stepping stone for later arrivals, just as do other immigrant communities. Since 1980, the Vietnamese have made small-scale entrepreneurship a major part of their strategy for survival in America. Ethnic entrepreneurship, however, is a field overwhelmingly dominated by first-generation immigrants. The children of those who own corner grocery stores and ethnic restaurants will be unlikely to follow in their parents' footsteps, especially those who are college-bound. The probable departure of the second generation from their ethnic communities will mean that these communities will remain the foothold of the first generation. Ethnic enclaves, such as Little Saigon and Versailles Village, will thus begin to contract if unreplenished by a sufficient quantity of new arrivals.

Vietnamese communities themselves will not disappear, nevertheless. These ethnic communities will continue to serve as home to those who have not made it to mainstream American society and will probably serve as symbolic centers for Vietnamese Americans who have moved into affluent suburbs. If middle-class suburban coethnics stopped returning to these centers, for business or pleasure, the ethnic communities then would be organized around small numbers of stores selling ethnic foods and other goods to tourists, and their residents may well be disproportionately the elderly and the unsuccessful. Ironically, the "over-Americanized" Vietnamese, who have acculturated into the marginal or underclass segment of American society, may be the least likely to be able to leave their ethnic communities. The dark scenario may be possible: the bifurcation of Vietnamese children may lead to the increasing ghettoization of Vietnamese neighborhoods, as the success stories move away and the dispirited, alienated members of the group stay and raise families. Consequently, these neighborhoods may become more and more similar to other troubled minority concentrations.

The end of Southeast Asian refugee flows to the United States also raises questions about the extent to which Vietnamese people will remain distinct from the rest of American society. We suggest that without a constant source of renewal a Vietnamese-American ethnicity, while it will not disappear in the foreseeable future, will become increasingly symbolic. Buddhist temples and Vietnamese Catholic churches will become permanent additions to the American landscape, but their adherents will cease to seem exotic or alien to others.

As the Vietnamese become more a part of mainstream American society, intermarriage with non-Vietnamese will become much more common. This trend will not necessarily mean that the Vietnamese as a group simply disappear into the melting pot. Instead, it will probably mean that Vietnamese Americans will have numerous family connections to non-Vietnamese or to people of mixed ancestry and that the boundaries between who is and who is not a member of this ethnic group will become more indistinct over time.

Vietnamese America is now a permanent part of American life. In the years to come, Vietnamese communities may evoke the same sorts of nostalgia as today's Irish and Italian urban villages—places that are still with us but seem to belong to a bygone era. The grandchildren and great-grandchildren of the Vietnamese adolescents whom we have studied may well visit Versailles Village, Little Saigon, or one of the many other Vietnamese communities and reflect that this is where their ancestors had once lived together and helped each other to become American.

SUGGESTIONS FOR FUTURE RESEARCH

Our study has attempted to show that, in the long journey to becoming American, the progress of immigrants depends heavily on the social structure of the host society and on the social structure of the immigrant group. As they are absorbed into different segments of American society, becoming American may not always be an advantage for young immigrants and children of immigrants. When immigrants enter middle-class communities directly or after a short transition, they may find it advantageous to acculturate and assimilate. When they enter the bottom of the ethnic hierarchy, where the forces of assimilation come mainly from the underprivileged, acculturation and assimilation are likely to result in distinct disadvantages, viewed as maladjustment by both mainstream society and by the ethnic community. In this case, young immigrants or children of immigrants may benefit from cultivating social ties within ethnic communities to develop forms of behavior likely to break the cycle of disadvantage and to lead to upward mobility.

Given certain disadvantages of ethnic group membership, then, continued research should focus on identifying the conditions that limit opportunities for members of an ethnic group and considering how group membership can help or hinder young people to make the most of the opportunities they do have. We suggest a number of interesting questions for further theoretical inquiry: Will members of a generation born or reared in the United States gradually be pulled away from a heritage vastly different from those of the Europeans who arrived over the course of this century? Will those who rebel against this heritage be the best-adjusted, socially and economically? Will racial barriers limit the participation of immigrant children in American life? How will being hyphenated Americans influence the ways in which young people become assimilated and why may some of these ways be more advantageous than others? Will the cultural distinctiveness of hyphenated Americans eventually melt down into a pot of Anglo-American homogeneity? Will immigrant families and ethnic communities persist in affecting the lives of children of the second generation? Each of these questions has theoretical as well as practical implications. Given the complexity of the ways in which second-generation members of new immigrant groups are becoming American, future studies are both urgent and necessary.

Notes

Introduction

1. We see Vietnamese children as part of the present-day's new second generation that includes not only U.S.-born children of contemporary immigrants but also foreign-born children who have arrived in the United States at young ages. For the Vietnamese children under study, we emphasize important differences between the 1.5 generation and the second generation. We broaden the Vietnamese second generation to include foreign-born children arriving at pre-school age (0 to 4 years) because these children share many linguistic, cultural, and developmental experiences with the U.S.-born. We further classify foreign-born children arriving between 5 and 12 years of age as 1.5-generation children and those arriving as adolescents (aged 13 to 17) as first-generation children.

2. In our detailed description in chapter 6, we group these 15 students at the magnet school with those at Jefferson High, since most of the Vietnamese students attending Jefferson High were also enrolled in the magnet program.

Chapter 2

1. Rumbaut's definition of the 1.5 generation included those arriving at adolescence. Since this book focuses on comparisons of different cohorts of children, adolescents here are categorized as the first generation in the 0 to 17 age group. Clearly, however, there is a qualitative difference between those who arrive as adolescents and those who arrive as adults.

Chapter 3

1. Although we did not have data on daily hours spent on homework by non-Vietnamese students in that school, the teachers we interviewed consistently reported that Vietnamese students generally worked harder and spent more time on homework than their American counterparts. Results from the San Diego Survey of 1992 on immigrant children showed that Vietnamese students spent an average of two hours daily on homework, compared with 1.16 hours for Mexicans, 1.56 for other Latins, and 1.97 for other Asians, as revealed in table 2.8 in Rumbaut 1996.

Chapter 4

1. This usage reflects traditional Vietnamese gender relations and the old association of teaching with masculinity. The feminine equivalent of *thay giao* is *co giao*.

Chapter 5

1. Our study used PUMAs (Public Use Microdata Areas) as proxies for coethnically concentrated Vietnamese neighborhoods. All PUMAs in the 1990 census 5-percent PUMS that contained at least one hundred Vietnamese families were selected. Because coethnically concentrated areas offer extensive opportunities for intraethnic contacts, we expected that Vietnamese children living in those areas should show greater Vietnamese language retention than those living elsewhere.

2. When there was a discrepancy between reported reading ability and reported writing ability, reading ability was always just slightly higher; the extremely strong association between the two items suggests that the reporting pattern is consistent.

Chapter 6

1. The data for this examination come from the 5-percent Public Use Microdata Sample (PUMS) of the 1990 U.S. census. We took a full sample of Vietnamese aged 16 to 19 ($N = 2265$) and a random sample of comparable size for whites ($N = 2500$), blacks ($N = 2500$), and Chinese ($N = 2500$). Our sample was limited to young people who were living with their parents or guardians. The high school dropout rates in this analysis are therefore somewhat more conservative than those found in the full U.S. census.

2. Because the dependent variable is dichotomous (students either are dropouts or they are not), logistic regression is felt to be the proper methodological approach. The interpretation of the effects of continuous variables (such as income) in logistic regression equations is straightforward; one unit change in family income will increase the log odds of being a high school dropout by its logit, controlling for all other independent variables. The logit coefficients of the noncontinuous, and particularly the dichotomous, independent variables are not sufficient to interpret the model, however, for it is difficult to grasp the magnitude of effects in a logarithmic scale (Alba 1986). For this reason, the logit parameters are translated into multiplicative parameters (that is, odds ratios). The odds ratios are then transformed into percentage differences, for example, the percent increase in probability of being a dropout for each unit increase in the independent variable. Extreme caution should, of course, be used in comparing percentage differences of variables with different numbers of categories, since very tiny percentage differences in

continuous variables (such as age) will reflect significant effects, while relatively large percentages in dichotomous variables may be insignificant. For the sake of comparability, then, we have sought to code variables as dichotomous wherever this is methodologically justifiable.

3. This variable was created by identifying those PUMS areas (PUMAs) in the 1990 census that contain at least one hundred Vietnamese households in the population and coding those who live in these areas as 1.

4. Estimates of dropout rates in this analysis may differ slightly from those in the full census, since these rates are based on the 5-percent PUMS and because only minors living with parents were included in our analysis.

5. These five survey items were: 1) What language do you speak at home with your parents? Possible answers were "Vietnamese," "English," or "other." 2) How well do you read and write Vietnamese? Possible answers were "quite well," "a little," or "not at all." 3) How do you identify yourself? Possible answers were "Vietnamese," "Vietnamese American," "Asian-American," "American," or "other." 4) What is the ethnicity of most of your close friends? Possible answers were "Vietnamese," "other Asian," "black," "white," or "other." 5) How likely do you think it is that you will marry someone of Vietnamese origin? Possible answers were "almost certain," "likely," "unlikely," "very unlikely," or "don't know."

6. Except for number of siblings, all the control variables are dummy variables.

Chapter 8

1. There is no breakdown of types of institutions by detailed race categories, but the census does give total numbers of institutionalized juveniles in the detailed race categories.

2. We used a 5-point scale in our questionnaire, ranging from 1 "dislike very much," 2 "dislike," 3 "indifferent," 4 "like," and 5 "like very much."

References

Airriess, Christopher, and David L. Clawson. 1991. "Versailles: A Vietnamese Enclave in New Orleans, Louisiana." *Journal of Cultural Geography* 12 (1):1–14.
———. 1994. "Vietnamese Market Gardens in New Orleans." *Geographical Review* 84 (1):16–31.

Alba, Richard D. 1986. "Interpreting the Parameters of Log-Linear Models." *Sociological Methods and Research* 16 (1):45–77.

Aldrich, Howard E., and Roger Waldinger. 1990. "Ethnicity and Entrepreneurship." *American Review of Sociology* 16:111–35.

Allen, Rebecca, and Harry Hiller. 1985. "The Social Organization of Migration: An Analysis of the Uprooting and Flight of Vietnamese Refugees." *International Migration Review* XXIII (22):439–51.

Allmen, Eva. 1987. "The Refugee Woman and Her Family." *Refugees* 6:8.

Ancel, David, and Kathleen Hamilton. 1987. "All Is Clear under the CO Sky." *Passage: A Journal of Refugee Education.* Special Galang Issue, 25–29.

Anderson, Elijah. 1990. *Streetwise: Race, Class, and Change in an Urban Community.* Chicago: The University of Chicago Press.

Averitt, Robert T. 1968. *The Dual Economy: The Dynamics of American Industry Structure.* New York: W. W. Norton.

Baldwin, C. Beth. 1982. *Capturing the Change: The Impact of Indochinese Refugees in Orange County, Challenges and Opportunities.* Santa Ana, Calif.: Immigrant and Refugee Planning Center.
———. 1984. *Patterns of Adjustment: A Second Look at Indochinese Resettlement in Orange County.* Orange, Calif.: Immigrant and Refugee Planning Center.

Bankston, Carl L. III. 1997. "Education and Ethnicity: Community and Academic Performance in an Urban Vietnamese Village." In *Beyond Black and White: New Faces and Voices in U. S. Schools*, edited by Lois Weiss and Maxine S. Seller. New York: State University of New York Press.

Bankston, Carl L. III, and Min Zhou. 1995a. "Effects of Minority-Language Literacy on the Academic Achievement of Vietnamese Youth in New Orleans." *Sociology of Education* 68 (January):1–17.
———. 1995b. "Religious Participation, Ethnic Identification, and Adaptation of Vietnamese Adolescents in an Immigrant Community." *The Sociological Quarterly* 36 (3):501–12.
———. 1996. "Go Fish: The Louisiana Vietnamese and Ethnic Entrepreneurship in an Extractive Industry." *National Journal of Sociology* 10(1):1–18.

247

Barringer, Herbert R., Robert W. Gardner, and Michael J. Levin. 1993. *Asians and Pacific Islanders in the United States*. New York: Russell Sage Foundation.

Blau, Peter, and Otis D. Duncan. 1967. *The American Occupational Structure*. New York: Wiley.

Bourgois, Philippe. 1991. "In Search of Respect: The New Service Economy and the Crack Alternative in Spanish Harlem." Paper presented at the Conferences on Poverty, Immigration, and Urban Marginality in Advanced Societies. Maison Suger, Paris (May 10–11, 1991).

Brimelow, Peter. 1995. *Alien Nation: Common Sense about America's Immigration Disaster*. New York: Random House.

Bronfenbrenner, Uri. 1979. *The Ecology of Human Development*. Cambridge: Harvard University Press.

Caplan, Nathan, Marcella H. Choy, and John K. Whitmore. 1991. *Children of the Boat People: A Study of Educational Success*. Ann Arbor: The University of Michigan Press.

———. 1992. "Indochinese Refugee Families and Academic Achievement." *Scientific American* (February):36–42.

Caplan, Nathan, John K. Whitmore, and Quang L. Bui. 1985. *Southeast Asian Refugees Self-Sufficiency Study: Final Report*. Office of Refugee Resettlement of the Department of Health, Education, and Welfare. Ann Arbor: Institute for Social Research, University of Michigan.

Caplan, Nathan, John K. Whitmore, and Marcella H. Choy. 1989. *The Boat People and Achievement in America: A Study of Family Life, Hard Work, and Cultural Values*. Ann Arbor: The University of Michigan Press.

Carnegie Council on Adolescent Development. 1992. *A Matter of Time: Risk and Opportunity in the Non-School Hours*. New York: Carnegie Corporation of New York.

Child, Irving L. 1943. *Italian or American? The Second Generation in Conflict*. New Haven: Yale University Press.

Coleman, James S. 1987. *Public and Private High Schools: The Impact of Community*. New York: Basic Books.

———. 1988. "Social Capital in the Creation of Human Capital." *American Journal of Sociology* 94:95–120.

———. 1990a. "Rawls, Nozick, and Educational Equality." In *Equality and Achievement in Education*, edited by James S. Coleman. Boulder, Col.: Westview Press.

———. 1990b. *Foundations of Social Theory*. Cambridge, Mass.: The Belknap Press.

Coleman, James S., E. Q. Cambell, C. J. Hobson, J. McPartland, A. M. Mood, F. D. Weinfeld, and R. L. York. 1966. *Equality of Educational Opportunity*. Washington, D. C.: U.S. Government Printing Office.

Conzen, Kathleen Neils. 1991. "Mainstreams and Side Channels: The Localization of Immigrant Cultures." *Journal of American Ethnic History* 11 (Fall): 5–20.

Cotter, Barbara S., and Patrick R. Cotter. 1979. "American Attitudes Toward Indochinese Refugees: the Influence of Region." In *Proceedings of the First Annual Conference on Indochinese Refugees,* compiled by G. Harry Stopp, Jr. and Nguyen Manh Hung. Fairfax, Va.: Citizens Applied Research Institute of George Mason University.

Covello, Leonard. 1972. *The Social Background of the Italo-American School Child.* Totowa: Rowman & Littlefield.

Cummins, Jim. 1991. "Language Shift and Language Learning in the Transition from Home to School." *Journal of Education* 173:85–98.

Darity, William A., Jr., and Samuel L. Myers, Jr. 1995. "Family Structure and the Marginalization of Black Men: Policy Implications." In *The Decline in Marriage among African Americans,* edited by M. Belinda Tucker and Claudia Mitchell-Kernan. New York: Russell Sage Foundation.

Davis, Mary. 1993. "The Gautreaux Assisted Housing Program." In *Housing Markets and Residential Mobility,* edited by G. Thomas Kingsley and Margrey Austin Turner. Washington, D. C.: Urban Institute Press.

DeBonis, Steven. 1995. *Children of the Enemy: Oral Histories of Vietnamese Amerasians and Their Mothers.* Jefferson, N.C.: McFarland.

De Vos, George A. 1975. "Ethnic Pluralism: Conflict and Accommodation." In *Ethnic Identity: Cultural Continuities and Change,* edited by George De Vos and Lola Romanucci-Ross. Palo Alto, Calif.: Mayfield Publishing Company.

Dickerson, Debra. 1996. "Who Shot Johnny?" *The New Republic* 214 (January 1):17–18.

Dornbusch, S. M., P. L. Ritter, P. H. Leiderman, D. F. Robert, and M. J. Fraleigh. 1987. "The Relation of Parenting Style to Adolescent School Performance." *Child Development* 55:1244–57.

Drucker, Peter F. 1993. *Post-Capitalist Society.* New York: Harper Collins.

Duiker, William J. 1989. *Vietnam Since the Fall of Saigon.* Athens, Ohio: Ohio University Center for International Studies.

Durkheim, Emile. 1951 [1897]. *Suicide: A Study in Sociology,* trans. by John A. Spaulding and George Simpson, edited by George Simpson. New York: The Free Press.

Ekstrom, Ruth B., Margaret E. Goertz, Judith M. Pollack, and Donald A. Rock. 1986. "Who Drops Out of High School and Why? Findings from a National Study." *Teachers College Record* 87:356–73.

English, T. J. 1994. *Born to Kill: America's Most Notorious Vietnamese Gang and the Changing Face of Organized Crime.* New York: Morrow.

Fainsten, Norman. 1995. "Race, Segregation, and the State." In *The Bubbling Cauldron: Race, Ethnicity, and the Urban Crisis,* edited by Michael P. Smith and Joe Feagin. Minneapolis: University of Minnesota Press.

Fernández, Roberto M., and Francois Nielsen. 1986. "Bilingualism and Hispanic Scholastic Achievement: Some Baseline Results." *Social Science Research* 15:43–70.

Fernández-Kelly, M. Patricia. 1995. "Social and Cultural Capital in the Urban Ghetto: Implications for the Economic Sociology and Immigration." In *The Economic Sociology of Immigration: Essays on Networks, Ethnicity, and Entrepreneurship*, edited by Alejandro Portes. New York: Russell Sage Foundation.

Finnan, C. R., and R. Cooperstein. 1983. *Southeast Asian Refugees Resettlement at the Local Level.* Washington, D. C.: Office of Refugee Resettlement.

Fordham, Signithia. 1996. *Blacked Out: Dilemmas of Race, Identity, and Success at Capital High.* Chicago: The University of Chicago Press.

Freeman, James M. 1989. *Hearts of Sorrow: Vietnamese-American Lives.* Stanford, Calif.: Stanford University Press.

Gans, Herbert J. 1992. "Second-Generation Decline: Scenarios for the Economic and Ethnic Futures of the Post-1965 American Immigrants." *Ethnic and Racial Studies* 15(2):173–92.

Gardner, Robert W., Bryant Robey, and Peter C. Smith. 1985. "Asian Americans: Growth, Change, and Diversity." *Population Bulletin* 40(4). Washington, D. C.: Population Reference Bureau Inc.

Gibson, Margaret A. 1989 *Accommodation Without Assimilation: Sikh Immigrants in an American High School.* Ithaca, N.Y.: Cornell University Press.

Gold, Steven J. 1992. *Refugee Communities: A Comparative Field Study.* Newbury Park, Calif.: Sage Publications.

Gordon, Linda W. 1989. "National Surveys of Southeast Asian Refugees: Methods, Findings, Issues." In *Refugees as Immigrants*, edited by David W. Haines. Totowa, N.J.: Rowman & Littlefield.

Gropp, Gerry. 1992. "In Orange County's Little Saigon, Vietnamese Try to Bridge Two Worlds." *Smithsonian* 23(5):28–32.

Hagerty, Elizabeth Ann. 1980. *Vietnamese in Southern California.* Ph.D. Diss., School of Human Behavior, United States International University. Ann Arbor, Mich.: University Microfilms International.

Haines, David W. 1981. *Refugee Settlement in the United States: An Annotated Bibliography on the Adjustment of Cuban, Soviet, and Southeast Asian Refugees.* Washington, D.C.: Office of Refugee Resettlement, Department of Health and Human Services.

———. 1985. "Toward Integration into American Society." In *Refugees in the United States: A Reference Handbook*, edited by David W. Haines. Westport, Conn.: Greenwood Press.

Hanh, Phung Thi. 1979. "The Family in Vietnam and Its Social Life." In *An Introduction to Indochinese History, Culture, Language and Life: For Persons Involved with the Indochinese Refugee Education and Resettlement Project in the State of Michigan*, edited by John K. Whitmore. Ann Arbor, Mich.: Center for South and Southeast Asian Studies, University of Michigan.

Harding, Richard K., and John G. Looney. 1977. "Problems of Southeast Asian Children in a Refugee Camp." *American Journal of Psychiatry* 134:407–11.

Hayakawa, S. I. 1979. "Keynote Address." In *Proceedings of the First Annual Conference on Indochinese Refugees*, compiled by G. Harry Stopp, Jr., and Nguyen Manh Hung. Fairfax, Va.: Citizens Applied Research Institute of George Mason University.

Hein, Jeremy. 1995. *From Vietnam, Laos, and Cambodia: A Refugee Experience in the United States*. New York: Twayne Publishers.

Herbers, John. 1986. *The New Heartland: America's Flight Beyond the Suburbs and How It Is Changing Our Future*. New York: Times Books.

Hernandez, Donald J. 1986. "Childhood in Sociodemographic Perspective." *Annual Review of Sociology* 12:159–80.

———. 1993. *America's Children: Resources from Family, Government and the Economy*. New York: Russell Sage Foundation.

Hickey, Gerald Cannon. 1964. *Village in Vietnam*. New Haven: Yale University Press.

Hitchcox, Linda. 1988. *Vietnamese Refugees in Transit: Process and Change*. Ph. D. Diss. Oxford University.

Hochschild, Jennifer L. 1984. *The New American Dilemma*. New Haven, Conn.: Yale University Press.

Hung, Nguyen Manh. 1985. "Vietnamese." In *Refugees in the United States: A Reference Handbook*, edited by David W. Haines. Westport, Conn.: Greenwood Press.

Jencks, Christopher, and Susan Mayer. 1990. "The Social Consequences of Growing Up in a Poor Neighborhood." In *Inner-City Poverty in the United States*, National Research Council. Washington, D.C.: National Academy Press.

Kao, Grace, and Marta Tienda. 1995. "Optimism and Achievement: The Educational Performance of Immigrant Youth." *Social Science Quarterly* 76(1):1–19.

Kasarda, John D. 1983. "Entry Level Jobs, Mobility, and Minority Unemployment." *Urban Affairs Quarterly* 19(1):21–40.

Kelly, Gail Paradise. 1977. *From Vietnam to America: A Chronicle of the Vietnamese Immigration to the United States*. Boulder, Co.: Westview Press.

———. 1986. "Coping with America: Refugees from Vietnam, Cambodia, and Laos in the 1970s and 1980s." *Annals of the American Academy of Political Social Science* 487 (September):138–49.

Keniston, Kenneth, and the Carnegie Council on Children. 1977. *All Our Children*. New York: Harcourt Brace Jovanovich.

Kibria, Nazli. 1993. *Family Tightrope: The Changing Lives of Vietnamese Americans*. Princeton, N.J.: Princeton University Press.

Kohl, Herbert. 1994. *"I Won't Learn from You" and Other Thoughts on Creative Maladjustment*. New York: The New Press.

Kuntz, Laurie. 1986. "Poetry at PASS." *Passage* 2(2):53–55.

Landale, Nancy S. 1996. "Immigration and the Family: An Overview." In *Immigration and the Family: Research and Policy on U.S. Immigrants*, edited by Alan Booth, Ann C. Crouter, and Nancy Landale. Hillsdale, N.J.: Lawrence Erlbaum Associates.

Lanphier, C. Michael. 1983. "Dilemmas of Decentralization: Refugee Sponsorship and Service in Canada and the United States." In *The Southeast Asian Environment*, edited by Douglas R. Webster. Ottawa, Ont.: University of Ottawa Press.

Lee, Seh-Ahn. 1992. "Family Structure Effects on Student Outcomes." In *Parents, Their Children, and Schools*, edited by Barbara Schneider and James S. Coleman. Boulder, Col.: Westview Press.

Liang, Zai. 1994. "On the Measurement of Naturalization." *Demography* 31(3):525–48.

Lichter, Daniel T. 1988. "Racial Differences in Underemployment in American Cities." *American Journal of Sociology* 93:771–92.

Light, Ivan. 1972. *Ethnic Enterprise in America: Business Welfare among Chinese, Japanese and Blacks*. Berkeley, Calif.: University of California Press.

Light, Ivan, and Edna Bonacich. 1988. *Immigrant Entrepreneurs: Koreans in Los Angeles*. Berkeley, Calif.: University of California Press.

Lindholm, Kathryn J., and Zierlein Aclan. 1991. "Bilingual Proficiency as a Bridge to Academic Achievement: Results from Bilingual/Immersion Programs." *Journal of Education* 173:99–113.

Liu, William T., Maryanne Lamanna, and Alice Murata. 1979. *Transition to Nowhere: Vietnamese Refugees in America*. Nashville, Tenn.: Charter House.

Lopez, David E. 1976. "The Social Consequences of Chicano Home/School Bilingualism." *Social Problems* 24(2):234–46.

———. 1996. "Language: Diversity and Assimilation." In *Ethnic Los Angeles*, edited by Roger Waldinger and Mehdi Bozorgmehr. New York: Russell Sage Foundation.

Los Angeles Times. 1994. *Los Angeles Times Poll: Vietnamese in Southern California*. Storrs, Conn.: The Roper Center for Public Opinion Research. Archive number USLAT94–331.

Louisiana Department of Education. 1992. *One Hundred and Forty Second Annual Financial and Statistics Report*. Session 1990–1991. Bulletin 1472. Baton Rouge, La.: Louisiana Department of Education, Office of Research and Development, Bureau of School Accountability.

Maciel, Timothy. 1987. "ESL Curriculum Development at PASS." *Passage: A Journal of Refugee Education* 3(1):34–37.

Massey, Douglas S. 1996. "The Age of Extremes: Concentrated Affluence and Poverty in the Twenty-First Century." *Demography* 33(4):395–412.

Massey, Douglas S., and Nancy A. Denton. 1987. "Trends in Residential Segregation of Black, Hispanics, and Asians: 1970–1980." *American Sociological Review* 52:802–25.

McDill, Edward L., Gary Natriello, and Aaron M. Pallas. 1985. "Raising Standards and Retaining Students: The Impact of the Reform and Recommendations on Potential Dropouts." *Review of Educational Research* 55(4):415–33.

Merton, Robert K. 1938. "Social Structure and Anomie." *American Sociological Review* 3:672–82.

Mishel, Lawrence, and Jared Bernstein. 1992. *The State of Working America: 1992–1993*. Washington, D.C.: Economic Policy Institute.

Montero, Darrel. 1979. *Vietnamese Americans: Patterns of Resettlement and Socio-economic Adaptation in the United States*. Boulder, Col.: Westview Press.

Moore, Joan, and James Diego Vigil. 1993. "Barrios in Transition." In *In the Barrios: Latinos and the Underclass Debate*, edited by Joan Moore and Raquel Pinderhughes. New York: Russell Sage Foundation.

Muller, Peter O. 1981. *Contemporary Suburban America*. Englewood Cliffs, N.J.: Prentice Hall.

Muzny, Charles. 1989. *The Vietnamese in Oklahoma City: A Study in Ethnic Change*. New York: AMS Press.

Nash, Jesse W. 1992. *Vietnamese Catholicism*. Harvey, La.: Art Review Press.

Natriello, Gary, Aaron M. Pallas, and Edward L. McDill. 1986. "Taking Stock: Renewing Our Research Agenda on the Causes and Consequences of Dropping Out." *Teachers College Record* 87:430–40.

New Orleans Indochinese Resettlement Task Force. 1979. *Impact Analysis of Indochinese Resettlement in the New Orleans Metropolitan Area: A Task Force Study*. New Orleans, La.: Mayor's Office of Policy Planning.

New Orleans School Board. 1993. *Norm-Reference Test Result of the New Orleans Public Schools: A Comprehensive Report on Their Relationship to Major Student Characteristics*. New Orleans, La.: Department of Educational Accountability, Division of Educational Programs.

Nhu, Tran Tuong. 1976. "The Trauma of Exile: Viet-Nam Refugees." *Civil Rights Digest* (Fall):59–62.

Ogbu, John U. 1974. *The Next Generation: An Ethnography of Education in an Urban Neighborhood*. New York: Academic Press.

———. 1983. "Schooling the Inner City." *Society* 21 (November/December):75–79.

———. 1989. *Cultural Models and Educational Strategies of Non-Dominant Peoples*. The 1989 Catherine Molony Memorial Lecture. New York: The City College Workshop Center.

———. 1991. "Immigrant and Involuntary Minorities in Comparative Perspective." In *Minority Status and Schooling: A Comparative Study of Immigrant and Involuntary Minorities*, edited by Margaret A. Gibson and John U. Ogbu. New York: Garland Publishing.

Ogbu, John U., and Maria E. Matute-Bianchi. 1986. "Understanding Sociocultural Factors: Knowledge, Identity and School Adjustment." In *Beyond Language: Social and Cultural Factors in Schooling Language Minority Students.* Sacramento, Calif.: California State Department of Education, Bilingual Education Service.

Ornstein, Allan C., and Daniel U. Levine. 1989. "Social Class, Race, and School Achievement: Problems and Prospects." *Journal of Teacher Education* 40:17–23.

Oropesa, R. S., and Nancy S. Landale. 1997. "Immigrant Legacies: Ethnicity, Generation and Children's Familial and Economic Lives." *Social Science Quarterly* 78(2):399–416.

Palmer, Ingrid. 1981. "Advancement Preparation and Settlement Needs of Southeast Asian Refugee Women." *International Migration Review* 19:94–101.

Park, Robert E. 1928. "Human Migration and the Marginal Man." *American Journal of Sociology* 33:881–93.

Perlmann, Joel. 1988. *Ethnic Differences: Schooling and Social Structure among the Irish, Italians, Jews, and Blacks in an American City, 1880–1935.* New York: Cambridge University Press.

Perlmann, Joel, and Roger Waldinger. 1997. "Second Generation Decline? Children of Immigrants, Past and Present—A Reconsideration." *International Migration Review* 31(4).

Piore, Michael J. 1979. *Birds of Passage: Migrant Labor and Industrial Societies.* New York: Cambridge University Press.

Portes, Alejandro. 1995. "Economic Sociology and the Sociology of Immigration: A Conceptual Overview." In *The Economic Sociology of Immigration: Essays on Networks, Ethnicity, and Entrepreneurship*, edited by Alejandro Portes. New York: Russell Sage Foundation.

———. 1996. "Introduction: Immigration and Its Aftermath." In *The New Second Generation*, edited by Alejandro Portes. New York: Russell Sage Foundation.

Portes, Alejandro, and Dag MacLeod. 1996. "The Educational Progress of Children of Immigrants: The Roles of Class, Ethnicity, and School Context." *Sociology of Education* 69(4):255–75.

Portes, Alejandro, and Rafael Mozo. 1985. "The Political Adaptation Process of Cuban and Other Ethnic Minorities in the United States: A Preliminary Analysis." *International Migration Review* 19:35–63.

Portes, Alejandro, and Rubén G. Rumbaut. 1996. *Immigrant America: A Portrait.* 2nd edition. Berkeley, Calif.: University of California Press.

Portes, Alejandro, and Richard Schauffler. 1994. "Language and the Second Generation: Bilingualism Yesterday and Today." *International Migration Review* 28(Winter):640–61.

Portes, Alejandro, and Alex Stepick. 1993. *City on the Edge: The Transformation of Miami.* Berkeley, Calif.: University of California Press.

Portes, Alejandro, and Min Zhou. 1992. "Gaining the Upper Hand: Economic Mobility Among Immigrant and Domestic Minorities." *Ethnic and Racial Studies* 15:491–522.

———. 1993. "The New Second Generation: Segmented Assimilation and Its Variants Among Post-1965 Immigrant Youth." *Annals of the American Academy of Political and Social Science* 530 (November):74–98.

———. 1994. "Should Immigrants Assimilate?" *Public Interest* 116 (Summer):18–33.

Purdham, Lois, Margo Pfleger, Rose Bowery, Karen Harrison, Susan Reynolds, and Barbara Wolf. 1987. "Preparing Refugees for Elementary Programs: The PREP Program." *Passage: A Journal of Refugee Education* 3(1):11–15.

Rahe, Richard H., John G. Looney, Harold W. Ward, Tran Minh Tung, and William T. Liu. 1978. "Psychiatric Consultation in a Vietnamese Refugee Camp." *American Journal of Psychiatry* 132:185–90.

Reich, Robert. 1992. *The Work of Nations: Preparing Ourselves for 21st Century Capitalism*. New York: Random House.

Reyes, Luis O. 1992. *Toward a Vision for the Education of Latino Students: Community Voices, Student Voices*. Interim report. New York City, N.Y.: Latino Commission on Educational Reform.

Reyes, Olga, and Leonard A. Jackson. 1993. "Pilot Study Examining Factors Associated with Academic Success for Hispanic High School Students." *Journal of Youth and Adolescence* 22:57–71.

Ritter, P. L., and S. M. Dornbusch. 1989. Paper presented at a conference of the American Educational Research Association, San Francisco, Calif.

Rodriguez, Richard. 1982. *Hunger of Memory: The Education of Richard Rodriguez*. New York: Bantam Books.

Rose, Peter I. 1981. Part I: Overview. "Some Thoughts about Refugees and the Descendants of Theseus." *International Migration Review* 15(1):8–15.

Rumbaut, Rubén G. 1991. "The Agony of Exile: A Study of the Migration and Adaptation of Indochinese Refugee Adults and Children." In *Refugee Children: Theory, Research, and Services*, edited by Frederick L. Ahearn, Jr., and Jean L. Athey. Baltimore, Md.: Johns Hopkins University Press.

———. 1994a. "The Crucible Within: Ethnic Identity, Self-Esteem, and Segmented Assimilation Among Children of Immigrants." *International Migration Review* 28(Winter):748–94.

———. 1994b. "Origin and Destinies: Immigration to the United States since World War II." *Sociological Forum* 9(4):583–621.

———. 1995a. "The New Californians: Comparative Research Findings on the Educational Progress of Immigrant Children." In *California's Immigrant Children: Theory, Research, and Implications for Educational Policy*, edited by Rubén G. Rumbaut and Wayne A. Cornelius. San Diego: University of California, San Diego. Center for U.S.-Mexican Studies.

———. 1995b. "Vietnamese, Laotian, and Cambodian Americans." In *Asian*

Americans: Contemporary Trends and Issues, edited by Pyung Gap Min. Thousand Oaks, Calif.: Sage Publications.

———. 1996. "Ties that Bind: Immigration and Immigrant Families in the United States." In *Immigration and the Family: Research and Policy on U.S. Immigrants*, edited by Alan Booth, Ann C. Crouter, and Nancy Landale. Hillsdale, N.J.: Lawrence Erlbaum Associates.

Rumbaut, Rubén G., and Kenji Ima. 1988. "Twelve Case Histories." In *The Adaptation of Southeast Asian Refugee Youth: A Comparative Study*. Washington, D.C.: U.S. Office of Refugee Resettlement.

Rumbaut, Rubén G., and John R. Weeks. 1986. "Fertility and Adaptation: Indochinese Refugees in the United States." *International Migration Review* 20(2):428–66.

Rumberger, Russell. W. 1983. "Dropping Out of High School: The Influence of Race, Sex, and Family Background." *American Educational Research Journal* 16:199–220.

Rutledge, Paul J. 1985. *The Role of Religion in Ethnic Self-Identity: A Vietnamese Community*. Lanham, Md.: University Press of America.

———. 1992. *The Vietnamese Experience in America*. Bloomington: Indiana University Press.

Sancton, Thomas. 1992. "How to Get America Off the Dole?" *Time* (May 25):44–47.

Schulz, Nancy. 1983. *Voyagers in the Land: A Report on Unaccompanied Southeast Asian Refugee Children, New York City, 1983*. Washington, D.C.: U.S. Catholic Conference, Migration and Refugee Services.

Schumacher, Chuck. 1987. "Work Orientation." *Passage: A Journal of Refugee Education*. Special Galang Issue, 29–34.

Shaker, Peggy, and Holmes Brown. 1973. *Indochina Is People*. Philadelphia: United Church Press.

Skinner, B. F. 1984. "The Shame of American Education." *American Psychologist* 39(9):947–54.

Skinner, Kenneth A. 1980. "Vietnamese in America: Diversity in Adaptation." *California Sociologist* 3(Summer):103–24.

Skinner, Kenneth A., and G. Henricks. 1979. "The Shaping of Ethnic Self-Identity Among Indochinese Refugees." *Journal of Ethnic Studies* 7(3):25–41.

Spence, Janet T. 1985. "Achievement American Style: The Rewards and Costs of Individualism." *American Psychologist* 40:1285–95.

Starr, Paul D., and W. Jones, Jr. 1985. *Indochinese Refugees in America: Problems of Adaptation and Assimilation*. Durham, N.C.: Duke University Press.

Starr, Paul D., and Alden E. Roberts. 1982. "Occupational Adaptation of Refugees in the United States." *International Migration Review* 13:25–45.

———. 1985. "Community Structure and Vietnamese Refugee Adaptation: The Significance of Context." *International Migration Review* 16:595–613.

Steele, Claude M. 1995. "Stereotype Threat and the Intellectual Test Performance of African Americans." *Journal of Personality and Social Psychology* 69:797–811.

Stein, Barry. 1979. "Occupational Adjustment of Refugees: The Vietnamese in the United States." *International Migration Review* 13(1):25–45.

Steinberg, Laurence. 1996. *Beyond the Classroom*. New York: Simon & Schuster.

Steinberg, Laurence D., Patricia L. Blind, and Kenyon S. Chan. 1984. "Dropping Out Among Language Minority Youth." *Review of Educational Research* 54:113–32.

Suárez-Orozco, Carol, and Marcelo M. Suárez-Orozco. 1995. *Transformations: Migration, Family Life, and Achievement Motivation among Latino Adolescents*. Stanford, Calif.: Stanford University Press.

Sue, Stanley, and Sumie Okazaki. 1990. "Asian American Educational Achievement: A Phenomenon in Search of an Explanation." *American Psychologist* 45:913–20.

Sung, Betty Lee. 1987. *The Adjustment Experience of Chinese Immigrant Children in New York City*. Staten Island, N.Y.: Center for Migration Studies.

Testa, Mark and Marilyn Krogh. 1995. "The Effect of Employment on Marriage among Black Males in Inner-City Chicago." In *The Decline in Marriage among African Americans*, edited by M. Belinda Tucker and Claudia Mitchell-Kernan. New York: Russell Sage Foundation.

Tienda, Marta, and Zai Liang. 1994. "Poverty and Immigration." In *Confronting Poverty: Prescriptions for Change*, edited by Sheldon H. Darzinger, Gary D. Sandefur, and Daniel H. Weinbers. Cambridge: Harvard University Press.

Tienda, Marta, and Ding-Tzann Lii. 1987. "Minority Concentration and Earnings Inequality: Blacks, Hispanics and Asians Compared." *American Journal of Sociology* 2:141–65.

Tolbert, Charles, Patrick M. Horan, and E. M. Beck. 1980. "The Structure of Economic Segmentation: A Dual Economy Approach." *American Journal of Sociology* 85:1095–1116.

Tollefson, James W. 1989. *Alien Winds: The Reeducation of America's Indochinese Refugees*. New York: Praeger.

Tran, Thanh V. 1991. "Sponsorship and Employment Status among Indochinese Refugees in the United States." *International Migration Review* 25 (3, Fall):536–50.

U.S. Bureau of the Census. 1984. *Census of the Population, 1980: Detailed Characteristics of the Population: U.S. Summary*. PC80-1D1-A. Washington, D.C.: U.S. Government Printing Office.

———. 1994. *Statistical Abstract of the United States: 1994* (114th ed.). Washington, D.C.: U.S. Government Printing Office.

U.S. Department of Education, National Center for Educational Statistics. 1994. *The Condition of Education, 1994*. NCES 94–149. Washington, D.C.: U.S. Government Printing Office.

U.S. Department of Health, Education, and Welfare (USHEW). 1975a. *Infor-

mation about the Indochina Refugee Resettlement Program. Washington, D.C.: U.S. Government Printing Office.

————. 1975b. USHEW Refugee Task Force. *Report to the Congress.* Washington, D.C.: U.S. Government Printing Office.

————. 1977. USHEW Refugee Task Force. *Report to the Congress.* Washington, D.C.: U.S. Government Printing Office.

————. 1978. USHEW Indochinese Refugee Assistance Program. *Report to the Congress.* December 31. Washington, D.C.: U.S. Government Printing Office.

U.S. Department of Health and Human Services (USHHS). 1993. "Report of the Office of Refugee Resettlement." *Migration World,* Vol. 21(1):24–25.

U.S. Department of State. 1975a. Office of Media Services, Bureau of Public Affairs. *Indochina Refugee Resettlement Program.* Special Report No. 21. Washington, D.C.: U.S. Government Printing Office.

————. 1975b. Interagency Task Force on Indochinese Refugees. *Report to the Congress.* Washington, D.C.: U.S. Department of State.

U.S. Immigration and Naturalization Service (USINS). *Statistical Yearbook of the Immigration and Naturalization Service,* 1975–1995. Washington, D.C.: U.S. Government Printing Office.

Vigil, James Diego. 1993. "Gangs, Social Control, and Ethnicity: Ways to Redirect." In *Identity and Inner-City Youth: Beyond Ethnicity and Gender,* edited by Shirley Brice Heath and Milbrey W. McLaughlin. New York, N.Y.: Teachers College Press.

Vigil, James Diego, and Steve C. Yun. 1990. "Vietnamese Youth Gangs in Southern California." In *Gangs in America: Diffusion, Diversity, and Public Policy,* edited by Ronald Huff. Beverly Hills, Calif.: Sage.

Wagenaar, Theodore. 1987. "What Do We Know about Dropping Out of High School?" In *Research on Sociology of Education and Socialization: A Research Annual,* edited by Ronald G. Corwin. Greenwich, Conn.: JAI Press.

Wagley, Charles, and Marvin Harris. 1964. *Minorities in the New World.* New York, N.Y.: Columbia University Press.

Waldinger, Roger. 1996. "Ethnicity and Opportunity in the Plural City." In *Ethnic Los Angeles,* edited by Roger Waldinger and Mehdi Bozorgmehr. New York: Russell Sage Foundation.

Waters, Mary C. 1996. "Immigrant Families at Risk: Factors that Undermine Chances of Success." In *Immigration and the Family: Research and Policy on U.S. Immigrants,* edited by Alan Booth, Ann C. Crouter, and Nancy Landale. Hillsdale, N.J.: Lawrence Erlbaum Associates.

Whitmore, John K. 1985. "Chinese from Southeast Asia." In *Refugees in the United States: A Reference Handbook,* edited by David W. Haines. Westport, Conn.: Greenwood Press.

Williams, Holly Ann. 1990. "Families in Refugee Camps." *Human Organization* 5(2, Summer):100–107.

Willig, Ann. 1985. "A Meta-Analysis of Selected Studies on the Effectiveness of Bilingual Education." *Review of Educational Research* 55:269–317.

Willoughby, Jack. 1993. *Vietnamese Gangs and Other Criminals.* Unpublished internal training aid. New Orleans, La.: New Orleans Police Department.

Wilson, William J. 1978. *The Declining Significance of Race: Blacks and Changing American Institutions.* Chicago: University of Chicago Press.

———. 1987. *The Truly Disadvantaged: The Inner City, the Underclass, and Public Policy.* Chicago: University of Chicago Press.

———. 1996. *When Work Disappears: The World of the New Urban Poor.* New York: Knopf.

Zhou, Min. 1992. *Chinatown: The Socioeconomic Potential of an Urban Enclave.* Philadelphia, Pa.: Temple University Press.

———. 1993. "Underemployment and Economic Disparities Among Minority Groups." *Population Research and Review* 12:139–57.

———. 1997a. "Growing up American: The Challenge Confronting Immigrant Children and Children of Immigrants." *Annual Review of Sociology* 23:63–95.

———. 1997b. "Social Capital in Chinatown: The Role of Community-Based Organizations and Families in the Adaptation of the Younger Generation." In *Beyond Black and White: New Voices, New Faces in U. S. Schools,* edited by Lois Weis and Maxine S. Seller. Albany, N.Y.: State University of New York Press.

Zhou, Min, and Carl L. Bankston III. 1994. "Social Capital and the Adaptation of the Second Generation: The Case of Vietnamese Youth in New Orleans." *International Migration Review* 28(4):775–99.

———. 1995. "Entrepreneurship." In *The Asian American Almanac: A Reference Work on Asians in the United States,* edited by Susan Gall and Irene Natividad. Detroit, Mich.: Gale Research.

Zhou, Min, and Yoshinori Kamo. 1994. "An Analysis of Earnings Patterns for Chinese, Japanese, and Non-Hispanic Whites in the United States." *The Sociological Quarterly* 35(4):581–602.

Index

Boldface numbers refer to tables and figures.

respect, as Vietnamese value: for elders, 167; as foundation of social relations, 94–96; parental authority and, 160, 167–70; for teachers, 169
Ritter, P. L., 147
Rodriguez, Richard, 13–14
Rumbaut, Rubén G., 29, 51–52, 140
Rutledge, Paul J., 38, 98, 143

sanctions, social control via, 105–6
San Diego, Vietnamese immigrants in, 137, 140
San Jose, Vietnamese community in, 18
Santa Ana Boys, 186
school clubs, delinquency and, 196, **197,** 198
schools, 220–21, 227; bilingual education in, 111; Chinese children in, **63,** 64; desegregation of, 132; English as a Second Language (ESL) classes in, 111; enrollment in, 137–39, **139;** failure in, 130; gang members absent from, 190–91; inadequacy of, 5; inequality and polarization in, 131–34; in Little Saigon, 75; performance in, 139–41, **140;** policy implications for, 238; poor learning environment in, 220; poverty among racial minorities in, 132–33; racial composition of, 132; resegregation of, 132, 133; in resettlement camps, 29; second-generation adaptation and, 7–8; Southeast Asian children in, **63,** 64; stratification in, 233, 236; U.S. government programs and, 31–32; in Versailles Village, 109, 111, 134–37, 141, 150–59, **153, 154, 156;** women and, *see* Vietnamese women, education of. *See also* college; *under* education; high school(s); school success
school success: blocked mobility and, 148; determinants of, 141–43; ethnicity and, 9–10, 143, 144, 145, 146, 228; minority children and, 8, 9–10; race and, 9–10
school success, Vietnamese children and, 5, 130–31; adaptation and, 233; adolescents and, 202, **203;** after-school classes and, 157–58; anti-intellectual youth subculture and, 133–34, 220–21; awards ceremony and, 158; community and, 145, 146, 147, 150–59, **153, 154, 156,** 227–28, 232–33; Confucianism and, 131, 143, 144, 146; culture and, 9, 20, 142–43, 144, 146; data sources for, 17; English-language proficiency and, 145; enrollment and, **63,** 64, 99, 137–39, **139;** ethnic involvement and, 9–10,

154, **154;** ethnicity and, 143, 144, 145, 146, 228; family and, 142, 147–48; family size and, 53–54, 142; family socioeconomic characteristics and, 141–42, 144, 145–46, **146;** family structure and, 142; family values and, 147, **153,** 153–55, **154, 156,** 223, 227–28; high school completion and, 137, 138–39, **140,** 144–47, **146;** language barrier and, 110; parental aspirations and, 41, 220–21, 223; performance and, 139–41, **140;** praise for, 223; relative functionalism and, 148; social capital and, 158–59; social organizations and, 157–58; social relations and, 145, 149–55, **152, 153, 154,** 223; upward mobility and, 3, 131, 138, 148, 149, 229; Vietnamese language literacy and, 115–29, **119, 120, 121, 123, 124, 126, 127,** 228; work ethic and, 227–28
Seattle, Vietnamese refugees in, 48
secondary internal migration, 45, **49,** 73–74
second generation: adaptation of, 6–14; Vietnamese children as members of, 4. *See also* children of immigrants; Vietnamese children
second-generation decline, 3–4
second-generation revolt, 4
segmented assimilation perspective, 236
segregation, minorities in low-income communities and, 219
selective Americanization, 224–27
self, respect for, 95, 96
serial migration, effect of on family, 55–56
sex ratio, of Vietnamese refugees, 49, **50**
shared obligations, immigrant cultures encompassing, 12
Singapore, boat people in, 27
Sino-Vietnamese refugees, 27, 74
social capital, 237; communities and, 54–55, 232–33; ethnicity as, 230; immigrant culture and, 12–14; school success and, 158–59; skills in parental native language as, 116; in Versailles Village, 81–83
social class, second-generation adaptation and, 7–8. *See also* socioeconomic characteristics
social control: from ethnic community, 221–23, 227; from family, 227; from immigrant cultures, 14; from integration, 105–7; over daughters, 177, 179–80, 181–84; over sons, 160, 168, 177, 179–80, 181, 182
social mobility. *See* upward mobility
social organizations. *See* community organizations

in, 53; family values in, 87–92, **89, 91, 990;** future and, 239; generalizability of, 18–19; interviews in, 15; Little Saigon *versus,* 18–19; occupational status in, **80,** 82; Orderly Departure Program and, 33; organizations in, 81–82, 102–3, 157–58; population of, 78, **79;** public assistance in, 80, **80;** reasons for settling in, 1; religious participation in, 18–19, 81, 95, 98–100, **100, 101, 102;** respect as value in, 95–96; schools in, 109, 111, 134–37, 141, 151–59, **152, 153, 154, 156;** social capital in, 81–83; social control in, 105–7, 222; sponsors of immigrants to, 78; surveys of students in, 15–16

Viet-Anh, Reverend Michael, 97

Vietnam: Amerasians in, 33–34, 43, **44;** Cambodia at war with, 26; China at war with, 26, 27; conditions in after war, 26; education in, 137; generational differences in orientation toward, 64–66, 70; hatred toward Communists of, 64–65; immigrants as temporary expatriates from, 64; normalization of feelings toward, 65–66; society-marginal family system oriented toward, 206, 210–11, **212;** trade embargo against, 66; Vietnamese children's thoughts of, 1, 2; women in, 171, 179

Vietnamese-American Voters' Association, 82, 102

Vietnamese children, 2, 4–6, 17; as Amerasians, 33–34, 43, **44;** cultural conflicts of, *see* bicultural conflicts; dependence of parents on, 40, 86, 165, 170; in family, 86, 87; in first generation, 4, 5; future of, 238–40; generational distribution for, 51–52, **53;** life in Vietnam as reality to, 38–39; maladaptation of, *see* delinquency of Vietnamese children; names of, 64, 65; obedience and, 175–76, 177; obstacles to success of, 4–5; in 1.5 generation, 4, 5, 39, 40, 51–52, **52,** 61, **62, 63;** parents and, *see* bicultural conflicts; religion and, 98–102, **100, 101, 102;** resettlement and, 38–41; social outlook of, 40–41; socioeconomic characteristics of, 61, **63,** 64; thoughts of Vietnam of, 1, 2; U.S.-born, 17, 24–25; U.S. government programs for, 31–32; as valedictorians, 225, *see also* school success, Vietnamese children and. *See also* Vietnamese daughters; Vietnamese sons

Vietnamese communities, 18; adaptation and, 20; dispersion of, 35, 45, **46–47,** 48; for-

mation of, 73–76; need for, 72–73; political prisoners in, 34–35; school success and, 145, 146, 147, 150–59, **153, 154, 156,** 227–28, 232–33. *See also* ethnic involvement; Versailles Village (New Orleans)

Vietnamese culture, school success and, 9, 20, 142–43, 144, 146

Vietnamese daughters: education for, *see* Vietnamese women, education of; housework by, 179; obedience from, 175–76, 177; social control over, 160, 168, 177, 179–80, 181–84

Vietnamese Educational Association, 82, 102–3, 104, 157–58, 159

Vietnamese family, 83–92; absent or partially absent, 206–7, **208;** children in, 86, 87; community-marginal, 206, 208–9, **209;** culture of, 13; grandparents in, 86; individualism *versus,* 165, 166–67; man in, 84, 85, 87; obligations to *versus* individualism, 165, 166–67; parental authority in, 167–70; reconstructed, 86–87; resettlement and, 32, 84–86; role reversals in, 86; school success and, 147–48; society-marginal, 206, 210–11, **212;** studies on, 6; support from in resettlement camps, 30, 32; traditional, 83–84, 87; woman in, 84, 85–86, 87. *See also* Vietnamese parents

Vietnamese family size, 52–54; school success and, 142

Vietnamese family, socioeconomic characteristics of: delinquency and, 194, **195;** English-language proficiency of children and, 114–15, 116; in 1980 and 1990, **57,** 59–61, **60;** poverty and, 40; in Versailles Village, **80,** 80–81; Vietnamese language literacy and school success and, 118, **119,** 123–25

Vietnamese family structure, 54–56, **55;** adjusted, 86–87; delinquency and, 194–95; high school dropout rate and, 138–39, **140;** school enrollment and, 138, **139;** uprooted, 84–86; in Versailles Village, **80,** 81

Vietnamese family values, 147, 151; school success and, 147, **153,** 153–55, **154, 156,** 223, 227–28; in Versailles Village, 87–92, **89, 90, 91**

Vietnamese fathers, daughter's education and, 175–78. *See also* Vietnamese parents

Vietnamese Fishermen Association, 68

Vietnamese immigrants: American public opinion toward, 37–38; educational attainment of, 137–38; naturalization of, 66–69; neigh-